insider CHINA

Lifeng Han

Emma Lejun Wu
Hua Cai

Published 2009 by Lexus Ltd
60 Brook Street, Glasgow G40 2AB
Scotland
www.lexusforlanguages.co.uk

contributing editors
Daniel Newman (who set the ball rolling), Esther Tyldesley, Yingxu Yin

Artwork
Elfreda Crehan, Øivind Hovland

Maps
Eugene Fleury

Design and typesetting
Elfreda Crehan

Lexus copy editors
Sophie Cadell, Jenny Wottrich

General editor
Peter Terrell

British Library Cataloguing in Publication Data
A catalogue record for this book is available from the British Library.

ISBN 978-1-904737-1-79

Printed and bound in Latvia by InPrint plc

This is a truly fascinating portrayal of Chinese life and culture. Here you have the real insider's knowledge of China and things Chinese, a vast range, both ancient and modern.

Introduction

This book offers a detailed picture of the sort of knowledge of China that an ordinary Chinese person may have simply by virtue of being Chinese, of having grown up in that culture. The overall theme of this book is insider knowledge of a different culture, with all its contradictions, good and bad, courteous and cruel, new and old, replacement and retention.

How to navigate around this book.

The articles are organized alphabetically, juxtaposing an emperor and a snooker player, a pirate and a romantic novelist, a Buddhist monk and a dumpling, simply by reason of their spelling. There is a topic index as well, which can be used for homing in on a particular area.

Spelling, cross-references, a.k.a.

The spelling, in English words, of Chinese names is no easy matter. The convention used is that known as "pinyin". (There is an article about this in the book). But even under pinyin there are differences. For example, both Qin Er Shi and Qin Ershi may be found in texts about China. And some Chinese people, emperors in particular, are often known by more than one name. There are birth names, courtesy names and titles of reign (articles about these in the book). Again, others – actors, performers, politicans – may be most commonly known by one name in Hong Kong and by another in the rest of China. In view of this complexity and in the interests of fullness of treatment, this book includes name variants and cross-refers them to each other as appropriate.

Red words in articles have their own alphabetical entry.

As for actual sequencing, this book alphabetizes on the first word. So, for example:

Hu Shi	Qi Xi
comes before	*comes before*
Hua Guofeng	qilin

How are dates entered?

If a date is before 1000AD, then it is given together with either the reference BC or the reference AD. This is done for clarity and serves also as a reminder of the antiquity of some of the subject matter of the book. If a given date is greater than 1000 and has no reference as to BC or AD, it will be AD.

Dynasties and Historical Periods

Chinese dynasties do not all follow in a neat chronological sequence. There are sometimes gaps and overlaps; and historians differ about the assignment of dates to some dynasties, especially the earlier ones. This is a list of the main dynasties only.

BC

before c.2100	*Three August Ones and Five Emperors*
c.2100-c.1600	*Xia*
1600-1046	*Shang*
1045–256	*Zhou*
1046-771	*Western Zhou*
770-256	*Eastern Zhou*
770-476	*Spring and Autumn Period (in the Eastern Zhou)*
475-221	*Warring States Period*
221-206	*Qin*
206BC-220AD	*Han*
206BC-9AD	*Western Han*

AD

9-23	*Xin*
25-220	*Eastern Han*
184-280	*Three Kingdoms*
256-420	*Jin*
265-317	*Western Jin*
317-420	*Eastern Jin*
420-589	*Southern and Northern Dynasties*
581-618	*Sui*
618-907	*Tang*
690-705	*Zhou*
907-979	*Five Dynasties and Ten Kingdoms*
951-960	*Later Zhou Dynasty*
960-1127	*Northern Song*
1127-1279	*Southern Song*
916-1125	*Liao*
1115-1234	*Jin*
1271-1368	*Yuan*
1368-1644	*Ming*
1644-1912	*Qing*

Maps of China

RUSSIA
KAZAKHSTAN
KYRGYZSTAN
TAJIKISTAN
AFGHANISTAN
PAKISTAN
INDIA
MONGOLIA
Qiqihar
Harbin
Changchun
Jilin
Siping
Tieling
Tonghua
Shenyang
Fushun
Urumqi
Kashgar
Turfan
TARIM BASIN
TAKLAMAKAN DESERT
Aiding Lake
Khotan
Jiayuguan
Datong
Baotou
Hohhot
Qinhuangdao
NORTH KOREA
SOUTH KOREA
Alashan Zuoqi
Beijing
Tianjin
Tangshan
Dalian
Yinchuan
Great Wall of China
Taiyuan
Shijiazhuang
Yantai
Weihai
Xining
Dongwan
Pingyao
Jinan
Weifang
Qingdao
Yellow River
Lanzhou
Yan'an
Handan
Qufu
YELLOW SEA
Tianshui
Luoyang
Kaifeng
Lianyungang
Xi'an
Zhengzhou
Xuzhou
HIMALAYAS
Yangzhou
Nanjing
Yangtze
Mianyang
Hefei
NEPAL
Shigatse
Lhasa
Deyang
Three Gorges Dam
Hankou
Shanghai
Chengdu
Neijiang
Yichang
Hangzhou
EAST CHINA SEA
BHUTAN
Fulin
Chongqing
Changde
Wuhan
Jingdezhen
Nanchang
Changsha
Wenzhou
INDIA
Liupanshui
BANGLADESH
Guiyang
Hengyang
Fuzhou
Dali
Kunming
Anshun
Ganzhou
Quanzhou
Taipei
Ruili
Guilin
Xiamen
Chaozhou
Jinmen
TAIWAN
Wuzhou
Guangzhou
MYANMAR (BURMA)
Nanning
Shantou
Jiangmen
Shenzhen
VIETNAM
Pingxiang
Yulin
Hong Kong
Zhuhai
Macao
Beihai
Zhanjiang
SOUTH CHINA SEA
LAOS
Haikou
Hainan
THAILAND
0 km 300
0 miles 200

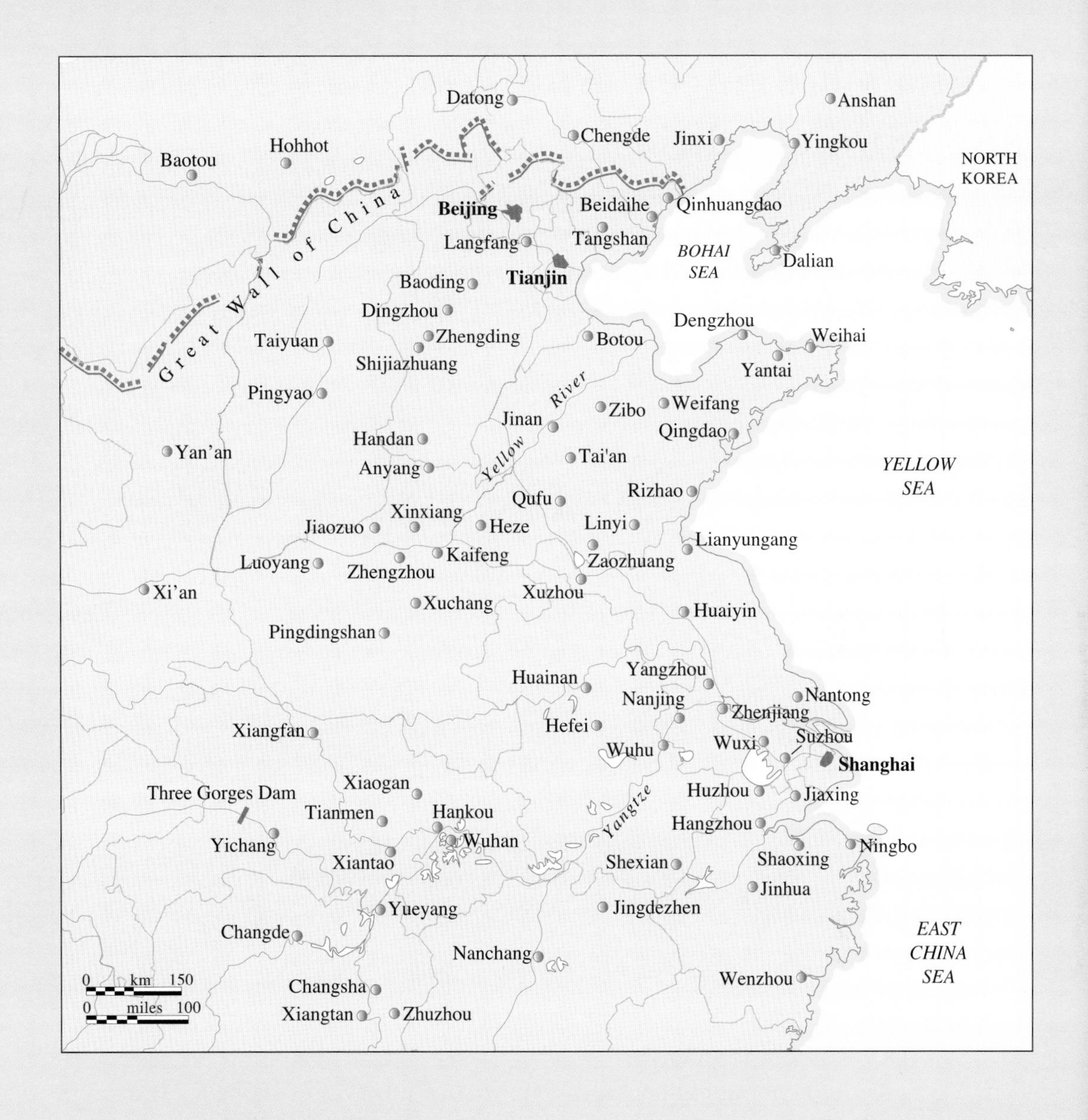
Datong
Anshan
Hohhot
Chengde
Jinxi
Yingkou
Baotou
NORTH
KOREA
Great Wall of China
Beijing
Beidaihe
Qinhuangdao
Langfang
Tangshan
BOHAI
SEA
Dalian
Tianjin
Baoding
Dingzhou
Dengzhou
Taiyuan
Zhengding
Botou
Weihai
Shijiazhuang
Yantai
Pingyao
Yellow River
Zibo
Weifang
Jinan
Qingdao
Handan
Yan'an
Tai'an
Anyang
YELLOW
SEA
Qufu
Rizhao
Xinxiang
Jiaozuo
Heze
Linyi
Lianyungang
Kaifeng
Luoyang
Zaozhuang
Zhengzhou
Xi'an
Xuzhou
Xuchang
Huaiyin
Pingdingshan
Yangzhou
Huainan
Nantong
Nanjing
Zhenjiang
Hefei
Xiangfan
Suzhou
Wuxi
Wuhu
Shanghai
Xiaogan
Three Gorges Dam
Huzhou
Jiaxing
Yangtze
Tianmen
Hankou
Hangzhou
Yichang
Wuhan
Ningbo
Xiantao
Shexian
Shaoxing
Jinhua
Yueyang
Jingdezhen
EAST
CHINA
SEA
Changde
Nanchang
0 km 150
Wenzhou
Changsha
0 miles 100
Xiangtan
Zhuzhou

China's Provinces, Autonomous Regions and Municipalities

AR = Autonomous Region

An autonomous region is an administrative subdivision of China, like a province, but with a large population of a minority ethnic group. There are five autonomous regions in China: Tibet for the Tibetan people, Guangxi for the Zhuang, Xinjiang for the Uygurs, Inner Mongolia for the Mongols and Ningxia for the Hui. Each autonomous region has its own local government and has more legislative powers than other provinces.

M = Municipality

There are four municipalities: Beijing, Shanghai, Tianjin and Chongqing. They are like provinces but with just one major city. The mayor of the main city has administrative responsibility for the whole municipality, being answerable only to the Communist Party leaders.

Topic Index

This index includes alternative names.

fashion & clothes

changshan; cheongsam; Chinese tunic suit; du dou; Han Fu; long pao; Mao suit; pyjamas; qi pao; Tang Zhuang; whitening cream; Zhongshan Zhuang

fashion designers

Ji Mi; Jimmy Liao; Mao Geping

festivals

Chinese New Year; Chinese New Year's Eve; Chong Yang Festival; Congee Festival; Double Ninth Festival; Dragon Boat Festival; Firebrand Festival; Ghost Festival; Ice Festival; Laba Festival; Lantern Festival; Magpie Festival; Mid-Autumn Festival; Moon Festival; New Year pictures; Night of Sevens; Qi Xi; Qing Ming Festival; Spirit Festival; spring couplets; Spring Festival; Tomb Sweeping Festival; Water Splashing Festival

flowers

lotus; peony

food

baozi; Buddha's delight; century egg; char siu; congee; dim sum; doufu; dough flowers; eating; Eight Great Traditions of Chinese cuisine; gong bao jiding; gourd; guotie; hot and sour soup; hot pot; jiaozi; kung pao chicken; mantou; mapo doufu; mianren; miansu; mooncake; noodles; Peking roast duck; pickled vegetables; placenta; stinky tofu; tea egg; toffee fruit; tofu; wonton; xiao long bao; youtiao; zongzi

games, chess & go

cricket fighting; mah-jong; Wu Qingyuan; Xie Jun; Ye Jiangchuan

geographical features

Aiding Lake; China and its regional differences; China's sorrow; Gulang; Jinggang Mountains; Taklamakan Desert; Yangtze River; Yellow River

gods

Budai; Cangjie; Chang'e; Da Yu; Daoji; Dizang; Eight Immortals; Erlang Shen; Four Emperors; Four Heavenly Kings; Gautama Buddha; Guan Yu; Guanyin; Heng'e; Houyi; Jade Emperor; Ji Gong; Kua Fu; Kuan Yin; Lin Moniang; Laughing Buddha; Matsu; Meng Po; Miao Shan; Monkey King; Ne Zha; Nüwa; Sakyamuni Buddha; Sun Wukong; Three August Ones and Five Emperors; Three Pure Ones; Three Sovereign Ones; Town God; Tu Di Gong; Wenchang; Xiaotian; Yu the Great; Zao Jun; Zhong Kui

implements

abacus; steelyard

inventions & discoveries

Cai Lun; Cangjie; Lunar Calendar; Pei Xiu; Shen Kuo; Yellow Emperor; Zhang Heng

language

Cantonese; classical characters; Hakka; Mandarin; Min dialect; pinyin; simplified characters; Wade-Giles; Wu; zhuyin, Taiwanese notation system

legendary beings

Ao Guang; Azure Dragon of the East; Bai Hu; Chinese Phoenix; Daji; dragon; Fenghuang; fox spirits; huli jing; Jingwei; Nian; Ox Head and Horse Face; peng; Phoenix; Pixie; Pixiu; qilin; Qing Long; Tao Tie; Xuan Wu; Yanluo; yaoguai; Zhu Que

literary & folklore

Afanti; Ah Q; All Men Are Brothers; Cao Xueqin; Cowherd and Weaver Girl; Dou E Yuan; Dream of the Red Chamber; Fengshen Yanyi; Investiture of the Gods; Jin Ping Mei; Journey to the West; Monkey King; Mudan Ting or the Peony Pavilion; Outlaws of the Marsh; Peony Pavilion; Romance of the Three Kingdoms; Romance of the West Chamber; Rulin Waishi; Scholars; Story of a Marital Fate to Awaken the World; Story of the Stone; Strange Stories from a Chinese Studio; Water Margin; Xingshi Yinyuan Zhuan; Xi Xiang Ji

martial arts

Huo Yuanjia; Wong Fei Hung; Shaolin Temple

medicine

acupuncture; common cold; cupping; moxibustion; traditional Chinese medicine

military

An Lushan; Ban Chao; Cao Cao; Chiang Kai-shek; Han Shizhong; Han Xin; Huang Gai; Jiang Jieshi; Lin Biao; Liu Bowen; Liu Huaqing; Ma Chao; Nian Gengyao; Nie Rongzhen; Sima Yi; Sun Ce; Sun Wu; Sun Zi; Xiao Daocheng; Ye Jianying; Yuan Chonghuan; Yue Fei; Zhang Fei; Zhang Xueliang; Zhang Zizhong; Zhao Yun; Zhou Yu; Zhu De; Zhuge Liang

models

Hu Bing; Ma Yanli; Mary Ma

music & musicians

A Bing; Anita Mui Yim-fong; Beyond; Cai Qin; Cantopop; C-pop; Cui Jian; Dao Lang; Deng Lijun; Dou Wei; Emil Chau; erhu; Faye Wong; guzheng; Hua Yanjun; Jacky Cheung; Jay Chou; Lang Lang; Liu Huan; Mei Yanfang; Nie Er; opera; pipa; rock; sheng; Tian Han; Tsai Chin; Twelve Girls Band; Wang Fei; Xian Xinghai; yangqin; Zhang Xueyou; Zhou Huajian; Zhou Jielun; Zhou Xuan

names

comrade; courtesy names; emperors' names; Middle Kingdom; names; title of reign; Westerners

philosophers & philosophy

Analects; Buddhism; Confucianism; Confucius; Daoism; Han Fei; Han Feizi; Kong Qiu; Kong Zhongni; Legalism; Mencius; Mohism; Mo zi; Neo-Confucianism; Taoism; Wang Yangming; Xun Zi; Zhu Xi; Zhuang Zi

poetry & poets

Ai Qing; Bei Dao; ci; Du Fu; Gong Zizhen; Li Bai; Ouyang Xiu; Qu Yuan; Su Dongpo; Su Shi; Wen Yiduo; Xu Zhimo; Zhao Zhenkai

politics & politicians

Chen Duxiu; Communist Youth League; Deng Xiaoping; Gang of Four; He Shen; Hu Jintao; Hu

A

A Bing, *a.k.a.* ***Hua Yanjun***

One of China's best-known musicians, A Bing (1893-1950) is remembered for his poignant erhu and pipa compositions and for his debauched lifestyle, that led to him contracting syphilis and losing his eyesight. In the year that he died, six of his original compositions were recorded by visiting musicians. It is through these recordings that his melancholy music is known to us today.

abacus

The abacus is still used by many Chinese traders. In the right hands, it can be used to calculate square roots and cube roots, and is often demonstrated to be a more efficient tool for addition, subtraction, multiplication and division than the modern calculator.

©iStockphoto.com/Yi Lu

Abbot Wang, *a.k.a.* ***Wang Yuanlu***

Wang Yuanlu (1849-1931), a Taoist priest, is generally remembered for discovering important ancient Buddhist scriptures in Dunhuang, Gansu Province, at the beginning of the 20th century. He sold some of the works to various European visitors and only a fraction of them are now kept in China. However, his discovery initiated a new era in the study of Chinese history.

Abode of Ghosts

Built on the northern bank of the Yangtze River near Chongqing more than two thousand years ago, the Abode of Ghosts was originally used as a temple in which people made offerings to the dead. Now, however, it has been done up for tourists and is stuffed full of devil mannequins.

acupuncture

A form of medicine used to unblock qi (energy) by inserting needles into particular points of the body, acupuncture has a history that can be traced as far back as 3000BC. Originally practised using blunt stone needles, it is now carried out with far less painful stainless steel implements measuring as little as 0.18 millimetres in diameter. Not only popular in China, acupuncture is now used all over the world as a means of treating a wide range of medical conditions, including allergies, arthritis, osteoarthritis and lower back pain. In modern China acupuncture is commonly offered, both in general hospitals and in special acupuncture clinics.

addresses

Addresses are normally written in the reverse order to that normal in the West, starting with the country and continuing with the province, town, street, number and name of the intended recipient. This would normally be written in Chinese characters, but pinyin can also be used, although this is likely to slow down delivery.

Afanti

A folk hero character found in Uygur folklore who uses his intelligence to outwit greedy bullies. He was famous for helping poor people. He is intelligent, wise and very funny and is almost always shown travelling with his donkey.

Ah Q

The protagonist of one of Lu Xun's most famous short stories, Ah Q is an archetypal village idiot whose cowardice and stupidity are used to convey the author's discontent with early twentieth century China. Today, his name is used to label the type of person who refuses to face up to reality and deceives himself into believing that he is successful all the time.

Ai Qing

Ai Qing (1910-1966) is now acknowledged as one of the greatest modern Chinese poets. As a young man he studied art and poetry in France. Returning to China at the age of 22, he was arrested and thrown into prison for opposing the Kuomintang. While in prison, he wrote some of his famous poems like "Da Yan River – My Babysitter". He was released in 1935 and later joined the Communist Party. However, in 1957 he became a victim of the Communist anti-rightist campaign and was sent to do hard labour on a farm. Ai Qing suffered at the hands of both the Nationalists and the Communists and yet his most famous poem, a favourite of many Chinese people, is *I love this land.*

Why my eyes are always filled with tears?
Because I love this land profoundly...

Ai Weiwei

An avant-garde artist, architect, exhibition planner and cultural and social critic, Ai Weiwei (born 1957), is the son of the famous poet Ai Qing and has been one of the most innovative figures in the Chinese art world for the past two decades. His work has contributed to shaping the course of Chinese art. He is widely exhibited in Europe, Asia and North America. From 2000 he started to concentrate mainly on architectural and urban development projects, including acting as artistic consultant for the Beijing Olympic Stadium for the 2008 Summer Olympics.

Aiding Lake

154 metres below sea level, this muddy plain in Xinjiang is the second lowest lake in the world. Its name derives from the Uygur word for moonlight, the colour of which can be seen in the shimmering reflections of the salt crystals lying on the bottom of the lake.

alcohol

It is quite common for guests in China to be offered large quantities of alcohol at formal dinners, and even the best of excuses will often fail to get you off the hook. In this case, your only hope is to bribe one of the waiters into secretly pouring you water. When toasts are drunk, the word ganbei is often screamed across the room at top volume. This literally means "***dry your glass***", and is a command to drain the glass in one go. Amongst the many types of alcohol in China are beer (pijiu) – which was introduced to China by thirsty German colonialists in the nineteenth century; rice wine – which tastes rather like Japanese sake past its sell-by date; and the infamously strong baijiu – which is distilled from sorghum grain to guarantee you a thumping headache the morning after.

All Men Are Brothers → *WATER MARGIN*

Alute

Alute was the daughter of a powerful Manchu family during the Qing Dynasty (1644-1912) who was married to Emperor Tongzhi. Surviving her husband by just two months, Alute (1854-1875) committed suicide at the age of 22 when the powerful Empress Dowager Cixi prevented her son from becoming the next emperor. Till this day, she is seen as one of the most talented and tragic empresses in Chinese history.

An Dehai

A eunuch in the Qing Dynasty, An Dehai (1844-1869) was favoured by Empress Dowager Cixi and became powerful in the imperial court. He was executed in 1869 for corruption.

An Lushan

A rebellious general of Turkish origin during the Tang Dynasty (618-907AD), An Lushan used his friendship with Yang Guifei to build a position of power in Emperor Xuanzong's palace. Attempting to take control of China, An Lushan (703-757AD) launched a rebellion and conquered the cities of Kaifeng, Luoyang and Xi'an, before declaring himself emperor. He was later assassinated by his own son.

Analects

The Analects is a record of the words and deeds of the philosopher Confucius and his disciples. Composed during the Warring States Period (475-221BC), it deals with humanistic concepts such as propriety, righteousness, loyalty and filial piety. The Analects' emphasis on strict hierarchical relationships is still apparent throughout East Asian society today.

Do not to others as you would not wish done to yourself.

The superior man thinks of virtue; the small man thinks of comfort.

Be not ashamed of mistakes and thus make them crimes.

He who chooses to secure the good of others has already secured his own.

A man without courtesy might quite as well cease to be.

He who chases two rabbits will catch neither.

ancestor worship

A practice based on the belief that ancestors have the ability to influence the lives of their relatives, ancestor worship is a common component of religious belief in many different societies. Few, however, can claim to take ancestor worship to the same extremes as the Chinese, who not only burn incense and paper money for deceased relatives, but also make offerings ranging from food and drink right through to toothbrushes, combs and slippers so that their ancestors will be as comfortable as possible in the afterlife.

Andy Lau, *a.k.a.* ***Liu Dehua***

A superstar in Hong Kong pop culture, Andy Lau is a successful singer, actor and film producer and has a huge fan base throughout Asia. He started his career as a TV actor in the 1980s. In the early 90s he was named as one of the "Four Kings" of the Hong Kong pop-music industry, along with Jacky Cheung, Leon Lai and Aaron Kwok. He has since starred in more than 100 films and has won more awards than any other male Cantonese pop star.

Ang Lee, *a.k.a.* ***Li An***

A Taiwanese filmmaker of eclectic talents whose most famous works include *The Wedding Banquet* (1993), *Sense and Sensibility* (1995), *Crouching Tiger, Hidden Dragon* (2000), *Brokeback Mountain* (2005) and *Lust, Caution* (2007). Ang Lee is the only Asian ever to have won an Oscar for Best Director.

©iStockphoto.com/Zubin Li

Mount Huangshan, Anhui Province

Anhui

A rugged eastern province, Anhui's poor agricultural conditions and regular flooding make it one of the poorest regions in eastern China. This may not be good news for the locals, but on the bright side it does mean that the province's natural beauty is yet to be pulverized into oblivion by the earth-moving equipment of the modern world. Highlights include the magnificent mountain ranges of Jiuhuashan and Huangshan and the ancient medicine-trading centre of Bozhou.

Anita Mui Yim-fong → *Mei Yanfang*

Anshi Rebellion

The Anshi Rebellion took place during the Tang Dynasty from 755 to 763AD. It was started by An Lushan, a powerful military commander in the north, who was favoured by Emperor Xuanzong's favourite concubine Yang Guifei. He made a move to usurp the throne and declared himself emperor after capturing Luoyang, the eastern capital of the Tang. The rebellion spanned the reigns of three Tang emperors. Though it was suppressed seven years later, the country was badly weakened economically and its centralized bureaucracy suffered. The great Tang Dynasty, in its remaining years, was never able to recapture its former glory.

Anshun

Famous for its colourfully dressed ethnic minorities and huge Sunday market, Anshun is one of Guizhou Province's most important trade centres, situated near Huangguoshu Waterfalls and Longgong Caves.

Anyang

Thought to be one of the earliest urban civilizations in China, this city in Henan has yielded up the oldest etchings and bronzes in China, which date back to the fourteenth century BC.

Anyuan coal mine

The Anyuan coal mine in Jianxi Province is famous for being the place where the young Mao Zedong inspired the miners with his ideas for a communist revolution that would remove capitalist oppression and create a new educated and liberated working class. Mao lived and worked there in the early 1920s and led a series of strikes that are seen as leading to the founding of the Chinese Communist Party.

Ao Guang

The Supreme Dragon King, who is said to have lived in a palace at the bottom of the Eastern Ocean, guarded by shrimp soldiers and crab generals. Possessing the ability to take on human form and manipulate the weather to his advantage, he was extremely powerful. However, he was eventually beaten in a fight by Ne Zha and turned into a snake.

Ayding Lake → *Aiding Lake*

Azure Dragon of the East → *Qing Long*

Ba Jin

Li Yaotang, better known by his pen name Ba Jin (1904-2005), is one of the most important modern Chinese writers. Born into a wealthy family in Chongqing, in the province of Sichuan, he received a good education in China. After graduating from college, he travelled to France in 1927 where he wrote his first novel *Destruction* (1929). Ba Jin is best known for his trilogy *Torrent* (the novels *Family*, *Spring* and *Autumn*) of which *Family* was wildly popular among young readers at the time. His other famous works include The Love Trilogy *Fog*, *Rain* and *Lightning*, a single novel *Cold Nights* and his memoirs *Random Thoughts*. During the Cultural Revolution, he was persecuted as a counter-revolutionary and was publicly humiliated. In 1977, however, he was rehabilitated and regained recognition in mainstream literary circles. He was elected head of the Chinese Writers' Association in 1981 and held this post until his death.

Bada Shanren → *Zhu Da*

Bai

The Bai are an ethnic group living mainly in Yunnan Province. Although Chinese is their written language, most Bai people speak the Bai language – which is generally believed to be part of the Tibeto-Burman language group. The Bai people, both men and women, like to wear white clothes, which is probably the reason why they are called the Bai, as bai in Chinese means white. They are famous for serving their "three-course tea", a traditional way of treating honoured guests. The first course is bitter tea, representing the hardship of life; the second course is sweet tea, meaning the happiness of life; and the third "aftertaste" tea is sweet and spicy, symbolizing a better understanding of life with all its ups and downs.

Bai Hu

Bai Hu, the White Tiger, is one of the four symbols of the Chinese constellations – a sacred beast representing the west (the compass direction, not the Western world) and the season of autumn. During the Han Dynasty, people believed that it took 500 years for a tiger to change its colour to white, thus making it holy. It is said that the immortals went to heaven by riding tigers. The White Tiger was also a historical symbol of military force, appearing in ancient times, for example, on the army's White Tiger flag or as an image on written military orders. In Chinese legends some famous generals are said to be the reincarnation of the White Tiger's Star.

Bai Xianyong, *a.k.a.* *Kenneth Hsien-yung Pai*

Bai Xianyong, a well-known contemporary writer, was born in Guilin, Guangxi, in 1937. His father is the famous Kuomintang general Bai Chongxi. In 1952 Bai and his family moved from Hong Kong to Taiwan after the KMT was defeated in the Chinese Civil War (1946-1950). He published his first short story *Madame Jin* in 1958 when he was studying at the National Taiwan University. Many of his other early works like *Jade Love* were published during his period as an undergraduate. He received an MA from the University of Iowa in the US and started to teach Chinese Literature at the University of California. A large number of his works have been turned into films, TV dramas or stage plays. Some of his writing has been translated into English – such as the collection of short stories *Taipei People* and *Crystal Boys: A Novel*. A lifelong devotee of Kunqu Opera, he has been deeply involved in the promotion of this elegant ancient genre of drama. His young people's version of Peony Pavilion has been staged in Taiwan, Hong Kong and major cities on the mainland.

baijiu

A generic term for any colourless, distilled spirit or liquor. In Chinese, jiu refers to any kind of alcoholic drink, while bai, which literally means whiteness, indicates the transparent nature of baijiu. Sometimes it is also known as shaojiu (the literal meaning of shao is burning), since baijiu generally has a high alcohol content and will burst into flames if lit. Unquestionably the most famous brand in China is Maotai, named after its place of origin – Maotai Town in Guizhou Province.

Ban Chao

Ban Chao (32-102AD) was an extraordinary general during the Eastern Han Dynasty (25-220AD), who extended the boundaries of Emperor Mingdi's empire further than had ever previously been achieved in Chinese history. During his early career, he not only defeated the restless Mongols and Xiongnu on China's northern borders, but also conquered the entire Tarim Basin. Following on from this, in 91AD, his troops arrived at the edge of the Caspian Sea, leaving only Parthia between China and Rome. Recognized as the Protector General of China's western regions, he played such an important role in the expansion of the Eastern Han Dynasty that China's power over Central Asia was weakened enormously immediately after his death.

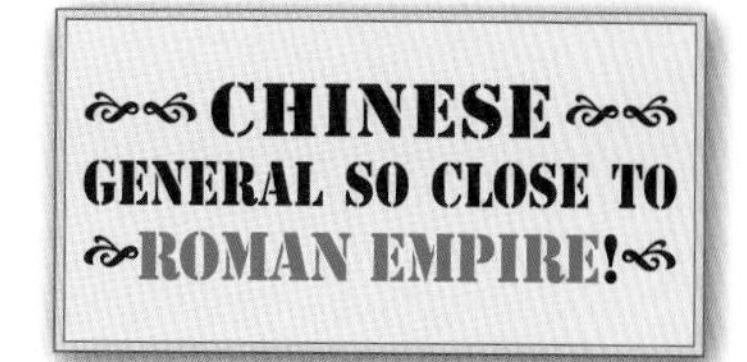

baozi

Bread rolls with savoury fillings eaten as a snack, usually for breakfast or for afternoon tea.

Cooking baozi, Suzhou

Bei Dao

Bei Dao was the penname of Chinese poet Zhao Zhenkai (born 1949). He is one of the most important of the so-called Misty (obscure) poets whose poetry takes obliquely imagist forms and was once officially denounced as obscure. In 1978 he and another poet Mang Ke founded *Jintian* (literally: today), an unofficial literary magazine, which became a cradle fostering the development of many young and talented Misty poets. The official criticism and controversy they aroused only made their work more appealing to young readers. *Jintian* lasted a brief two years before it was banned. Having developed a new language for poetry, Bei Dao, especially in his early works, engaged in veiled social criticism and a ceaseless quest for truth and love, struggling against the darkness of violence and lies. He was exiled in 1989 after the Tiananmen Square demonstrations where his famous poem *The Answer* was widely quoted. He continued to write in exile and taught at many institutions of higher learning. He has several times been nominated for the Nobel Prize in Literature.

Baseness is the secret knock of the base,
Integrity the epitaph of the noble,
Look how the gilded sky drifts full of
The inverted crooked reflections of the dead.

Beijing

Also known as Peking by some of the Western world, Beijing, situated in the northwestern part of China, is the political and cultural centre of the People's Republic of China. It has been the capital city for more than seven centuries. With Beijing's dialect being the standard form of Mandarin, it's considered as the best place to learn Chinese.

©iStockphoto.com/
Frank van den Bergh

Beijing traffic and neon lights. The sign tells the drivers not to set off fireworks in the city centre.

Beyond

Beyond, founded in 1983, was a unique Hong Kong rock band that made a niche for themselves in the Chinese musical industry with their creativity in melody and lyrics allied to their strong sense of social responsibility. Starting out as an underground band, they soon gained widespread popularity after some of their major songs were released (*Boundless Oceans Vast Skies*, *Glorious Years*, *Amani*). (Amani is Swahili for "peace" not a typo for a fashion designer). These songs, focusing on social issues, human rights and peace, stood out strongly in the Hong Kong music scene, where sugary sentimental love songs prevailed. The tragic death of lead vocalist Wong Ka Kui in 1993 was a tremendous loss to the band and to the Hong Kong music world. Beyond was disbanded in 2005 after their world tour. Now each member is pursuing his own career (Wong Ka Kui – lead vocals, guitar; Yip Sai Wing – vocals, drums; Wong Ka Keung – vocals, bass; Paul Wong Koon Chung – vocals, lead guitar).

Bing Xin

Bing Xin (1900-1999), whose real name is Xie Wanying, is a respected writer, poet and translator. Educated at Yanjing University in Beijing and at Wellesley College in the United States, she devoted her life to writing, education and cultural exchange. She contributed greatly to children's literature.

To my young readers, a collection of essays in the form of correspondence, is one of her most popular works. Her writing mostly expresses her inner feelings, praise of nature and motherhood and is characterized by a flowing, concise language which was later recognized as "Bing Xin Style". Her life spanned exactly one century, experiencing two world wars, the Chinese Civil War (1946-1950) and the havoc of the Cultural Revolution. Yet she always kept faith in beauty and truth as we can feel through all her works.

bird cage economy → ***Chen Yun***

Bo'ao Forum

The Bo'ao Forum for Asia is a non-governmental international organization designed as a high-level discussion platform for Asian and Australasian government officials, entrepreneurs and scholars. Its aims are to promote economic collaboration within and beyond Asia as well as to foster communication in important issues relating to economy, technology, society and the environment. It is headquartered at Bo'ao, a scenic coastal town in Hainan Province.

Bozhou → ***Anhui***

Bruce Lee

Bruce Lee (1940-1973), born in the United States and raised in Hong Kong, is regarded as one of the greatest masters of martial arts in the 20th century. He was also an actor and the founder of the combat form Jeet Kune Do. He made a great contribution to the improvement of modern fighting methods and to martial arts movies. The adoption of the word "kung fu" in English may be credited to his success in the movie industry. He died suddenly in 1973, leaving several books of his treatise on martial arts and his philosophy of Jeet Kune Do.

Budai → ***Laughing Buddha***

Buddha's Delight

Buddha's Delight (or luohan zhai) refers to the vegetarian dishes which are traditionally enjoyed by Buddhist monks. Since killing is strictly banned in Buddhism, monks and Buddhist disciples have to abstain from eating any kind of meat. In Chinese, luohan is synonymous with Buddha, while zhai means vegetarian food. The specific ingredients (as many as 35 different ingredients in the most elaborate recipes) used in Buddha's Delight usually vary tremendously from region to region. It tests the creativity of chefs. Quite a few specialities are made of doufu or tofu, which, with the right seasonings, can actually taste like meat.

Buddhism

Buddhism is one of the traditional religions of China, along with Taoism and Confucianism (which is strictly speaking an ethical system rather than a religion). Like all religions, Buddhism was distrusted and discouraged by the atheist Communist Party when it came to power in 1949. It remained popular, particularly with rural people, but it was attacked during the Cultural Revolution (1966-1976) as a feudal superstition and many temples and monasteries were closed down or even destroyed. In the post-Mao era, many temples have reopened and some are now training priests and nuns. New temples have also been built for the tourist trade. But the government remains ambivalent towards Buddhism. The Chinese Buddhist Association maintains ties with Buddhist communities abroad and there are showpiece monasteries like the one in the Lama Temple, Yonghegong in northeastern Beijing. If you visit temples like those in the Western or Fragrant Hills near Beijing, you will see offerings of coins, small denomination notes and sometimes fruit next to the Buddha's statue or in his outstretched hand.

Wen Shu Monastery in Chengdu – one of the four most sacred monasteries in China – Sichuan Province

Women practising a traditional fan dance on the Bund

Bund

The Bund, known in Chinese as Waitan (literally: the outer beach) is a famous and fashionable riverside area in Shanghai. It stretches for one mile along the bank of the Huangpu River and is lined with dozens of buildings of various (European) architectural styles such as Romanesque, Gothic, Baroque and Art Deco. Nowadays these buildings are mostly banks and luxury hotels and the area has some of the highest real estate prices in China. Known also as the Wall Street of the East, the Bund was formerly the Shanghai International Settlement where, from the late nineteenth century on, many foreign banks and trading companies operated. Today it is the most popular tourist destination in Shanghai. Couples will meet there to stroll along the riverside and take in the exotic atmosphere and beautiful river views.

Cai Lun

Cai Lun (?-121AD) was a eunuch during the Eastern Han Dynasty (25-220AD) who is generally remembered as the inventor of paper. In fact, the technology of papermaking already existed before his time, but it was Cai who significantly reformed the art of papermaking by adding new materials to the pulp. Cai's paper was thinner, stronger and cheaper so it could be mass-produced. The technique was introduced into Europe over a thousand years later in the 12th century. As one of the most important inventions in history, Cai Lun's work can be regarded as a turning point in the process of world civilization.

CHINESE PAPERMAKING TECHNOLOGY 1000 YEARS AHEAD OF THE WORLD!

Cai Qin → *Tsai Chin*

Cai Yuanpei

Cai Yuanpei (1868-1940) was a pioneering educator who served as Education Minister for the provisional national government when the Republic of China was founded in 1912. He was later chancellor of Beijing University. He introduced some aspects of Western education into China and promoted co-education for boys and girls. During his tenure at Beijing University, together with his colleagues – famous thinkers such as Chen Duxiu and Li Dazhao – he initiated the New Culture Movement, which exerted a profound influence on modern Chinese history. Today, in his hometown of Shaoxing, in Zhejiang Province, a middle school and a primary school have been named after him.

©iStockphoto.com/Yenwen Lu

The characters mean "living peacefully"

calligraphy

Calligraphy is one of the four basic skills of the Chinese literati, together with painting (hua), playing stringed musical instruments (qin) and board games (qi). Fundamentally, this art form can be divided into five categories: the seal script (zhuan shu), official script (li shu), regular script (kai shu), running script (xing shu) and cursive script (cao shu). Within each style there are various schools. To learn calligraphy, one has to know how to use the tools, namely a brush, paper, ink stick and ink stone, commonly referred to as the Four Treasures of the Study. Calligraphy manifests the basic characteristics of all Chinese art forms and its impact can be observed throughout the realm of art, from classical poetry to architecture. It is a mental exercise rather than a physical one, and requires harmonious coordination of the mind and body. It is relaxing yet highly disciplined for both physical and spiritual well-being. Most calligraphic artists live to a ripe old age.

Cang Wu Wang → *LIUSONG HOUFEI DI*

Cangjie

A legendary figure who is believed to be the inventor of Chinese characters. There is no solid evidence to determine when he actually lived. Some guess that Cangjie was the historian of the Yellow Emperor. Some thought Cangjie must have been a ancient wise man who standardized the characters that had already been in use. The Chinese computer input method, the Cangjie system, is named after him.

Cantonese

Cantonese, a major dialect of Chinese, is spoken by most people in Guangdong, Guangxi, Hong Kong, Macau and some overseas Chinese communities. Historically, Guangdong Province was called yue, so Cantonese is also known as yue yu (the language of yue). It is estimated that there are over 90 million people using Cantonese worldwide. Cantonese, like many other Chinese variants, has quite a different pronunciation from the standard Mandarin, and is usually unintelligible for people outside this linguistic community. While Mandarin has four tones, most scholars agree that Cantonese has nine.

Cantopop

Hong Kong pop music.

Cao Cao

A great statesman, military strategist and poet in the Three Kingdoms Period, Cao Cao (155-220AD) rose to power when he was appointed Chancellor of the Eastern Han Dynasty and made the Emperor Han Xiandi his political puppet. He built up his military forces in northern China and laid the foundations for what was to become the Kingdom of Wei, one of the three great kingdoms at the end of the Han. In the classic novel Romance of the Three Kingdoms, Cao Cao is depicted as a cruel and suspicious villain, an image so popular and widespread that it overshadowed the real Cao Cao, who, according to historical records, was an outstanding ruler and poet.

Cao Xueqin → *DREAM OF THE RED CHAMBER*

Cao Yu

Originally named Wan Jiabao, Cao Yu (1910-1996) is regarded as the most important Chinese playwright in the first half of the 20th century. His drama trilogy – *Thunderstorm*, *Sunrise* and *The Wilderness* – is a monument of Chinese theatre and secured his fundamental position in the history of modern Chinese drama. Applying modern Western play-writing skills to the creation of Chinese plays, Cao contributed greatly to the formation and maturity of the modern Chinese "spoken theatre" (hua ju).

century egg

The century egg, also known as the thousand-year egg, is made by a special process. Ducks' eggs are pasted with a mixture of lime, straw ash, salt and clay, and then preserved in air-tight pots for 15-30 days. Since the alkaline material in the paste reacts with the egg white and yolk, the yolk gradually turns into a dark-green creamlike substance with a distinctive odour while the white becomes a dark-brown transparent curd. Sometimes fine and irregular patterns like cypress branches (song hua) may appear on the surface of the white (a reason for another name for this food: Songhua egg). Just take off the shell and eat as an appetizer.

Chang'e, *a.k.a.* ***Heng'e***

A goddess in Chinese mythology, she lives on the moon. There are various stories about Chang'e and how she ended up living on the moon. The popular version is that she was a beautiful daughter of the emperor Ku in ancient times. She married Houyi, the great archer who was known for shooting down the nine suns out of the ten that had been scorching the earth. Houyi got the pill of immortality from the Queen Mother of the West. Chang'e stole the pill and swallowed it. Then she started to float up into the sky and finally landed on the moon. Legend says that she was not completely alone on the moon. She was accompanied by a jade rabbit who was constantly making herbal medicine, and the woodcutter Wu Gang who kept on cutting a cassia tree that would instantly grow back the minute he chopped it down. Chang'e is a familiar figure in traditional Chinese literature, generally connected with the beauty of the moon. She also symbolizes the painful isolation of women in their secluded, harem-like quarters.

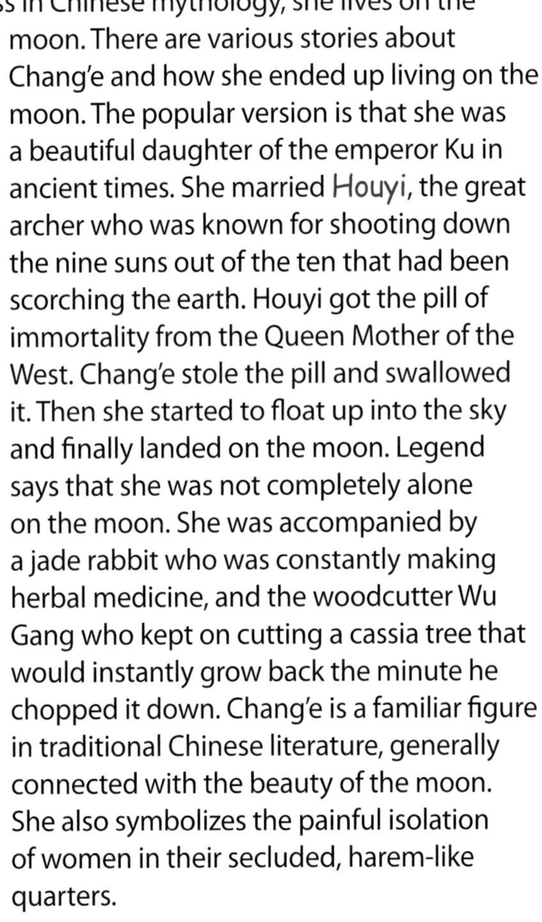

changshan → *HAN FU*

char siu

Char siu is a spiced, Cantonese honey roast pork, popular all over China. It can be eaten either by itself, or used as an ingredient for other dishes like noodle soups and fried rice. The meat, typically a shoulder of pork, is seasoned and skewered with long forks and placed in a covered oven or over a fire. The traditional cooking method uses metal S-hooks.

Chen Daoming

A famous actor known for his superb acting, intellectual temperament and modest personality. His performances in the TV series *The Last Emperor* (1984), *Fortress Besieged* (1990) and *Chinese Divorce* (2004) were acclaimed by both public and critics. He has won numerous awards in China, including the Best Actor for 2003 Golden Rooster Award, Best Actor for 1988 and 2002 Golden Eagle Award.

Chen Duxiu

An educator, philosopher and politician, Chen Duxiu (1879-1942) played various roles in Chinese history. He was one of the political leaders of the Xinhai Revolution in 1911, which led to the collapse of the Qing Dynasty. Along with other thinkers of the time, he initiated the New Culture Movement. The vernacular Chinese periodical *New Youth* that he set up became the base for advocating science and democracy. He was a co-founder of the Chinese Communist Party (CCP) in 1921 and worked as its first chairman and first General Secretary. Increasingly resentful of the influence of the Comintern over the Chinese Communists, he gravitated to the Trotskyist left and opposed many of the Comintern policies. This association caused him to be expelled from the CCP in 1929 and for the last years of his life he was unable to regain any influence in the party.

Chen Jingrun

A famous Chinese mathematician, Chen Jingrun (1933-96) graduated from the Mathematics Department of Xiamen University. Hua Lougeng, another prominent Chinese mathematician and Chen's mentor-to-be, invited him to become a member of the Chinese Academy of Sciences. Chen's most distinguished accomplishment lay in the field of number theory and the progress he achieved on Goldbach's conjecture. In the early 1980s he was set up as a role model by the government. Some thought him an eccentric who led a life of austerity to the exclusion of all interests bar mathematics. But he didn't care about this and consistently pursued his dream. In his later years, he suffered from Parkinson's disease and died in 1996.

Chen Kaige

Chen Kaige (born 1952), along with Tian Zhuangzhuang, Zhang Yimou and others, is one of the so-called Chinese fifth-generation directors whose films offer a profound reflection of China's national fate and fresh angles of storytelling. His most famous works are *Yellow Earth, The King of Children, Life on a String* and *Farewell My Concubine. Concubine*, the best-known to Western viewers, is an epic film spanning 50 years from the early part of the 20th century to the tumultuous Cultural Revolution. It won the 1993 Palme d'Or at the Cannes Film Festival. Chen excels in analyzing the influence and restrictions that history and tradition exert on people's minds and in depicting complex feelings. In 2002, Chen made his first English-language film, *Killing Me Softly*, a thriller featuring Hollywood stars Heather Graham and Joseph Fiennes. His attempt to be international was a failure. In recent years, he has returned to historical epics.

Chen Ning Franklin Yang → *YANG ZHENNING*

Chen Yun

Chen Yun (1905-1995) joined the Communist Party of China in 1925 and was actively involved in the development of the Chinese Communist movement until his death in 1995. From 1949 onwards he held senior posts within the Party and gradually entered the inner circle of top decision-makers. Known for his conservatism within the Chinese Communist Party,

Chen always persevered with his Marxist beliefs, though he advocated adjusting the economic system of rigid central planning and adopting a market-based system so as to allocate resources for economic development after the Cultural Revolution. Differing from Deng Xiaoping's reform concept of abandoning the planned economy and creating a market-orientated system, Chen Yun viewed planning as fundamental to socialism and the market only as a secondary means to assist the planned economy. He generalized his idea as the "bird cage economy": the bird (economic system) needs to fly and cannot be held down by a human hand; but it must be kept in a cage (state planning) otherwise it will fly away; the cage, however, needs to be adjusted to the right sort of size to allow the bird to fly. Chen's views were shared by some other senior members of the CCP, who together formed a counterbalance to Deng Xiaoping's socialist market economy reforms in the 1980s. From the 1990s onwards his influence waned.

BIRD CAGE ECONOMY

Cheng Long → *Jackie Chan*

Chengdu

The capital of Sichuan Province and the economic and cultural centre of China's southwestern region, Chengdu, on the fertile Chengdu Plain, has been the most populous and prosperous city in this region throughout China's long history. Often referred to as the "kingdom of heavenly residence", it is an industrial and transportation hub with a great many tourist attractions. Chengdu is also famous for its hot and spicy food that belongs to Sichuan cuisine, one of the most popular regional culinary styles in China.

An open-air restaurant in Chengdu

©iStockphoto.com/Sining Zhang

cheongsam → *QI PAO*

Chiang Kai-shek, *a.k.a.* ***Jiang Jieshi***

Chiang Kai-shek (1887-1975), known in Taiwan as Jiang Zhongzheng, was the former leader of the Kuomintang and President of the Republic of China. In his early years he trained at military academies both in China and Japan. He became a supporter of Sun Yat-sen, the leader of the republican revolution, in 1911. He served as the head of the Huangpu Military Academy in 1924, a position which helped him win support from the military élite in the future. After Sun's death in 1925 Chiang manoeuvered successfully and emerged as the new leader of the Kuomintang. He defeated the Communist army and forced the survivors to make their famous Long March, retreating to the northwest; Chiang eventually established a government in Nanjing. During the second Sino-Japanese War (1937-1945) his government lost control of the coastal regions and most of China's major cities. Chiang found himself forced to collaborate with Mao Zedong and his Communist guerrilla forces. As soon as the Japanese surrendered, the conflicts between the two parties became intense and civil war broke out in 1946. Chiang's army was defeated in 1949 and Chiang was forced to flee to Taiwan where he was president until his death in 1975.

September 1945, Chiang Kai-shek (left), Chairman of the Nationalist government, standing side by side with Communist leader Mao Zedong

©iStockphoto.com/Xin Zhu

Shanghai skyline at night – the Pudong district

China and its regional differences

Because all China is a single country, it is very easy to think of it as all one thing – one uniform, homogeneous country. This is very far from the truth, unsurprisingly, as China is larger than the whole of western Europe. In fact, where a person lives – whether north or south, east or west, in the town or in the countryside – has a profound influence on the life this person leads.

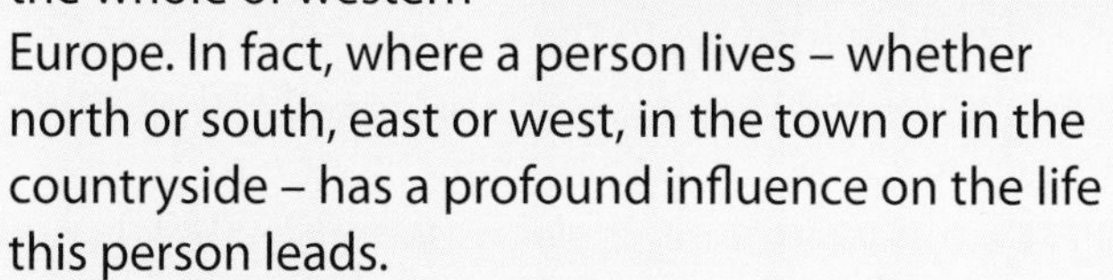

north and south

The climate of China's northernmost regions is Siberian, and the south is tropical, with a huge variety of climate in between. Even fundamental things like central heating depend on where you live – built-in central heating is expected in homes and offices north of the Yangtze river, but not to the south, even in places that can get quite cold in winter.

Different climates are home to different kinds of plants and animals, so the north-south divide also affects food. Northern Chinese cooking is wheat-based, and noodles, dumplings, flatbreads and pancakes are eaten much more than in the south, where the staple is rice.

These differences even extend to regional stereotypes – the most common image of the northern Chinese personality is bluff, open, honourable and occasionally rather naïve, whereas the stereotype of a southerner will be charming, glib and not entirely trustworthy.

east and west

There is also a strong east-west divide in China – which is not surprising as more than 3250 miles separate China's easternmost point from its westernmost point.

The most obvious difference is population density – some of the most densely populated cities in the world, including Shanghai, are to be found on China's east coast, whereas in parts of Tibet and the deserts of Xinjiang in the far west the population density is around three people per square mile, or even less. There is also a great difference in wealth between the economic powerhouses of the eastern coastal cities and the poorer, more backward west of the country. This has partly to do with ease of travel – there is a comprehensive network of roads and motorways in the more developed eastern regions, whereas many villages in some of the western parts, where travel tends to be difficult due to natural obstacles such as mountains or deserts, can be reached only by dirt tracks.

There is also far more ethnic diversity in the west of the country. Parts of these regions were occupied relatively late in China's history, and are still the home of the majority of China's fifty-one minority groups.

As China continues to develop economically, much of the west of the country has lagged behind. The Chinese government, concerned about this inequality, has put in place a series of policies to open up the economy of the western regions. These have had a certain success, but the gap is still great.

Zhangjiajie National Forest, Hunan Province

cities and countryside

©iStockphoto.com/George Clerk

Shanghai disappears into the smog

However, in China the biggest differences are often not between the different regions, but between the towns and countryside. Even allowing for regional differences, the standard of living in big cities is pretty much the same all over China – while some cities are richer than others, and urban poverty certainly does exist, the overall standard of living tends to be much higher in cities, and the gap is still growing.

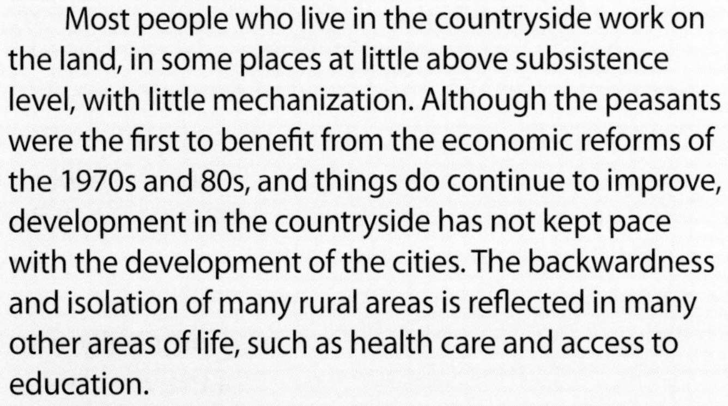

Most people who live in the countryside work on the land, in some places at little above subsistence level, with little mechanization. Although the peasants were the first to benefit from the economic reforms of the 1970s and 80s, and things do continue to improve, development in the countryside has not kept pace with the development of the cities. The backwardness and isolation of many rural areas is reflected in many other areas of life, such as health care and access to education.

The government is concerned about this situation and has put in place a variety of poverty alleviation measures such as abolition of the agricultural tax and a variety of subsidies.

A small village near Tingri in the Tibetan Highlands, with Mount Everest and Cho Oyu in the background

©iStockphoto.com/ Guenter Guni

China's sorrow → *photograph at Yellow River*

A name for the Yellow River, which often floods, wreaks havoc and claims lives. But the river is also known as "China's pride", since it brings water to irrigate the land and grow crops. In some years China's sorrow has failed to reach the sea.

Chinese Civil War

The Chinese Civil War, or the War of Liberation – a term used in Chinese Communist media – was a war between the Kuomintang (KMT) and Chinese Communist Party (CCP) which lasted from 1946 to 1950. The ideological clash between the KMT and CCP had started in 1927. When Chiang Kai-shek rose to power, he ended the KMT-CCP coalition and started to purge CCP members. The clash soon escalated to armed conflict. Chiang defeated the Communist armies and forced the survivors to start their famous Long March, retreating to the rural areas of the northwest. The war was temporarily interrupted by the Second Sino-Japanese War, when the two parties combined against the Japanese. But immediately after the Japanese surrender the power struggle intensified and full-scale civil war broke out in 1946. The CCP took over the mainland and established the People's Republic of China in October 1949. The KMT was forced to retreat to the island of Taiwan and proclaim Taipei as its temporary capital.

Chinese courtyards

Most urban Chinese used to live in siheyuan, which are formed by inward-facing houses on four sides, enclosed by walls. Such a residence offers space, comfort, quiet and privacy. The central courtyard would be planted with shrubs and flowers, thus becoming a garden. Children used to live with their parents even after they got married: the parents lived in the main house facing south and the children and their family lived in the side houses, while the unmarried daughters, or sometimes female servants would live in the rear building behind the main house.

The traditional Chinese courtyard house would have a brick screen just inside the main gate. This was to keep out evil spirits – who can only travel in a straight line. There was also a sill at the entrance, put there so that demons would stumble over it – although more mundane considerations might also have had a role to play in its use. The screen wall and doorsill also have a feng shui role – to prevent the wealth of the household from flowing away to the outside world.

From the size and style of a siheyuan you could tell whether it belonged to ordinary people or to a rich and powerful individual. The simple house of an ordinary person had only one courtyard whereas the mansion of a titled or very rich family would have two or more courtyards, one behind the other. The biggest courtyard in China is the Forbidden City.

©iStockphoto.com/William Perry

Chinese New Year decorations, Ditan Park, Beijing

Chinese New Year → ***SPRING FESTIVAL***

Chinese New Year's Eve

The Chinese New Year's Eve falls on the last day of the twelfth month in the Chinese Lunar Calendar. It is a day symbolizing the turning over of a new leaf and the birth of new hopes, as is universal in most cultures. In China it is an important occasion for family reunion. Dinner on New Year's Eve is the most precious quality time of the whole year for all family members to be together. Before the dinner, people may put spring couplets on the door and hold rituals of ancestor worship. There are usually fireworks and firecrackers, a custom dating back to ancient times when the purpose was to scare away the man-eating monster Nian. In mainland China, most families gather in front of the television in the evening to watch the Spring Festival Gala and stay up until midnight to greet the New Year. Celebrations of New Year's Eve vary from region to region, but the general mood is unmistakably jubilant.

Chinese Phoenix → ***FENGHUANG***

Chinese tunic suit → *ZHONGSHAN ZHUANG*

Ching Shih, *a.k.a.* ***Zheng Yi Sao***

Ching Shih (1785-1844) was a famous woman pirate during the Qing Dynasty. She worked as a prostitute on a floating brothel in Canton before marrying Zheng Yi, a pirate whose family had been in the pirating business for more than a century. The couple organized an alliance of Cantonese pirate forces and succeeded in putting together a formidable fleet of more than 1500 ships, known as the Red Flag Fleet. After Zheng Yi's death, Ching Shih worked her way up the pirate hierarchy to become the new leader. The Chinese government was unable to crush the fleet, an inability shared by both the Portuguese and the British. However, in 1810, Ching accepted an amnesty from the government and gave up her piratical career. Some historians say that she was the "best woman pirate who ever lived".

Chiung Yao

Born Chen Zhe in 1938, Chiung Yao is a commercially successful Taiwanese romantic novelist. Her autographical novel *Outside the Window* (1963) marked the beginning of her prolific writing career. She wrote over 60 books many of which were adapted for the screen and for TV series – massive hits in both Taiwan and mainland China. With unusual, fluctuating plots and poetic language, her sentimental love stories have attracted a large number of readers, mostly teenagers. Though her works don't carry much weight in terms of literary merit, her success is undoubtedly a miracle of the culture industry.

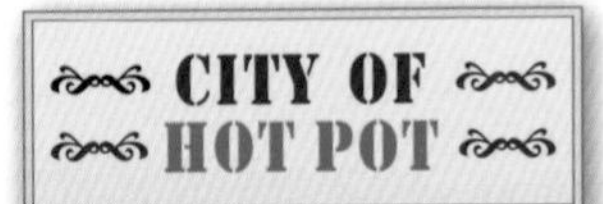

Chongqing

Chongqing once belonged to Sichuan Province and is now the largest of the four municipalities in China. Situated in the southwest on the upper reaches of the Yangtze River, Chongqing is known as the "mountainous city". It is a city rich in history and culture whose origin can be traced back over 3000 years. It was also the first inland trading port to open to foreigners in 1891. During the second Sino-Japanese War (1937-1945), Chongqing became the provisional capital of the Kuomintang's government and suffered bombing by the Japanese Air Force. Chongqing is famous for its Chuanju Opera which features the unique face changing performance. It is said that hot pot, the popular way of cooking and eating, originated in Chongqing, for which reason the city is also known as the "City of Hot Pot".

Chong Yang Festival

Chong Yang Festival, also known as the Double Ninth Festival, falls on the ninth day of the ninth month in the Chinese Lunar Calendar. The number 9 is considered auspicious in Chinese culture because it is the largest number and because it is pronounced jiu – a word which can also mean "longevity and eternity". A traditional activity on this day is to climb up into the mountains and drink chrysanthemum wine, which is, it should be said, not a strong drink at all, but rather something that is recommended by traditional Chinese medicine as a means of expelling cold from the body. Traditionally, the festival is also a day to observe the custom of caring for the elderly. But these days, especially in the big cities, the festival is losing its cultural significance.

Chow Yun-Fat → *photograph at Gong Li*

A talented and charismatic Chinese actor who has a large fan base in Asia and the West. Born into a poor family in 1955, he started out as a TV actor and owed his initial success and fame to a leading role in the hit series *The Bund*. Later he gravitated towards film acting. His successful collaboration with the famous action movie director John Woo propelled them both into the limelight of the "heroic bloodshed" genre. At the end of the 20th century he went to America seeking to enhance his career. After a few not-so-successful Hollywood movies, he returned to the Asian cinema circuit and starred in Ang Lee's martial arts epic *Crouching Tiger, Hidden Dragon*, which became an international success and won the Academy Award for Best Foreign Language Film. Ironically, Chow is mostly seen in Westerners' eyes as a cool gunslinger. His association with Woo, though fruitful, has practically obscured his ability in drama and comedy.

Christianity

Most scholars believe that Christianity first spread to China during the Tang Dynasty (618-907AD) when it was called Jing Jiao (Nestorianism). The next contact between China and Christianity probably took place during the Yuan Dynasty (1271-1368) when the Catholic Church sought an alliance with the Mongols against the Muslims who dominated Central Asia and Eastern Europe. From the late Ming Dynasty (1368-1644) onwards, major sects of Christianity gradually built up their influence in China with the arrival of more missionaries, such as Matteo Ricci the Italian Jesuit. The impact of Christianity can also be found in China's largest peasant uprising – The Taiping Rebellion. Their leaders borrowed some Christian ideas to incite the poor to revolt against the corrupt regime of the Qing Dynasty. The legality of Christianity was officially recognized after 1949 under the principle of "freedom of religion" and the guidance of the Communist government. In China, Christianity is generally understood by the public as a term referring to any of the Christian sects, Protestant or Catholic (the Chinese do not distinguish). The exact number of Christian believers is hard to estimate, but surveys conducted by some foreign agencies assert that followers might reach 50 million in China.

ci → *Su Shi*

Cixi → *Empress Dowager Cixi*

classical characters

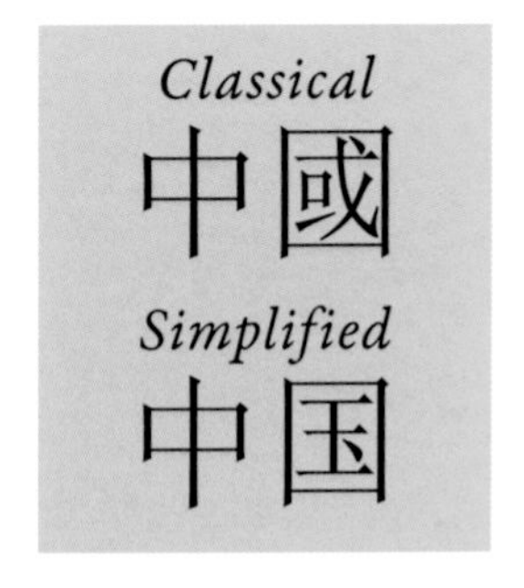

The Chinese for "China" written in both simplified and classical characters

Classical characters (or traditional characters) are the set of Chinese characters used in Taiwan, Hong Kong, Macau and many overseas Chinese communities. Compared with simplified characters, they may appear intricate and pedantic. However, there are those who think that the classical characters truly preserve the quintessence of Chinese tradition and should be honoured as the "standard" or "orthodox" Chinese characters. Such academic debates might well last for some time yet, but many Chinese regret the fact that the co-existence of two parallel writing systems causes some confusion to foreigners and is not helpful in promoting the Chinese language worldwide.

colours

©iStockphoto.com/Ma Liang

Red is traditionally associated with things Chinese. Red is used on festive occasions such as the Spring Festival and weddings. It symbolizes good fortune and happiness.

Yellow is historically viewed as the royal colour and was strictly used only by emperors since the Tang Dynasty. Yellow is also valued by Chinese Buddhism as representing the power of the spirit free from worldly cares. It has been used as the colour of temple architecture and Buddhist robes.

White is traditionally associated with death and will always be seen at funerals.

Black is also often used at funerals and since the 1950s people who have lost a relative wear a black armband at the funeral.

common cold

The Chinese have a slightly different attitude to the common cold. Rather than staying in bed, or bravely soldiering on, as Westerners tend to do, the Chinese see the common cold as a reason for a visit to the hospital.

Communist Revolution

The Communist Revolution, known in China as the Liberation War, refers to the final phase of the Chinese Civil War (1946-1950) when the Communist Party emerged victorious after defeating the Kuomintang and established the People's Republic of China on 1st October 1949 under the leadership of Mao Zedong.

Communist Youth League

This is the junior branch of the Communist Party. Members are aged 14-28. Membership of the Youth League is not compulsory, but most students do join because it is considered an honour and because most of their classmates are members.

There is a variety of social activities connected with the Youth League – such as decorating the dedicated spaces at the back of each classroom with inspiring messages, collecting money to help disaster victims and the occasional outing or trip. At university, most members of the Students' Union tend to be active Youth League members. However, equally important is the way in which the Youth League acts as a link between the members of a school class and the school's Party leadership.

Membership of the Youth League is also an essential first step to full membership of the Communist Party. However, the majority of Youth League members never make this step, as it is not easy to become a Party member, and not everyone wants to be one. Youth League membership lapses automatically at the age of 28.

comrade → *NAMES*

concubine → *MARRIAGE*

Confucianism

Confucianism, the cornerstone of traditional Chinese culture, is more a system of social and ethical philosophy than a religion. Created by Confucius, it was built on an ancient religious foundation to establish the social values, institutions and ideals of traditional Chinese society. It focuses on the importance of adhering to tradition in matters concerning etiquette and ritual and aims at the moral cultivation of human beings. Emperor Wudi of the Han Dynasty declared it the "state religion", and it has remained such through the history of imperial China, dominating people's minds for over 2000 years. Unlike major religions such as Christianity or Islam, Confucianism does not have an independent religious institution. Neither does it involve the worship of a deity. Combining aspects of politics and ethics, it values ancestor worship, filial piety, loyalty, benevolent government and faithfulness to the monarch. A new school called Neo-Confucianism, combining Taoist and Buddhist ideas with existing Confucian doctrine, emerged in the Song Dynasty, which gave this learning system renewed vigour. In modern times, Confucianism was attacked by the New Culture Movement from 1915 under the banner of science and democracy. During the Cultural Revolution it once again came under attack. Today people see signs of a revival of Confucianism in mainland China. Books and lectures concerning Confucian classics are becoming popular. People tend to turn to those ancient classics of wisdom to find ways of relieving the pressure and perplexity of modern society. Outside China, Confucianism also exerts a strong influence in other East Asian countries, such as Japan, Korea and Singapore.

Confucius, *a.k.a.* ***Kong Qiu or Kong Zhongni***

Known to his disciples by the honorific term Kong Fuzi (Master Kong), Confucius (551-479BC) was a great thinker and educator who lived during the Spring and Autumn Period (770-476BC). His ideas made up the essence of traditional Chinese ideology. Despite having a generally frustrating political career – his one notable achievement was being appointed Justice Minister of the State of Lu for a couple of years – he achieved far greater things working as a teacher and philosopher. His teachings were revolutionary in many ways. For instance, he claimed to "educate all despite their social status", in stark contrast to the then prevailing tradition that only the aristocracy should enjoy the privilege of education. The goal of his teachings is to create "gentlemen" who behave with grace, stand up for righteousness and demonstrate integrity in all things. Confucius' teachings demonstrate little of a religious character. Though maintaining the significance of performing traditional rites and sacrifices, he suggests it is wise "to keep distance from the gods and spirits" or "if you are not able even to serve man, how can you serve the spirits?" He is said to have had three thousand disciples, seventy-two of whom developed his thoughts into a system of philosophy known as Confucianism. The collection of his sayings The Analects has now existed for almost 2500 years and still impresses its readers with the wisdom of this remarkable man.

Statue of Confucius in the Confucius Temple, Suzhou

Confucius Institutes

Confucius Institutes are not-for-profit educational institutes, platforms for cultural communication and exchange, aiming specifically to promote the teaching of the Chinese language and of Chinese culture around the world. The first Confucius Institute opened in 2004 in Seoul, Korea. By 2010 the Chinese plan to have 500 Confucius Institutes all over the world.

congee

As an everyday meal, congee has many regional variations in China. It can be made from rice or other types of grain, such as cornmeal, millet or barley, and has a porridge-like consistency. Multigrain congee mixes are sold in the health food sections in supermarkets. Congee is also considered to act as a natural remedy and is used as a medicine, especially in southern China.

A special type of sweet congee with eight different kinds of grains and nuts, called ba bao zhou (literally: 8 treasure porridge), is traditionally eaten on the eighth day of the twelfth month. This custom has a long history and goes back over 1000 years. Legend has it that Buddha achieved Nirvana on this day. Buddhists would serve ba bao zhou in the temples in commemoration and emperors would instruct ba bao zhou to be given out to the people.

Congee Festival → *LABA FESTIVAL*

courtesy names

According to ancient Chinese tradition, when a person (usually a man) reached his twentieth year he would be given a courtesy name to be used as form of address by his peers and colleagues in order to gain respect and to show obedience to the social hierarchy. His true given name would only be used by his elders or by very good friends.

Besides the given name and courtesy name that were chosen by the elders, some ancient Chinese – especially educated people and the literati – also chose for themselves another name, the pseudonym.

Let's take the famous poet and scholar, Su Shi, also known by his courtesy name Zizhan. The courtesy name was used among friends. His pseudonym, Dongpo Jushi (and people might have more than one pseudonym) was used for his writings. His official name, Su Shi, was used in official contexts, on official documents etc. However, to complicate matters further, he is often referred to by a combination of these names: Su Dongpo!

The practice of using courtesy names has faded away since the **May Fourth Movement** in 1919, and it is seldom seen in modern Chinese society except among some artists who still persist with this cultural tradition.

Cowherd and Weaver Girl → *Qi Xi*

C-pop → Cantopop

cricket fighting

Cricket fighting has a long tradition going back over a thousand years. Enthusiasts can go to the marketplace to buy their crickets and there are books and DVDs on cricket keeping and cricket pedigrees. In Beijing, the Association for Cricket Fighting is responsible for organizing cricket fighting events.

crosstalk

A comedy technique involving two comedians, one of whom talks with the other being the stooge. The art form goes back centuries but is still popular.

Cui Jian

Known as the Father of Chinese Rock'n'Roll, Cui Jian is a skilled trumpet player, guitarist and composer from northern China. Growing up in Beijing, he started his musical career at the age of 14. In the early 1980s he set up his first rock band and explored new musical styles with each album he produced. His hit song *I Have Nothing* became the anthem of the famous Tiananmen Square protests of 1989, and incurred the

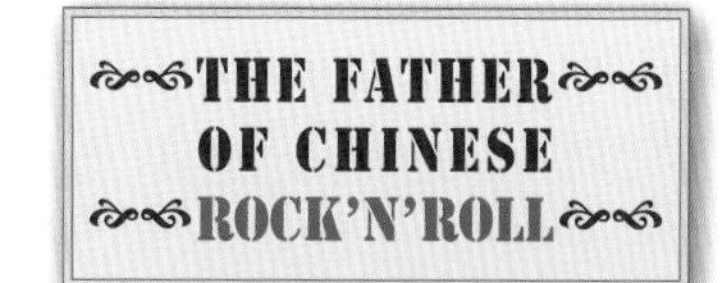

Cui Jian performs at his concert on June 3, 2005 in Wuhan, Hubei Province

©China Photos/Getty Images

government's disapproval. Not long after, he began his first tour "Rock'n'Roll on the New Long March" during which he performed the song *A Piece of Red Cloth* with a red cloth wrapped around his eyes. Such an obvious political gesture quickly caused the tour to be stopped by the Chinese authorities. He didn't appear again in large-venue performances until the new millennium. Today, though he still does the occasional gig, he keeps a low profile and is not well-known to younger audiences.

Cultural Revolution

The Cultural Revolution was a massive political and social upheaval affecting all levels of Chinese society from 1966 to 1976. It was put in motion by Mao Zedong, Chairman of the Chinese Communist Party, who aimed to identify political opponents and remove them from his revolutionary new China and so strengthen the power of the Communist Party. It is widely recognized (including by the Chinese themselves) as the most turbulent and disastrous period in China's history since the foundation of the People's Republic of China in 1949. It is called the "ten-year catastrophe". During the Cultural Revolution, millions of people died, were persecuted or imprisoned. People from all walks of life, from high-ranking officials to the ordinary man on the street, but especially intellectuals, teachers, writers and artists or people who had contacts with foreign countries. Long lines of the so-called "oxes, ghost snakes and spirits", mostly intellectuals being persecuted and forced to wear tall white pointed hats, were paraded through the streets.

One of the underlying causes of the movement was a fear of Western ideologies and other ideas different from Communist thought. Even talking about ideas like free enterprise or freedom of the press were activities likely to land you in a labour camp, if you should be overheard by a Red Guard.

Another of the aims of the Cultural Revolution was to do away with Confucianism and anything related to Confucianism, such as historical antiques and books. People were not allowed to wear qi pao (traditional Chinese-style clothes) or Western-style clothes which were thought of as a symbolic image of feudalism and capitalism.

A description of the personal impact of the Cultural Revolution:

"My uncle was the principal of a senior school. He was forced to stop teaching. He was humiliated, he had to stand wearing a big hat, his head bowed, writing all the time about what he had done wrong. He was isolated in a single room in the cold winter with little food and no heating. After that he was half dead, he could never work again."

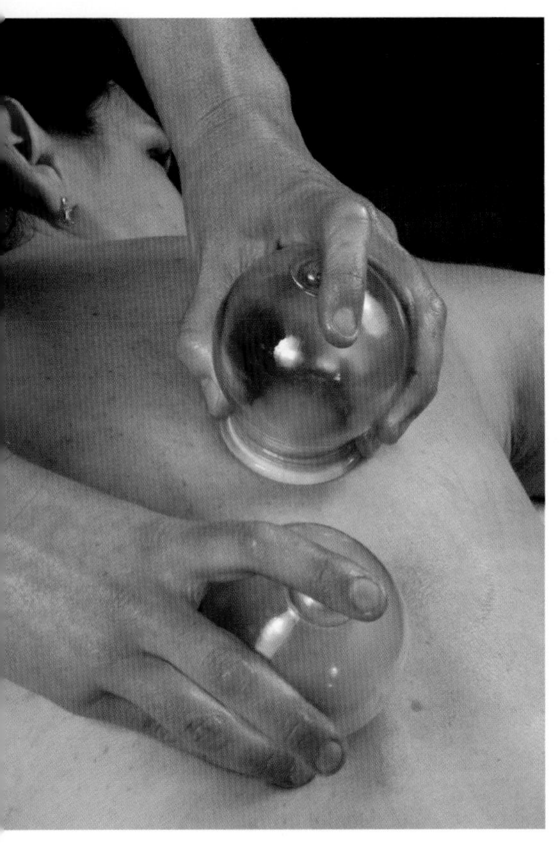

cupping

As a means of physical treatment, cupping (or ba guan) has been around for a long time in China and remains very much in use today. It involves placing glass, pottery or bamboo cups on the skin with a vacuum beneath. The therapy is used to relieve what is called "stagnation" in traditional Chinese medicine, that is ailments such as rheumatism, bronchitis, headaches, dizzy spells and the common cold. Cupping can be done by the individual at home or it can be done professionally by a special masseur in a special cupping clinic.

Da Yu, *a.k.a.* ***Yu the Great***

A mythical figure who is said to have controlled and channelled China's watercourses and relieved a great flood. According to legend, he was the son of Gun who was appointed by King Yao in ancient times to control the great deluge. Gun was either executed or demoted because of his failure, and his son was recruited by the next ruler, King Shun, to carry on the project. Yu dredged the rivers and created outlets through which the water could drain away and be used to irrigate farmlands. His feat was such that King Shun passed the throne to Yu instead of his own son. Yu thereafter founded the first recorded Chinese dynasty, Xia (probably c.2100-c.1600BC).

Dai

The Dai live mostly in the frontier regions in the south of Yunnan Province. In terms of culture, they are closely related to the people of the nearby countries – Laos, Burma and Thailand. They have developed their own written language, calendar, medicine and operas over thousands of years. Most Dai people believe in Hinayana, the more conservative and orthodox school of Buddhism. The Water Splashing Festival, similar to that in Thailand, is their most important festival, celebrating New Year according to the Dai Calendar. People, both adults and kids, go out into the street and throw buckets of water over each other.

Daji → *HULI JING*

Dalai Lama

This supreme spiritual leader of Tibetan Buddhism is widely believed by Tibetans to be the living incarnation of Buddha. The dominant sect of Tibetan Buddhism, also known as Dge-lugs-pa (Yellow Hat), was founded in the 14th century, and one of its chief leaders at Lhasa (another leader Panchen Lama has his seat at Rikaze) received the title of Dalai Lama from Altan Khan in the 16th century. It is believed that when the incumbent Dalai Lama dies his soul enters into a new-born baby and a host of elaborate and precise instructions (divine signs) must be followed before a successor can be identified. The present 14th Dalai Lama came to the throne in 1940 at the tender age of 5. He fled into exile in 1959 after a separatist conspiracy against the Chinese central government failed. The Chinese government sees the Dalai Lama as a political dissident who is largely responsible for the disturbances in Tibet and strongly objected to his being awarded the 1989 Nobel Peace Prize. In spite of this, efforts have never ceased to persuade him to return to reunite his people under the guidance of the Chinese government.

Dalian

A coastal city and major port at the end of the Liaodong Peninsula. From the early 1900s, it was occupied by the Japanese for nearly half a century. Nowadays Dalian has developed into an important industrial centre. It is also an attractive summer resort for many Chinese. Dalian is known as "The City of Football", its local football clubs having won eight national championships. The city is also a fashion and design centre in China and hosts the annual Dalian International Fashion Festival.

Dao Lang

A pop singer (1971-), originally called Luo Lin, Dao Lang owes his sudden rise to fame to his hit album *The First Snows of 2002*. He integrated into his music many elements of Uygur folk songs and performed modern adaptations of some famous old songs.

Daoism → *Taoism*

Daoji, *a.k.a.* ***Ji Gong***

Daoji (1130-1209), commonly known as Ji Gong (Master Ji), was a Buddhist monk at the Ling Yin Temple near Hangzhou during the Southern Song Dynasty (1127-1279). Legend says that he was a kindly mad monk with magical powers, always ready to help the common people, though he appeared to act in bizarre ways. Unlike traditional Buddhist monks, he ate meat and drank wine. Soon he was kicked out of the monastery for constantly breaking the rules of Buddhism. Daoji wandered around the country and helped people whenever he could. After his death he was honoured as a popular deity.

death

The Chinese view of death reflects the influence of Taoism, Buddhism and Confucianism. Traditionally, the Chinese attach great importance to the enjoyment of a simple earthly life. As Confucius said, "how can we know death if we don't know life". Death, like the changing of the seasons, is natural and inevitable, and so neither is it something to be feared nor should it cause feelings of pity. If a person dies naturally at an age of over 80, his funeral will be called xisang (a happy funeral). His family is not supposed to show grief and the funeral can be as boisterous as a wedding, with a band playing and people holding big outdoor banquets.

AS CONFUCIUS SAID, "HOW CAN WE KNOW DEATH IF WE DON'T KNOW LIFE"

Buddhists believe in an afterworld, but their afterworld is not characterized by an absolute dichotomy between Heaven and Hell, as in Christianity. Rather they view death as a liberation from all the pains of this earthly world and as a necessary preparation for rebirth.

PAPER MODELS OF HOUSEHOLD ITEMS ARE BURNT AT THE FUNERAL

In Taoism, people seem not to care about death; Taoist disciples are believed to be able to achieve immortality by developing their spiritual side.

Chinese people hold the dead in great reverence. They are meticulous in choosing a burial ground and will use a feng shui expert to help them choose the most auspicious location and layout. In times past, delicate household items, furniture and treasures used to be buried with the dead to ensure that they could still enjoy the afterlife. Nowadays cremation has become compulsory. So the Chinese have found another way of giving the dear departed a gift of objects from the material world which they are leaving: paper models of household items are burnt at the funeral or at the graveside. The mourners will set fire to paper televisions, paper chairs or paper kitchen tables. Most of the commoner paper models can be bought from special stores. Special requests for more elaborate goods to take to the afterlife, like houses or cars, take a bit longer and will have to be ordered in advance.

Deng Lijun

THE QUEEN OF CHINESE POP NEVER PERFORMED LIVE IN MAINLAND CHINA

Deng Lijun (1953-1995) had a voice that was pure and natural. In the 1980s and 90s she was, without any doubt, the queen of Chinese pop, but never actually performed live in mainland China. Out of 40 albums, 30 are platinum. Her songs are well-known in Asia and in Chinese communities all over the world. Lots of them are still firm favourites in karaoke bars. As well as being a talented singer, Deng could speak 6 languages and 3 Chinese dialects. She never married. For a time she had a relationship with Jackie Chan. She once got engaged to a man from a rich family, but broke it off because her future parents-in-law disapproved of her occupation as a singer and insisted on her abandoning her singing career to become a housewife. It took her a few years to recover. So immense was her popularity in China when pop music was new that it was said that Deng Xiaoping ruled by day, but when night came it was the other Deng who took over.

DENG XIAOPING RULES BY DAY, AT NIGHT THE OTHER DENG TAKES OVER

Deng Xiaoping

Deng Xiaoping (1904-1997) was a supreme leader and China's most prominent statesman when Mao Zedong's predominance waned. He is regarded as the chief designer of China's political and economic reforms which were launched in the 1980s. As one of the founders of the People's Republic of China, Deng's military career was no less glorious although he declined the honour of being made a Marshal. In the 1950s, he was appointed the Vice-Premier and General Secretary of the CCP (Chinese Communist Party). In the following years Deng and Liu Shaoqi tried to implement a series of mild, pragmatic reforms to stabilize China's economy. Maoist fanatics accused him of taking a "capitalist road". Subsequently he was purged and dismissed from all positions. In 1974, with the help of Zhou Enlai, he was restored to the vice-premiership. However, after Zhou's death in 1976, he was again ousted by the radical leftist group later referred to as the Gang of Four. His second rehabilitation took place one year later when the Gang of Four was crushed by Hua Guofeng and Ye Jianying. In the following years, he consolidated his authority in the CCP with the help of his followers Hu Yaobang (General Secretary of the CCP) and Zhao Ziyang (Premier). As de facto leader in the post-Mao era he initiated the massive-scale reforms which changed many aspects of China's social and economic life and paved the way for China's rapid rise as a great power in the new millennium. The strongest criticism against Deng might come from his iron-fisted handling of the political disturbances in 1989. When Jiang Zemin succeeded Zhao Ziyang as the General Secretary of the CCP, he gradually resigned from all his positions, a symbolic transfer of power to the new leadership. Deng died on the 9th February 1997, six months before the return of Hong Kong to China, which came about under his innovative One Country Two Systems guideline.

Mourners pay their last respects to China's Deng Xiaoping in Tiananmen Square, displaying his portrait during the funeral service in the Great Hall of the People

©iStockphoto.com/Hywit Dimyadi

dim sum

Dim sum is a Cantonese term for a variety of Chinese pastry or snack, usually eaten at breakfast or as refreshments. In most Chinese restaurants dim sum is shown on the menu as a snack or dessert, although there are some restaurants that make a feature of dim sum and do not offer other dishes.

Ding Junhui

A promising Chinese snooker player, Ding (born 1987) became a household name after the 2005 China Open in Beijing, when he astounded the snooker world by defeating then world No. 3 Stephen Hendry. Ding is the second youngest player ever to win a ranking title. He was soon called "Snooker Prodigy", and became a new sports star in China.

Dizang

Dizang or Dizang Pusa, a Bodhisattva in Chinese Buddhism, is second in popularity only to Guanyin. He is widely worshipped for his resolution to save all living beings in hell and liberate them from suffering before he himself achieves Buddhahood. Legend says that Dizang was reincarnated as the former Korean prince Jin Qiao Jue (696-794AD) who came to China to study Buddhism during the Tang Dynasty. He chose Jiuhua Mountain in Anhui Province as the place to go to endure austerity and attain enlightenment. He had a temple built there. He passed away at the age of 99. His body was kept in a big jar, which was opened three years later only to reveal him still well-preserved and without any sign of decomposition. People believe that Jiuhua Mountain is the sacred seat of Dizang. Along with Putuo Mountain, Wutai Mountain and E'mei Mountain, it is known as one of the great four mountains of Buddhism in China, which attract millions of pilgrims.

Dou E Yuan *or* The Injustice to Dou E

A famous play written by the playwright Guan Hanqing in the Yuan Dynasty (1271-1368). The story tells of a girl Dou E whose father sold her to Cai to be his wife since he needed money to enter the Imperial Civil Examination. Two years later her husband died. A local bully, Zhang Lu'er, resentful at Dou E's rejection of his marriage proposal, accused her of murdering his father. Dou E was sentenced to death by beheading. On the execution site she swore her innocence and asked for three signs from heaven to prove her innocence: 1. blood splashing onto a white scarf instead of to the ground; 2. snow in the middle of summer; 3. a drought for three years. All of these did occur. After three years of drought, Dou's father, then a government official, re-inspected the case as his daughter's ghost had revealed the truth to him. And the real murderer was brought to justice.

Dou Wei

A rock musician born in Beijing in 1969, he began with a rock band Hei Bao (Black Panther). As the lead vocalist, he is remembered for the hit songs *Ashamed* and *Don't Break My Heart*. When Hei Bao was disbanded, Dou pursued his own musical career in composition and producing. He has now faded from the limelight, sometimes even working in a local bar to make a living. But he has never stopped experimenting with new musical styles. His music tends to be obscure and mystical and focuses more on expressing inner feelings.

Double Ninth Festival → *Chong Yang Festival*

doufu, *a.k.a.* ***tofu***

Doufu, or literally bean curd, is made from soy milk. It is rich in protein. To make doufu, the soy milk is first coagulated in a process a bit like the production of cheese from milk. Then the coagulated curd is cut into small cubes. Doufu is whitish, almost tasteless and scentless and can be cooked in various ways: stewed, boiled, fried or eaten raw with seasonings.

There is a huge variety of doufu products to be found in China – soft doufu, stinky tofu, fermented doufu and many interesting regional doufu variants.

dough flowers

Dough flowers, or mianren (dough people) or miansu (dough sculptures) are sweet to the taste and a work of art to look at. The dough is sometimes mixed with glutinous rice for extra stickiness. They are normally made in the shapes of flowers, fruits, small animals or people. The most common dough flowers are in the shape of a peach – a symbol of longevity – and are served up at older people's birthdays. They can often be seen in New Year Pictures or on top of birthday cakes.

dragon

The dragon is a sacred creature in Chinese culture, symbolizing power (not evil, as in the West). So Chinese often consider themselves "the descendants of the dragon". Chinese emperors thought they were real dragons and the sons of Heaven. Dragons – in various forms – can be seen everywhere in the imperial palace. Traditionally, dragons are also held to be the forces governing water and weather. The kings of the dragons live in dragon palaces under the ocean and they have the power to decide where and when rain should fall. The dragon also plays an important role in Chinese Festivals. Festivities often involve dragon dancing – dancing with dragon puppets accompanied by drums and music. At the Dragon Boat Festival, the biggest celebration is dragon boat racing, which is now becoming a popular international event.

Dragon statue in the Summer Palace

Dragon Boat Festival

The Dragon Boat Festival, which falls on the fifth day of the fifth month in the Chinese Lunar Calendar, can be a lively and thrilling spectacle when thousands of people line up along the waterway, cheering and screaming for the rowing team they support. As to the origin of the Dragon Boat Festival, it is generally thought that the festival is to commemorate the great poet Qu Yuan (c.339-279BC) who, exiled and disillusioned, drowned himself in the Miluo River on the fifth day of the fifth month. Local people are said to have gone out in boats to retrieve his body – the origin of boat racing. They also threw packets of rice into the water for the fish to eat instead of gnawing away at his body – from this comes

Dragon boats on Daming Lake, Jinan

the other traditional practice – eating zongzi at the Dragon Boat Festival. Another activity commonly found in the past was to drink xiong huang jiu (realgar wine) to ward off disease or exorcize evil. It was not until 2007 that the Dragon Boat Festival was made an official public holiday.

Dream of the Red Chamber, *a.k.a.* ***The Story of the Stone***

A masterpiece of Chinese fiction written by Cao Xueqin who lived in the mid 18th century during the Qing Dynasty. It is usually listed as one of the Chinese Four Great Classical Novels (the other three being Romance of the Three Kingdoms, Water Margin, Journey to the West). The book, with detailed and precise depiction, allows the reader to enter the world of an aristocratic family in 18th century China that is believed to mirror the author's own life. The story begins with a stone in Heaven that wishes to spend time on earth to learn human emotions. It turns into a jade amulet falling into the hands of the spoiled youngest son of a rich and powerful Mandarin family, the Jias. Following him, along with some thirty main characters and over four hundred minor ones, we witness the fall of the Jias from the height of power and wealth to financial and moral ruin. The author also reveals the harem-like existence of women in old China, the hierarchies among female family members, their pleasures, silly squabbles, intrigues and tragedies. *The Dream* can be read on many levels: a love story, a social history, a philosophical reflection on human existence, or the literary treasure of Chinese classical artistic forms.

du dou

The du dou, which translates literally as "tummy cover", is a type of ancient Chinese female underwear garment equivalent to a bra. It's made of a piece of silk usually edged with brocade and with ribbons that tie around the neck and back. Women wore it through many dynasties and it became very popular in the Ming and Qing Dynasties. Nowadays it's in vogue for young girls to wear the du dou with no outer layers. It has also inspired some fashion designers in their exotic oriental summer collections.

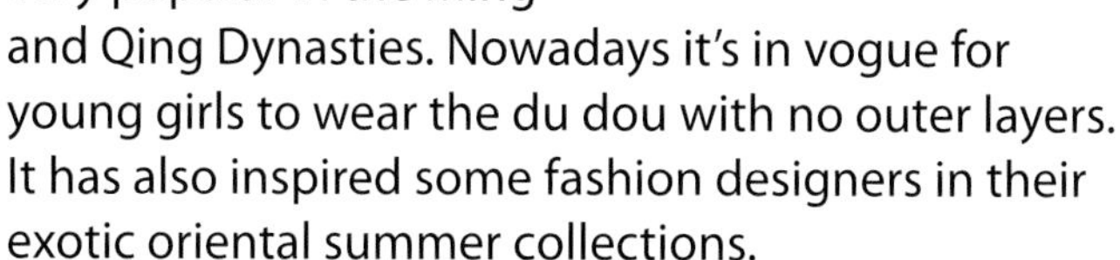

Nowadays, however, the du dou is more commonly a type of loose underwear top for babies.

Du Fu

A great poet in the Tang Dynasty, Du Fu (712-770AD) lived through the Anshi Rebellion, witnessing the collapse of China to a state of disastrous turmoil. The strong sense of history that permeates his work has led to his being known as the Poetic Historian. Like his country, Du Fu himself suffered from poverty and unrest during the last fifteen years of his life. His work is very diverse, but his most prominent poems are those about the war and its impact on his own life. In his *Advent of Spring*, he wrote:

The city has fallen: only the hills and rivers remain.
In Spring the streets were green with grass and trees.
Sorrowing over the times, the flowers are weeping.
The birds startled my heart in fear of departing.

dual-track pricing

This was a system introduced on the basis of an idea of Professor Zhang Weiying. It enabled the continuation of a system under which prices were set by the government in tandem with a system which allowed the market to determine prices. During the late 1980s both systems were in force, with market-controlled prices gradually coming to the fore. A pragmatic and realistic approach to an issue which other countries all too often see as an either/or.

Dunhuang

A historical city in Gansu Province famous for being the hub of the central and eastern silk routes in ancient times. With the flourishing trade along the Silk Road, Dunhuang had become one of the important centres for cultural exchanges between West and East. The art treasures kept in the Mogao Caves in Dunhuang are a reminder of its former glory. Mogao, also known as the Caves of the Thousand Buddhas, contains some of the best Buddhist art in China, notable for the artistic frescos. At the beginning of the 20th century, the Taoist Abbot Wang discovered in one of the caves a large quantity of Buddhist manuscripts on which the learning of Dunhuang Studies was based.

The Mogao Caves, Dunhuang

eating

The Chinese mostly eat with chopsticks, for the use of which there is no general etiquette. It is normal for people sitting around a table to eat all out of the same central dish using their own chopsticks. Don't be surprised if people spit bones out onto the table. China is rightly famous for its eight major cuisines. But there are some other dishes which might be less appetizing to the Westerner. Snakes, worms and dogs may appear on the menu, and cats are also eaten. Human placenta is considered a special food which is generally good for the health, although it is not that easy to come by and you will need a good relationship with hospital staff if you want to get hold of some.

> HUMAN PLACENTA IS CONSIDERED A SPECIAL FOOD WHICH IS GENERALLY GOOD FOR THE HEALTH

education

All Chinese children are required by law to attend school from the first year of primary school, which they start at six or seven, to the final year of junior middle school (14-15). Compulsory education is supposed to be free, although in practice a lot of the "better" schools charge for their services, and the final bill can be considerable, especially in private schools.

In China's history, as now, education was seen as the best way to get on in life, and parents are generally very supportive of education, in a way that most Western parents would not consider – it is not uncommon for extended families to take on considerable debts in order to see one family member through university.

©EIGHTFISH/Getty Images

primary school

Primary school begins at the age of 6-7. Classes are large with usually 40-50 pupils to a class. Because of large class sizes, discipline can seem very strict. The Chinese writing system requires that each character be memorized individually, so there is a lot of rote learning from an early age. However, there are also opportunities for singing, dancing and volunteer work after class. This can take the form of street sweeping, helping the elderly or planting trees as well as jobs in the school, like tidying up the classroom. Children in primary school begin each day (usually at 8.00 or 8.30) with morning exercises to music, and again at break, when they also do facial massage to protect their eyesight. From an early age, Chinese schoolchildren elect class leaders, who are in charge of organizing the collection of homework and class activities of various sorts. School usually ends between 3.30 and 4.30. From the third year of primary school, students join the Young Pioneers, who can be easily recognized by a red scarf round the neck.

junior middle school

Students attend junior middle school from the ages of 12 to around 15. The curriculum is much the same as at a Western secondary school, with the exception of politics, which is compulsory. The average class size is about 50, although in overcrowded schools or where there are not enough teachers, numbers can be much greater. There are not many after-school clubs or hobby-related activities, but students are expected to take part in "Evening Study", where they do their homework under the supervision of a teacher. A lot of emphasis is placed on voluntary work and helping others – students regularly have days off school to plant trees and do volunteer work. Some students will join the Communist Youth League while in junior middle school – most of the rest will join when they reach senior school.

Attendance at junior middle school is compulsory, although some places enforce this rule more rigorously than others.

After junior middle school, students can either leave school to find work, or continue their studies in either vocational or senior middle school.

senior middle school

Unlike students in vocational schools, who are being trained for a particular trade or profession, the main goal of senior middle school students is to pass the gaokao examinations to gain university entrance. Pressure is intense in these three years of senior school, especially in the third year. Classes begin early (often 7.30), finish late (between 5.00 and 6.00) and there are often supplementary classes for weaker or more ambitious students. This "late individual study" is organized by the school for senior middle school students to continue their schoolwork in the evenings after their evening meal.

All senior school students study the same subjects for the first year, but in the second year they are split into two groups, one with a greater emphasis on sciences, the other on arts subjects. Chinese, maths, English and politics are compulsory for both groups.

Many students find their time in senior school very tough, many have to go short on sleep to get all their schoolwork done, but most consider the sacrifice worthwhile if they can make it onto a university course. In 2006 roughly 23% of students got into university, with more going on to further education, and others retaking their final year of senior school in the hope of doing better next year.

tertiary education

The most common form of this is the university, but a variety of high-level vocational schools also exist, such as teachers' colleges.

> **FAMILY WILLINGLY PLUNGES INTO HUGE DEBT TO FUND EDUCATION**

Fees vary from university to university, but few are really cheap. Agricultural, teacher training and military universities do not usually charge a fee, and are a popular choice among students from poorer backgrounds. Financial help is available for less well-off students in the form of bursaries or loans, though many students also supplement their income through part-time work.

Student dormitories are cramped, with between three and twelve people sharing a room, sleeping in bunk beds. Some students who crave privacy or quiet choose to rent accommodation outside the university.

As well as their main course of study, students are expected to take certain other subjects, such as politics, English and PE.

There is generally a lot more contact time in Chinese universities than in their Western counterparts, particularly in the arts subjects. At some vocational schools students are expected to attend Evening Study – this is a system where students are supposed to turn up and spend a couple of hours doing homework in their classrooms – a teacher will be on duty and check that everyone is there. This isn't as crazy as it sounds when you consider that dormitories are cramped (unless you are very well-off) and library space is limited – it provides a space for students to get their academic work done without distraction.

Classes are large (about 30-50 students per class), and students in a class will spend a lot of time together and take most of their lessons together. For this reason, the bonds between classmates are often very strong.

Increasingly, a university education is seen as the only route to a successful, white-collar career. However, there are many more university places than there used to be and, while this has relieved pressure on students taking the gaokao exam, it has also resulted in large numbers of graduates flooding the market, and élite jobs are consequently harder to find. Many students now aspire to a postgraduate degree, feeling that this will increase their chances in an increasingly competitive job market.

Eight Great Traditions of Chinese cuisine

The Eight Great Traditions of Chinese cuisine are eight major regional cuisines. The regions are Anhui, Canton, Fujian, Hunan, Jiangsu, Shandong, Sichuan and Zhejiang. Amongst these Shandong cuisine ranks first.

Eight Immortals

The Eight Immortals are the eight mythical Taoist deities of Chinese folklore. They are:

Zhang Guolao an old man riding a donkey
Han Zhongli a fat man with a bare belly holding a fan
Han Xiangzi a handsome young man with a flute
He Xiangu a female immortal with her magic lotus flower
Lan Caihe a teenager carrying a floral basket (sex not established, but generally portrayed as male)
Li Tieguai a lame beggar with a stick and a gourd
Lu Dongbing a middle-aged man carrying a magic sword
Cao Guojiu a middle-aged man of royal origin and always shown in fine court garments

(Mary Evans Picture LIbrary

The Eight Immortals cross the sea, each using their own particular magic charm. The story is used as a proverb for there being many ways to accomplish a task.

The Eight Immortals are popular figures in almost all genres of Chinese art, representing longevity and happiness. The most famous story is *The Eight Immortals Crossing The Sea*. It tells how they use their magic powers to cross the sea on their way to a magic peach party held by the Queen Mother of the West (the peach is a symbol of longevity). The Eight Immortals enjoy great popularity with the Chinese and there are many folktales about how they encourage people to lead good lives and punish those who are greedy and evil.

Eileen Chang, *a.k.a.* ***Zhang Ai-ling***

Eileen Chang (1920-1995), one of the best Chinese writers of the 20th century, was born into a famous Shanghai family. Her grandmother was the daughter of Li Hongzhang, an influential official in the late Qing Dynasty. Despite her unhappy and eventful childhood, she displayed great literary talents as a teenager. She was educated at the University of Hong Kong. However, Hong Kong's fall to the invading Japanese in 1941 forced her to end her studies before graduating. She returned to Shanghai where she shot to stardom as a writer with many hugely popular novels, plays and essays. Most of her best works, like *The Golden Cangue* and *Love in a Fallen City* were written during this period. After the Communists' takeover of China, she managed to emigrate first to Hong Kong and then to the United States. She married the playwright Ferdinand Reyher in 1956, but then lived as a recluse until her death in Los Angeles in 1995. Chang's fiction is loved by her readers for revealing the true flavour of the charms of old Shanghai. She excelled in depicting the tension between men and women in love and is considered unique for her truthful rendering of human experience, however painful.

Emil Chau → *ZHOU HUAJIAN*

emperors' names

There were hundreds of Chinese emperors over a period spanning thousands of years. The earliest emperors merge into myth and legend in the ancient times before the Xia Dynasty (2100-1600BC). They were the mythic ancestors of the Chinese people. The last emperor, Puyi, abdicated his throne in 1912.

There are different ways of naming Chinese emperors. They can be referred to by their dynastic titles, which usually end with di, zu or zong. Since emperors with the same titles existed in different dynasties, the name of the dynasty is usually put before the title in order to differentiate. Take Han Wudi, for instance. Wudi is the emperor's dynastic title and Han is the name of the dynasty he belongs to. In this book we use the form:

Han Wudi
Liusong Wendi
Sui Wendi
Han Gaozu *etc*

Different conventions exist as to the actual word order of the names. You may also come across:

Emperor Wu of the Han
Emperor Wen of the Liusong
Emperor Wen of the Sui
Emperor Gao of the Han *etc*

Emperors can also be named by their "title of reign", a practice more popular for the emperors in the Ming and Qing Dynasties, since starting from the Ming each emperor used only one title of reign (before the Ming period a emperor could have several titles of reign). For example, Puyi is also known as Emperor Xuantong, as Xuantong was his title of reign.
In addition to these variants, emperors can also be known by their personal names. For example, Yuan Shizu is also Kublai Khan.

Empress Dowager Cixi

Cixi (born 1835) was the de facto ruler of the Qing Dynasty from 1861 until her death in 1908. Born into a middle-class Manchu family, she entered the palace as a specially chosen beauty. Due to the favour of Emperor Xianfeng, she was honoured as a high-ranking imperial concubine, and then became Empress Dowager after her son, Emperor Tongzhi, inherited the throne at the age of five. Adept at court politics, she manoeuvered herself into a position as decision-maker of the empire. This was the start of her "ruling from behind the curtains". Though she

Portrait of the Empress Dowager Cixi (1835-1908) (oil on canvas) Summer Palace, Beijing

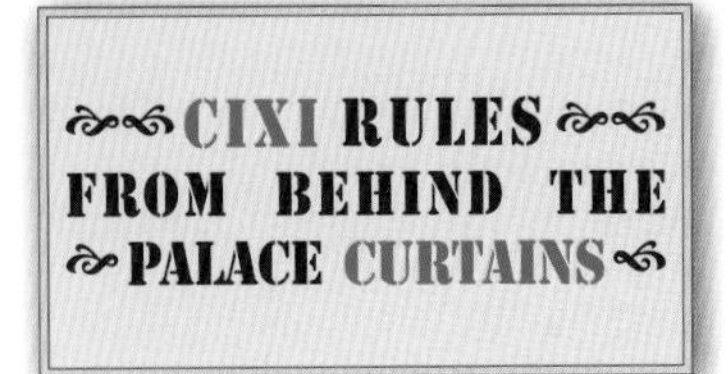

later seemed to hand over power to Tongzhi and his successor, Emperor Guangxu, she continued to rule behind the scenes. She is notorious in history for being conservative and autocratic. Many historians believe that it is she that should bear the blame for the fall of the Qing Dynasty.

Empress Dowager Longyu

Empress Dowager Longyu (1868-1913) was the Empress Consort of her cousin Emperor Guangxu of the Qing Dynasty. She was also Empress Dowager Cixi's niece. After the death of her husband and of her powerful aunt in 1908, she, like Cixi, though not as experienced, began to "rule behind the curtains" with the child Emperor Qing Xuantong (also known as Puyi) as the nominal ruler. She signed the abdication on behalf of Puyi in 1911, officially ending the rule of the Qing Dynasty – a signature which brought about the end of imperial China.

Empress Dowager Lü

Lü Zhi (241-180BC), commonly known as Empress Dowager Lü, was the wife of Liu Bang, the first emperor of the Han Dynasty. Power-hungry and a skilled political tactician, she was considered one of the three most powerful female rulers in Chinese history (the other two being Wu Zetian and Empress Dowager Cixi). She was described as a cruel and malicious woman who tortured her late husband's favourite concubine Qi by chopping off her limbs, making her deaf and blind and keeping her locked in a toilet, while naming her Ren Zhi (human pig). However, she showed great political skill in helping her husband eliminate the threat of the principalities by having the famous generals Han Xin and Peng Yue executed on a charge of conspiracy. Though notorious for largely favouring the members of her own clan, she proved herself to an able regent of the empire, which began to recover after the endless turmoil of war.

Empress Dowager Wu, *a.k.a.* ***Wu Zetian***

(Mary Evans Picture LIbrary

Empress Dowager Wu and a suitor

A highly controversial female politician and the only female emperor in Chinese history. She also founded her own dynasty, the Zhou (690-705AD). Wu Zetian (625?-705AD) was originally a concubine of Emperor Taizong of the Tang Dynasty and was made a concubine of Taizong's son, the Emperor Gaozong, after Taizong's death. In order to seize the position of empress, she was said to have killed her own infant daughter to frame the former empress and finally tortured the empress to death. After her husband suffered a crippling stroke, she became the de facto ruler of the country. Through a long series of intrigues she managed to secure her power behind the throne and later succeeded to the throne herself. Traditional historians described her as ruthless in her rise to power and accused her of murdering many innocent people including one of her own sons. During her reign, however, many of her policies were of great benefit to the country and people continued to prosper.

Empress Dowager Xiaozhuang

Empress Dowager Xiaozhuang (1613-1688), the mother of Emperor Shunzhi and grandmother of Emperor Kangxi in the Qing Dynasty, was highly regarded by historians for her virtue and political competence. After her husband Huang Taiji's sudden death, there was a fierce struggle for the throne. Xiaozhuang managed to buy the support of Dorgon, Huang Taiji's brother, and made her son Shunzhi the successor. There have been many anecdotes about the love affair and marriage between Xiaozhuang and Dorgon and a lot of TV series nowadays are based on these. One anecdote is this: it is said that Dorgon fell in love with Xiaozhuang before she married his brother Huang Taiji. After Huang Taiji's death, Dorgon was the most powerful contender for the throne. But Xiaozhuang persuaded him to make her son the successor and Dorgon himself the regent. Only for this price could he have his marriage.

Although capable of ruling the country, she never tried to usurp power. She devoted herself wholeheartedly to her family and exerted a sound influence during the reigns of her son and grandson.

Empress Jia

The Empress Jia (256-300AD), named Jia Nanfeng, the wife of Emperor Huidi of the Jin Dynasty, was notorious for her ruthlessness and cruelty. Though very ugly, Jia Nanfeng became the wife of the crown prince. She owed a lot to the influence of her father, Jia Chong, who was a founding father of the Jin Dynasty and held great power at court. When the crown prince became emperor, Jia was his empress. Emperor Huidi, a man generally lacking in intelligence, particularly lacked the ability to control court affairs. So Empress Jia seized that opportunity to secure her position behind the scenes by killing off not only Huidi's mother, the Empress Dowager Yang, but also Yang's clan and all the court officials who supported the Yang clan. Empress Jia's autocratic rule finally provoked the opposition of the princes Liang and Zhao who broke into the palace with their troops and killed her. More princes got involved in the struggle for the throne and that was the start of the "Eight Princes Rebellion" which heralded the downfall of the Jin Dynasty.

EMPRESS GIVES GRAIN HANDOUTS TO HARD-UP FARMERS

Empress Ma

The Empress Ma (1331-1382) was the wife of Emperor Zhu Yuanzhang (a.k.a. Ming Taizu), the first emperor of the Ming Dynasty. She married Zhu Yuanzhang in the midst of their rebellion against the Yuan Dynasty. She is seen as the model of humility and austerity, expert at maintaining harmonious relations with the other court concubines and the court officials. She also showed concern for the welfare of farmers by encouraging her husband, the emperor, to distribute grain reserves to farmers in need. Emperor Zhu Yuanzhang respected her and often listened to her suggestions about the empire's administrative affairs. On her death her husband was so grief-stricken that he refused to take a new empress in her place, a very unusual decision in the history of imperial China.

Empress Zhangsun

Zhangsun was the wife of Emperor Taizong of the Tang Dynasty and a respected empress. Frugal and modest, she set a perfect example of showing how to be a "good assistant to the emperor", serving as an intelligent adviser and critic for her husband.

Empress Zhao Feiyan

Zhao Feiyan (?-1BC), the empress of Han Chengdi during the Western Han Dynasty, is commonly known for her beauty and skills as a dancer. It was said that she could dance gracefully on a crystal plate. Slender and supple as a willow, she seemed at risk of being blown away by the slightest breath of wind. If Yang Guifei, the well-rounded concubine of Emperor Xuanzong, represented the beauty of the Tang Dynasty, Feiyan certainly set the standard for that of the Han.

SHE COULD DANCE GRACEFULLY ON A CRYSTAL PLATE

erhu

A two-stringed instrument, played by inserting the bow between the strings and drawing it backwards and forwards. This makes the unique whining tone, similar to that of a violin but thinner due to the smaller sound box, which is traditionally covered with snakeskin. The erhu is typically used for Chinese folk music.

Erlang Shen

A god in popular Chinese belief who has, in the middle of his forehead, a third magical eye with which he is able to see truth. In some legends, his job is said to be to control floods. According to the mythical novels of the Ming Dynasty, the *Investiture of the Gods* and *Journey to the West*, Erlang Shen is the nephew of the *Jade Emperor*. He appeared as a warring deity, with a three-pointed knife in hand and Xiaotian the Dog by his side.

eunuchs

REPORT TO PALACE CASTRATION DEPARTMENT

In imperial China eunuchs were generally regarded as servants or even slaves and their participation in politics was forbidden. The ban, however, tended to be broken in almost every dynasty, for a combination of reasons, and sometimes a eunuch, working as he did at the very seat of supreme power, could become powerful enough to control his emperor.

Servants of the Emperor and the Empress had to be castrated in China so that the Emperor could be absolutely sure that any sons or daughters, but especially sons, were his and his alone (or at least not fathered by a servant).

Poor families would send their sons to the palace recruitment office, seeing this as a good career move.

Some adults would voluntarily report to the castration section of the palace in order to get a job. And sometimes men would get themselves castrated in advance in order to qualify, although this route was later banned.

F

face changing

©iStockphoto.com/Michael Chen

Face changing is a famous technique used in Chinese Sichuan Opera. The performers change the colours and types of their facial makeup in a quick series of motions to reflect the character's moods and feelings. Expert artistes are said to be able to change faces in just one second. There are normally four types of face-changing skills: makeup wiping, colourful powder blowing, silk mask string-pulling and the taichi breathing trick. Face changing first appeared in Sichuan Opera during the Qing Dynasty, at which time performers could only change between a couple of faces. Nowadays, after generations of research and development, professionals can change between over 18 faces.

Face changing in Sichuan Opera in Chengdu

©iStockphoto.com/Michael Chen

The skill of face changing is a traditional art treasure in China. Custom requires that the secret may not be revealed to anyone outside the world of Sichuan Opera and that the skills may only be passed on to a faithful male apprentice. However, some underground face-changing activities have come into existence in recent years and some performers started to teach the technique to outsiders and even sold the secret overseas.

facial makeup

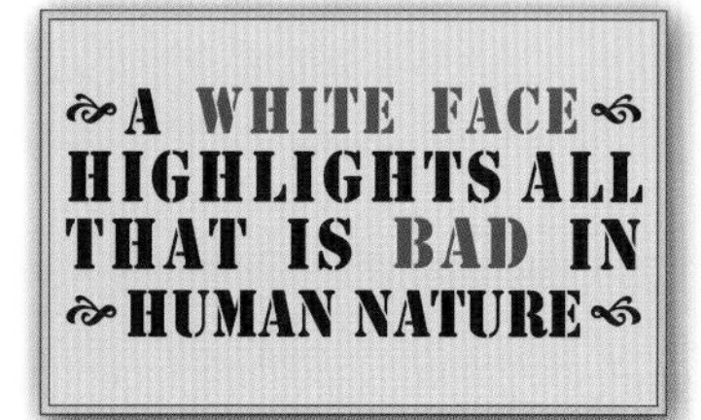

Various designs with lines and coloured patches are painted on the faces of certain operatic characters. They follow traditionally fixed patterns for specific types so that the audience can immediately tell whether they are heroes or villains, kind or wicked. For example, a red face shows bravery, uprightness and loyalty. A black face indicates either a rough and bold character or an impartial and selfless personality. A white face, on the other hand, highlights all that is bad in human nature: cunning, craftiness and treachery.

Falun Gong

Falun Gong is a hybrid of Buddhism and Qigong (a system of Chinese meditation exercises and breath control). Public fanaticism about Qigong started in the late 1980s when many Qigong masters, who allegedly possessed special powers, sprang up overnight. However, all of them were proved to be frauds. Falun Gong was introduced by Li Hongzhi in the heat of Qigong-mania in 1992, so people had every reason to be sceptical about what lay behind it. The real panic from the government started in April 1999. Some 10,000 Falun practitioners, instructed by Li, appeared suddenly out of nowhere and lined up silently outside Zhongnanhai, the headquarters of the Communist Party, petitioning for legal recognition. Two months later, the Chinese government declared Falun Gong an illegal political organization opposed to the Communist Party of China and the central government.

Although there seems nothing wrong with the Falun Gong advocacy of such ideas as truthfulness, compassion and forbearance, doubts arose when people came to question whether Li really believed in what he preached – and the fact that large sums of money, donated by his followers, remained unaccounted for did nothing to help his credibility. In a non-Christian cultural context, it all looked more like fraud and pseudoscience than faith. When Falun Gong was declared illegal most people voluntarily abandoned it (after all, for them it was more of a Qigong than a belief, and they did have many other alternatives to it). But some would not abandon their adherence. Thus there are reports from the Western world that practitioners are persecuted and are regarded as martyrs. Such reports were never confirmed, but neither have they stopped.

family → *FILIAL PIETY*

Faye Wong → *WANG FEI*

feng shui

Feng shui, literally "wind water", is mainly concerned with understanding the relationships between nature and human beings. It draws together a wide mix of geographical, religious, philosophical, mathematical, aesthetic and astrological ideas to ensure that lives can be lived in harmony with the environment. It has become a kind of architectural acupuncture: feng shui specialists can be hired as consultants. They might advise where bathrooms should go, which way doorways should face, where mirrors should hang, which direction the head of the bed should face. They can consult on a good site for your grandparents' tomb or give advice in real estate decisions about land purchase. They decide these things on the basis of their feel for the flow of the good or bad "energy".

Feng Xiaogang

A Chinese film director, born in 1958, who is known as a trail-blazer of the New Year Celebration film genre. He excels in making comedies with typically Beijing-type dialogues and is considered a top box office director in mainland China.

Feng Zikai

Feng Zikai (1898-1975) was a well-known cartoonist, writer, educator and translator in modern China. His main and most enduring work lay in the field of cartoons. He was generally regarded as the founder of the modern cartoon in China with the publication of *Zi Kai Cartoons* in 1924. His style was casual and he liked to draw everyday scenes from the lives of ordinary folk, adding humorous touches. His art was nonetheless rooted in a traditional Chinese philosophy of life centering on peace, contentment and natural simplicity.

Fenghuang, *a.k.a.* ***Chinese Phoenix***

Unlike the phoenix in ancient Greek and Egyptian mythology, which is closely associated with sun worship and the idea of rebirth, the Fenghuang in Chinese mythology is an immortal and holy bird that is generally regarded as a symbol of harmony and good luck. The Fenghuang is said to reign over all other birds – Feng refers to the male and Huang the female, and when combined together, they symbolize the union and harmony of yin-yang forces. However, such distinctions of gender have gradually blurred, and nowadays the Fenghuang is usually represented as a female bird – an imaginary composite of many different birds (the tail of a peacock, the head of a pheasant, the body of a mandarin duck, the talons of a hawk, the legs of a crane). And in painting or decoration, it is often paired with a dragon (representing male qualities and royal dignity) to symbolize marital harmony and bliss.

A phoenix on the walls of a tower used for burnt offerings, Tian Hou Temple, Shenzhen, Guangdong

Fengshen Yanyi, *a.k.a.* ***The Investiture of the Gods***

An important mythical fiction written in the Ming Dynasty which describes a group of heroes who fought against the tyranny of the Shang Dynasty (1600-1046BC) and founded the Zhou Dynasty (1045-256BC). The story begins when King Zhou of the Shang offends Nüwa, the ancient Chinese goddess, who sends three spectres to bewitch the king. The kingdom soon falls into chaos and civil war breaks out. Gods, spirits and spectres take sides in the war and mingle with human beings. In the end, at the downfall of the Shang, the feudal Zhou Dynasty is established. Many of the deceased heroes are made into deities.

filial piety

Filial piety, one of the fundamental virtues advocated in Chinese tradition, refers to the obligations owed to one's parents – showing respect, being obedient, taking care of them in their old age and when they are sick, arranging a proper funeral and mourning for a certain period of time (three years used to be standard). Most important of all, a son has to make sure that the family line will be continued. Dying without a son is, therefore, one of the greatest violations of the concept of filial piety. In olden times, being "unfilial" was regarded as a hideous crime and, as such, deserving of severe punishment (although failing to produce a son was not in itself punished). Numerous exemplars of filial conduct are to be found in Chinese history. Some of them may look like the cultivation of religious asceticism where sons undergo great hardship, or even sacrifice their lives, in order to look after their sick parents or save parents in danger. This is one reason why ancestor worship is practically a religious belief unshakable in Chinese tradition. Though the exercise of filial piety is not that strictly required in today's China, it is still deeply rooted in people's minds.

Firebrand Festival → *Yi*

→ *Yi*

five poisons

Five animals were traditionally thought of as poisonous: the snake, scorpion, centipede, toad and lizard. In ancient times, Chinese people would paint the image of five poisons (or these five poisonous animals) on pieces of paper and hang them up in their homes or they would carve the images on pieces of jade and tie these to their clothing. This would happen especially in the month of June when the poisonous animals started to become more problematic. The purpose of using the five poisons image was to combat the pestilent sources, which derived from the concept "fighting poisons with poisons" in Chinese culture.

foot binding

A NECESSARY PRACTICE IN ORDER FOR WOMEN TO BE CONSIDERED MARRIAGEABLE

Foot binding is an ancient Chinese custom practised on females in order to achieve what was perceived as beauty. How it originally started is not fully known. It is generally considered that the practice of foot binding began in the Song Dynasty (960-1279AD), reportedly to imitate an imperial concubine who danced gracefully with her feet bound. The practice became widespread and more

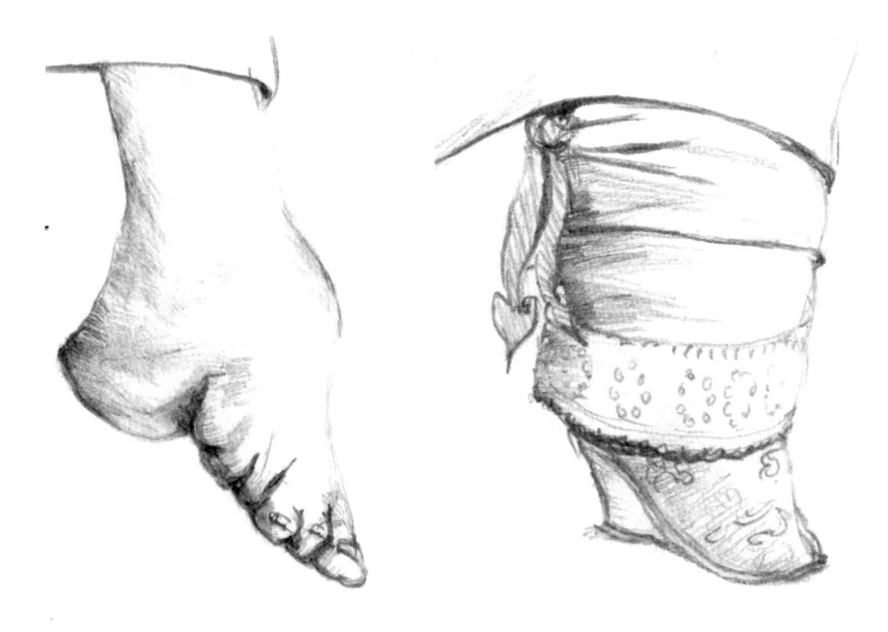

severe during the Ming and Qing Dynasties. It was no longer a mere matter of fashion but a necessary practice in order for woman to be considered marriageable and hence achieve a good life. Having crippled Chinese women for nearly a thousand years, it was officially banned in 1912 when the New Republic was founded.

Forbidden City

The Forbidden City, built in the heart of Beijing from 1406-1420, was the royal palace of the Ming and Qing dynasties and was the home of 24 emperors from Emperor Yongle of the Ming to the last emperor of China, Puyi of the Qing. It is "Forbidden" because nobody was allowed to enter the site without the Emperor's permission. The world's largest existing palace, it consists of 980 buildings and some 8700 rooms. It now houses the Palace Museum displaying a wide range of late imperial collections of artwork and antiquities. It was made a world cultural heritage site in 1987.

An alleyway in the Forbidden City

©iStockphoto.com/Izabela Habur

Four Emperors

The Four Emperors, namely Mid-Heaven Emperor of the Pole Star, Long-life Emperor of the South Pole, Upper-Palace Heavenly Emperor of Gouchen and the Empress of Earth, are the four Gods of the Taoist religion who rank below the Three Pure Ones. It is said that they assist the Jade Emperor in ruling the Kingdom of Heaven.

Four Heavenly Kings

The Four Heavenly Kings, commonly known as the Four Great Jin Gang in Chinese Buddhism, are Buddhist guardian gods who watch over the four cardinal points of the earth. Statues of these gods are common in Buddhist temples throughout China.

The Heavenly King of the South is dressed in blue with a sword in hand; the Heavenly King of the East is in white with a pipa; the Heavenly King of the North is often in green and carrying an umbrella; the Heavenly King of the West is in red with a dragon. As a group they are also known in China as Feng Tiao Yu Shun, which means "favourable weather", the precursor of a good harvest.

Statue of one of the Four Heavenly Kings, Lingyin Temple, northwest of Hangzhou, Zhejiang Province

Four Treasures of the Study

These are brush, paper, ink stick and ink stone (a stone which yields ink when water is dripped onto it and the ink stick is ground in). They are the essential tools for calligraphy.

fox spirits → *HULI JING*

Friendship Stores

Friendship Stores don't exist any more; they had their day from the 1950s to the early 1990s. They were department stores cum supermarkets in the larger cities intended specifically for expatriate foreign residents such as diplomats and journalists, and tourists. They sold Western goods which were, at the time, not available in ordinary shops - instant coffee, teabags and Scotch whisky for example - luxury items and high quality handicrafts. Goods could only be paid for with Foreign Exchange Certificates or by credit card, so the vast majority of the Chinese were excluded from them, and even if they got hold of some Foreign Exchange Certificates, they were likely to have been turned away by the police or security guards. Times have changed.

fu

Fu is a Chinese character meaning "good fortune" and "happiness" which is put up on walls, doors and doorposts during the Spring Festival to express good wishes and blessings for the coming year. According to folk tradition, the character fu is normally displayed upside-down.

Fu the right way up

There is a nice story about the upside-down fu. In the Qing Dynasty a senior servant of Prince Gong instructed other servants to put up the character fu outside their house on the eve of the Spring Festival. One illiterate servant put the fu upside-down on the gate. When Prince Gong saw this he was furious and, in his fury, decided to have the unfortunate illiterate severely punished. The senior servant, who was very wise, suddenly had an idea how he could save his subordinate (and presumably his own face for allowing this to happen). Because the Chinese for "upside-down" sounds the same as "arrive" in Chinese and fu had been put up upside-down it can there be read as a very subtle way of saying "fu arrives" – which would obviously be a good omen for the whole family. So it wasn't a mistake at all, it was deliberate.

The upside-down fu – wishing good luck for the new year

Prince Gong was very pleased by his senior servant's explanation and cancelled the punishment. Since then it has been a folk tradition for Chinese people to display the upside-down fu at Chinese New Year.

QUEEN OF DIVING MARRIES FINANCE SECRETARY

Fu Mingxia

A Chinese diver and Olympic champion who dominated the sport of diving for nearly a decade, Fu Mingxia (1978-) became the youngest world champion ever in this sport in 1991 – a record unlikely to be challenged because shortly afterwards, as a result of her stunning performance and out of consideration for the protection of teenage athletes, an age-limit requirement of 14 was imposed on divers in certain international events. Fu just met this requirement for the 1992 Barcelona Olympics and thus became China's youngest Olympic champion. Four years later she won gold medals for both platform and springboard events at Atlanta. After a retirement of about 2 years, she had a convincing comeback at the 2000 Athens Olympics and captured another gold and a silver. In her prime she was dubbed the "Queen of Diving". Fu married Leung Kam Chung, former Financial Secretary of Hong Kong, in 2002.

Gang of Four

The Gang of Four were an extreme leftwing group in the Chinese Communist Party led by Mao Zedong's last wife Jiang Qing and her close associates, Zhang Chunqiao, Yao Wenyuan and Wang Hongwen. They rose to power during the Cultural Revolution and were blamed for the social chaos and humanitarian disasters of that ten-year period. The removal of the group from power in 1976, a month after Mao's death, marked the end of the Cultural Revolution. In 1981 they were all convicted of anti-party activities at a public trial. Jiang Qing and Zhang Chunqiao were both sentenced to death, though this was later commuted to life imprisonment. Wang Hongwen was sentenced to life imprisonment and Yao Wenyuan was given 20 years.

Gao Lishi

A powerful eunuch official during the reign of Emperor Xuanzong of the Tang Dynasty. Gao Lishi (684-762AD) is regarded as a loyal and trusted friend of Xuanzong and had run much of the empire during Xuanzong's decrepit later years. He introduced the famous beauty Yang Guifei to Xuanzong and played an important role in their love affair, which is a favourite theme in the works of many poets and writers. During the Anshi Rebellion, the mutinous imperial guard blamed Yang and her family for the upheaval and demanded her death. Upon Xuanzong's approval, Gao either strangled Yang or witnessed her suicide. Gao maintained a life-long loyalty to Xuanzong. That's probably why he was praised in historical records for his moral integrity despite his participation in politics as a eunuch.

gaokao

The Gaokao or National Matriculation Test is a standardized higher education entrance examination. The test results decide whether the candidate can enter a higher education institution or win a place at a top university. Most examinees are third-year students in secondary schools, though there is no age restriction. The exam takes place every June and lasts three days. Three subjects are mandatory: Chinese, mathematics and a foreign language – usually English. Candidates also have to take two other exams on subjects chosen either from three sciences – physics, chemistry, biology – or from three humanities – history, geography and political education. The requirements may vary from province to province. The examination system has been under constant criticism for causing severe anxiety among young students and their parents.

Gaoshan

The Gaoshan people are the indigenous inhabitants of Taiwan. They have various origins but now live in the mountains and on the plains along Taiwan's eastern seaboard. The Gaoshan are made up of a dozen smaller tribes, each of which has its own distinctive cultural heritage. They have differing languages and live in different regions. A remarkable fact is that they do not have written languages. Most of the Gaoshan are still engaged in such traditional activities as farming, hunting and fishing and so lead increasingly hard lives in the face of commercialism and economic globalization.

Gautama Buddha, *a.k.a.* ***Sakyamuni Buddha***

The founder of Buddhism, whose original name was Siddhartha Gautama. He lived in northern India in the 6th century BC and his father was the ruler of the kingdom of Sakyas (in modern Nepal). As a prince, he wanted for nothing in his luxurious palace. But all of a sudden, confronted with the reality of life and the suffering of mankind, he decided to find a solution – the way to overcome the universal suffering of old age, illness and death. At the age of 29 he left his palace and began his quest through a life of asceticism. After wandering for six years he attained Enlightenment one evening while meditating under a pipal tree (or Bodhi tree). Gautama, since then, has been known as the Buddha, "the Enlightened One". And he started to expound his teachings to all men and women who were ready to follow. At the age of 80, he attained nirvana.

Ghost Festival

The Ghost Festival is celebrated on the night of the fifteenth day in the seventh month of the Chinese Lunar Calendar. According to folklore, on that night ghosts, spirits and the souls of the deceased rise from the underworld to visit the living. People are supposed to burn joss paper and make food offerings to appease the hunger of the spirits.

Burning joss paper at Ghost Festival

ghost money → ***SPIRITUAL MONEY***

giant panda

The giant panda can only be found in the mountains of mid-west China. They live almost exclusively on bamboo and have a very long reproductive cycle. Regarded as China's national treasure, wild pandas are extremely rare. Many conservation areas have been set up to protect their habitat, the most famous of these being located in Wolong, Sichuan Province.

God Worshipper → ***HONG XIUQUAN***

Golden Eagle Award → ***MEDIA AWARDS***

Golden Rooster Award → ***MEDIA AWARDS***

gong bao jiding, *a.k.a.* ***kung pao chicken***

This spicy Sichuan dish is considered a Chinese delicacy by most people. The most important ingredient is handfuls of Sichuan peppercorns and red chillis, which lends authentic gong bao jiding its distinctive mouth-numbing flavour. You can order the dish in just about any restaurant, even vegetarian ones where chicken is replaced by some specially prepared tofu.

Gong Li

A famous Chinese actress and multiple awards winner, her success is largely attributable to director Zhang Yimou, who picked her to star in *Red Sorghum* – the Golden Bear winner in Berlin 1988. The following years witnessed her intimate collaboration (both professional and private) with Zhang in his distinctive movies such as *Ju Dou* (1990), *Raise the Red Lantern* (1991) and *The Story of Qiu Ju* (1992) which won her the Best Actress Award at the 1992 Venice Film Festival. However, this seemingly immaculate partnership unexpectedly ended in 1995. Gong Li gained wider international recognition for her role in *Farewell My Concubine*, the 1993 Cannes Palme d'Or winner

(Left to right) Zhang Yimou, Gong Li and Chow Yun-Fat

directed by Chen Kaige. Maybe the most famous Chinese actress in the Western world, she is a regular of many international film festivals.

Gong Zizhen

A poet, scholar and great thinker in the late Qing dynasty, Gong Zizhen (1792-1841) was born into a prestigious family of scholars and officials in Hangzhou. His life-long ambition to serve the nation was constantly frustrated by his bad luck with the Imperial Civil Examination. He remained a minor government official, retiring two years before his death. With numerous poems and essays to his credit, he also wrote extensively, as a reformist, on social and political problems, particularly on government policies. His ideas had a great impact on the reformers of later generations, such as Kang Youwei and Liang Qichao who led the influential, though unsuccessful, Hundred Days of Reform in 1898.

gourd

Gourds (or hulu in Chinese) have many uses in China. Farmers often cut the gourd into two and use them as ladles or wine containers. The gourd can also be made into a wind instrument called a sheng. The ancient Chinese regarded the gourd as a symbol of prosperity and it can be found in many decorative designs. A few ethnic groups even ascribed totemic status to them, believing their ancestors were born from gourds. It is a Chinese tradition to hang a gourd at your front door during the Dragon Boat Festival, since it is also claimed to offer protection against natural disasters.

Grand Canal

The Grand Canal runs from Beijing to Hangzhou in Zhejiang Province, a distance of almost 1300 miles. It passes Tianjin, crosses the Yellow River and the Yangtze and runs through the centre of Suzhou.

The central purpose of the Grand Canal was the transport of tax revenue, in the form of rice, to cities which have been China's capital: Chang'an (now Xi'an), Kaifeng, and then Beijing. Work was started under Emperor Sui Yangdi in the Sui Dynasty (581-618AD), the first dynasty to unite China since the Han Dynasty (206BC-220AD).

The Sui Dynasty engineers employed an immense workforce. They linked together rivers and lakes and cut new channels. The banks of the Canal were secured with tree planting. It is said that some two million labourers were used during construction work and many lives were lost.

The northernmost point was fed from rivers in the hills beside Beijing. The highest point, to the west of the mountains in Shandong Province, was reached by locks, with water supplied from reservoirs. Gates were used to secure the Canal where it crossed rivers.

The achievement of the Grand Canal is all the more spectacular in view of the restlessly changing course of the Yellow River, which today flows into the sea to the north of the Shandong Peninsula but which at times has flowed south of the Peninsula and joined the Huai River. The Huai River itself now joins the Yangtze River.

The Grand Canal was at its maturity in the Ming (1368-1644) and Qing (1644-1912) Dynasties. It went into decline in the nineteenth century, but is now in full operation again.

Great Leap Forward

The Great Leap Forward was an economic plan in 1958 designed by Mao Zedong to modernize China's economy so that its industrial production would surpass that of the UK and US within 15 years and China would make the transition from socialism to communism at the same time. A major shift from a largely rural economy to a steel-based production economy was targeted. The movement had two major fronts: a mass steel production campaign and the formation of people's communes. All over China small backyard furnaces were built and everybody from farmers to students pitched in working in around-the-clock shifts. In order to meet demand for steel production, they melted down everything that was made of iron – cooking utensils, door handles or even metal artefacts. The quality of this production was so poor that the so-called steel was completely useless. And mass production proved to be disastrous for the environment.

In tandem with this, communes were formed. People had to renounce their rights to property ownership since everything was now owned by the commune. The commune provided all that was needed – free food in dining halls; schools and nurseries were provided; the elderly were moved to the "houses of happiness" to be specially cared for. The campaign went horribly wrong and by 1959 even Mao admitted this. Economic failure and damage to the environment were followed by a series of natural disasters over the years 1959-1961 and it has been estimated that more than 40 million people died in the ensuing famine.

Great Wall of China

The Great Wall of China is an ancient Chinese military structure made of stones and bricks that stretches some 4188 miles over the vast territory of China from Heilongjiang Province in the northeast to Xinjiang in the west. (A comparative figure: the USA at its widest is some 3300 miles across). Since the days of the Spring and Autumn Period and the Warring

HE WHO HAS NEVER BEEN TO THE GREAT WALL IS NOT A TRUE MAN

States Period (770-221BC) ancient Chinese rulers and emperors like Qin Shi Huang used huge resources of manpower to build sections of walls to protect China from invaders to the north. The construction of the wall continued until the Ming Dynasty (1368-1644). The most famous stretch of the Great Wall is the Badaling Great Wall built in the Ming Dynasty and located northwest of Beijing.

When Chinese people think of the Great Wall they think of both architectural grandeur and the historical significance of the construction. It is said "He who has never been to the Great Wall is not a true man". In 2007 the Great Wall of China was voted one of the 7 New Wonders of the World.

©iStockphoto.com/Robert Churchill

The Great Wall of China at sunrise, Badaling, near Beijing

Guan Yu

Guan Yu, whose courtesy name was Yunchang, was the most respected military general in the ancient Three Kingdoms era (184-280AD). His fictional life depicted in the classic novel Romance of the Three Kingdoms is more popular than his real one. One of the sworn brothers of Liu Bei, Lord of the Kingdom of Shu, Guan Yu observed life-long loyalty to Liu even during his short service to Cao Cao, Lord of the Kingdom of Wei, who tried every means to buy Guan over. There are many widespread stories praising his courage and faithfulness: *Riding Alone for Thousands of Miles, Crossing Five Passes and Slaying Six Generals, Scraping the Bone to Treat the*

Poisoned Arm, to name but a few. Out of negligence and arrogance he was defeated in the war against the Kingdom of Wu. Refusing to surrender, he was finally executed. Numerous honourable posthumous titles were given to Guan through later dynasties. He was made a saint and was – and still is – generally worshipped as Emperor Guan or Lord Guan. Nowadays he is regarded as a guardian god and the God of Fortune. Temples and shrines dedicated to him can be found everywhere in China and some other East Asian countries.

Guangzhou

The capital of Guangdong Province on the Zhujiang River Delta near the South China Sea, Guangzhou has been an important sea port and trade centre since the days of the Tang Dynasty (618-907AD). It was one of the first sea ports forced to open to British colonists in the wake of the First Opium War (1839-42). In the late Qing Dynasty (1644-1912), it was the centre of Sun Yat-sen's democratic movement and later the headquarters of the Northern Expedition (1926-27), a military campaign to speed up the national revolution. These days Guangzhou is the largest city in southern China.

guanxi

Guanxi is the use of personal relationships to gain advantage or favours. The family is the primary source of connections and these are then supplemented by connections made at school and university. Economic and political relationships also depend on informal networks, which extend beyond families. Some guanxi is simply networking, as it would be understood in the West. But it can also be used to circumvent and avoid regulations or simply to speed through various formal permissions. To gain this support might involve gifts or owing a favour, which can be reclaimed later. So to set up a hotel, for example, could involve bringing various groups on side, such as local officials and police.

Guanxi might also relate to academic life. As two Chinese people comment:

> Even for academic entrance for masters, PhD, everything, people are trying to get a relationship with the academic staff – any people who can help. So parents will phone and say "Oh, do you know this professor, what does he like, what could we give him as a present?". Also if you need an operation, people try to find a better doctor through guanxi.
>
> It is very common for students to visit lecturers before examinations to give them song li (a present). Lecturers often come up to me and say "this student must pass and this one" because they have some complicated relationship with the family. If the students' relatives are powerful in the university, then teachers will be very pleased to help in this way, because you do a favour for the powerful person and maybe next time he can do a favour for you.

Thanks to: www.gla.ac.uk/centres/mediagroup/ for this article

Guanyin

Guanyin, also known as Guan Shiyin, is a Bodhisattva of Mercy who was believed to save people from all types of suffering. One of the Four Great Bodhisattvas – the other three being Wenshu, Puxian and Dizang – Guanyin is greatly revered for her kindness and compassion and has the biggest base of believers in China. Originally Guanyin appeared in male form. It was not until the Song Dynasty that Guanyin was worshipped as a female. In Chinese folk belief, she is regarded as a guardian of women and children and a fertility goddess who has it in her power to allow a woman to have a baby. Guanyin is usually represented as a beautiful woman wearing white garments, sometimes with "a thousand arms".

Legend says that Guanyin was originally a princess called Miao Shan who was driven out of the palace to a temple when she disobeyed her father's order to marry a wealthy man. Later, her father suffered from a severe illness that could only be cured by a medicine made out of a person's eye and the flesh on their arms. Miao Shan offered her arms and eyes without hesitation. The Buddha, moved by her filial deed, granted her a thousand arms and a thousand eyes, and helped her attain Buddhahood.

This huge statue of Guanyin is in Gui Yan Si (temple), Wuhan

Gulang → *XIAMEN*

Guo Moruo

A well-known scholar, poet, playwright, archaeologist and thinker in modern Chinese history, Guo Moruo (1892-1978) was educated in Japan. He was an influential figure in the New Culture Movement in the early 20th century. His anthology *The Goddesses*, written in vernacular Chinese, laid the cornerstone for the development of a new verse genre in Chinese literature. Besides poetry, his writings cover a wide range of literary forms, plays, autobiographies, translations, and monographs on Chinese history and philosophy. As a member of the Communist Party of China, he held important government offices in the People's Republic of China, including the first presidency of the Chinese Academy of Sciences. He abandoned his literary activities in the Cultural Revolution to avoid persecution and suggested that all his publications should be burned. He was subsequently severely rebuked for his great eagerness to please Mao Zedong and the authorities and for his failure to maintain his own moral integrity.

Guo Shoujing

An astronomer, mathematician and engineer during the Yuan Dynasty (1271-1368), Guo Shoujing (1231-1316) developed the Shoushi calendar system and calculated the year to be 365.2425 days, the same as the Gregorian calendar which came into use more than 300 years later. He built 27 observatories in China and took charge of large-scale surveys and observation projects. He also designed and improved many astronomical devices from the gnomon (sundial arm) to the armillary sphere (a spherical model of the universe). He was also an expert in water conservation and is famous for constructing the Kunming artificial lake in Beijing, a reservoir near to which the Summer Palace was later built.

MOUNTAIN ON THE MOON NAMED AFTER 13TH CENTURY CHINESE GENIUS

In commemoration of his contributions in the field of astronomy a mountain on the moon and asteroid 2010 have both been named after Guo.

guotie

Guotie, literally "pan stick", is a kind of shallow fried jiaozi or dumpling. They are popular as street food, appetizers or as a side order in Chinese restaraunts. To cook guotie, first make your dumplings or jiaozi. Then pan-fry them with vegetable oil. When they turn golden brown, a few minutes' steaming is necessary to get the flavour right. And if prepared correctly, they don't actually stick as much as their name suggests.

guzheng

The guzheng is a plucked instrument similar to the zither. It is one of the main instruments used in traditional Chinese music.

Ha'erbin, *a.k.a.* ***Harbin***

The largest city in Heilongjiang Province and the capital city of that province, Ha'erbin was originally a small fishing village on the Songhua River. Its rapid growth is largely attributable to Russian railway building in the late 19th century. It was once the largest settlement for Russian refugees and was occupied by Japanese troops from 1932 to 1945. Since 1949, Ha'erbin has developed into the chief industrial base in northeastern China. It is also a famous sightseeing city with its well-preserved Russian and European-style architecture. Ha'erbin is also a winter sports centre as well as being the home of the annual Ice Festival to which visitors from China and abroad come every January to see the amazing internally illuminated ice sculptures and take part in various types of sport on ice.

Classical Russian architecture in Harbin

Hainan

Hainan (capital: Haikou) is the most southerly of China's provinces. A tropical island, about the size of Holland, it was only made a separate province from Guangdong in 1988. With a January average temperature of 18 degrees celsius and its splendid palm-fringed beaches, Hainan is a very popular winter holiday destination. The hills in the south rise to almost 6000 feet and are clad with luxuriant primary forest. The island has three rice crops a year and is famous for its pineapples.

ISLAND FOR EXILES BECOMES HOLIDAY DESTINATION

The earliest inhabitants, from very early times, are the Li minority people – there are still over one million Li in Hainan today.

Hainan used to be China's back of beyond. Disgraced officials were sent here, sometimes courageous men who had spoken out at court, the most famous of these exiles being the Song poet Su Dongpo, who opened a school in Hainan.

Hakka

Hakka is a term referring to either a Chinese dialect or the group of people who speak this dialect. The Hakka people live mainly in parts of Guangdong, Guangxi and Fujian Provinces. It is believed that the Hakka people originated in the north around the Yellow River valley and migrated to the south seeking refuge from war, especially during the fall of the Southern Song Dynasty to the Mongols at the end of the 13th century. They were called Hakka (meaning "guests" in Cantonese) so as to distinguish them from the local inhabitants. Hakka preserves many older Chinese forms of pronunciation and sounds quite different from standard modern Chinese.

Han

The Han Chinese make up over 90% of the population of China. There are also about 40 million overseas Han Chinese worldwide, mostly in Southeast Asia. Their official language is Mandarin Chinese. The ancestry of the Han can be traced back to the Huaxia people, who lived along the Yellow River some four or five thousand years ago when the Yan Emperor (Yan Di) and the Yellow Emperor (Huang Di) united them. Chinese people sometimes refer to themselves as the Descendants of Yan Huang. Except for two periods, the Yuan and Qing Dynasties (totalling 400 years) the Han have been dominant in China since China became a united empire in 221BC. Although the current Chinese government promotes atheism, many Han still hold traditional beliefs, with Taoism and Buddhism having a wide grass-roots base. Recent years have seen a revival of Confucianism and the number of believers in Christianity is also growing steadily.

Han Aidi

Emperor Aidi who ruled from 7-1BC in the Western Han Dynasty (206BC-9AD) was so obsessed with his gay lover Dong Xian that he gave him State seals and offered to abdicate in his favour.

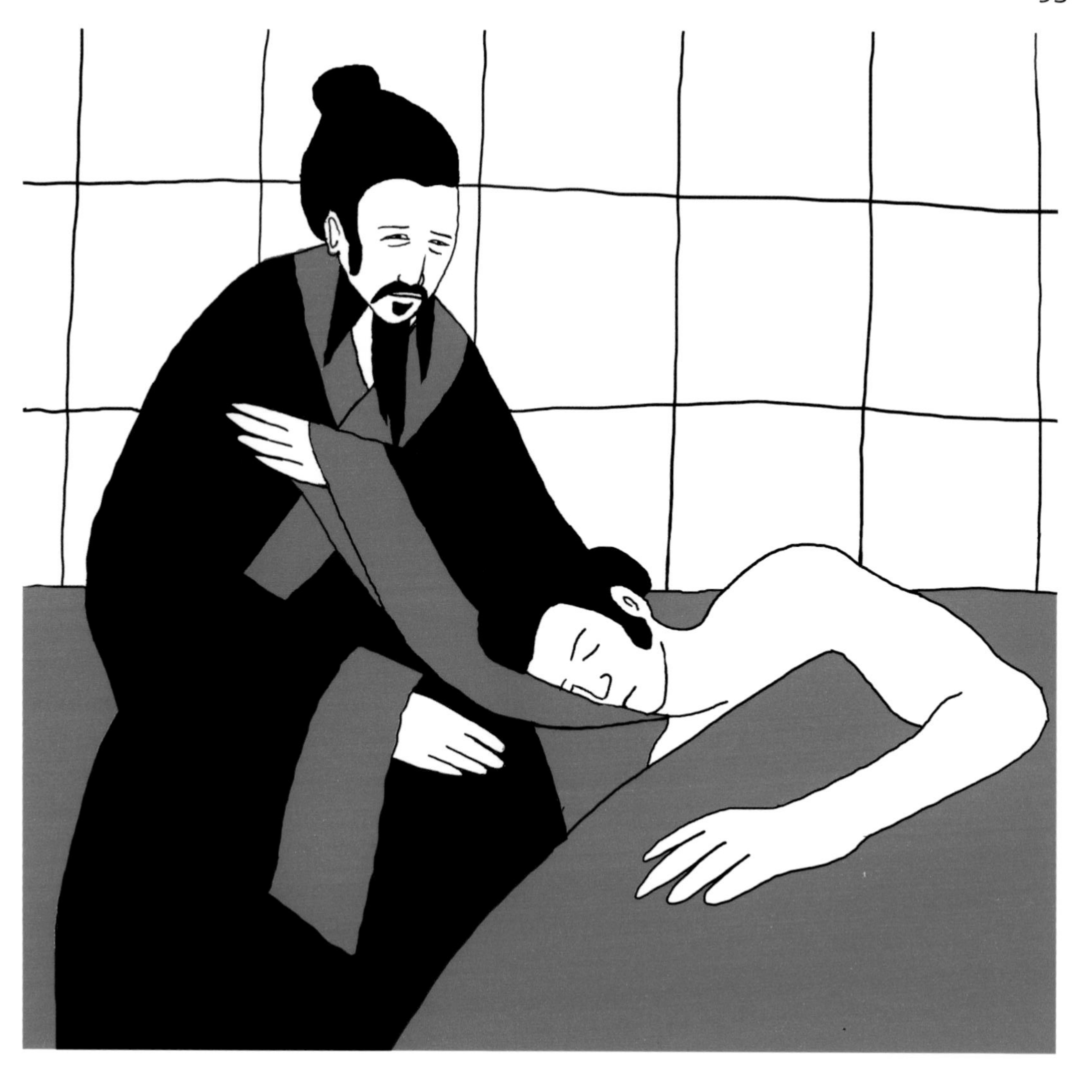

THE PASSION OF THE CUT SLEEVE

There is a well-known Chinese idiom which originates from a story about Emperor Aidi and his lover. One day the Emperor and Dong Xian both fell asleep on the same bed. Now Chinese costumes in those days had long voluminous sleeves and Dong Xian was lying right on top of the Emperor's sleeve. The Emperor woke up and found he couldn't move. But rather than wake up his lover, the Emperor cut off his own sleeve, so that he could slip off the bed. Chinese historians referred to Emperor Ai and his lover's relationship as "the passion of the cut sleeve". This expression is still used today, 2000 years later, to refer to a gay relationship.

Han Chengdi

The last Emperor to exercise any real control over the Western Han Dynasty (206BC-9AD), Chengdi (51-7BC) came to power shortly after his eighteenth birthday. Acting his age rather than his rank, he often sneaked out of his palace in disguise to enjoy himself in the city and watch cockfighting.

Married at an early age, Chengdi later fell in love with a concubine known as Flying Swallow (who later became Empress Zhao Feiyan), and then with her sister Zhao Hede. Neither of the Zhao sisters bore Chengdi a son, and are thought to have persuaded their emperor to kill his male heirs in order to protect their own positions of power. Consequently, Chengdi had no direct heir and appointed his nephew as crown prince.

Han Fei, *a.k.a.* ***Han Feizi***

Han Fei (c. 280-c. 233BC) was a philosopher who lived during the Warring States Period (475-221BC). He was a prominent figure representing the School of Law or Legalism. Han Fei was a prince in the royal family of the state of Han. He studied with the Confucian Xun Zi. A fellow student of his, Li Si, became chancellor of the state of Qin and, having grown jealous of Han's great talents, persecuted him and forced him to commit suicide by drinking poison. Han Fei's philosophy is encapsulated in his book *Han Feizi*, a superbly powerful piece of writing with flawless logic. Unlike Confucians, who tend to emphasize moral discipline, Han Fei advocates severe legal sanctions. To run the country by law is to punish the wrong and reward the right. Only in this way can the ruler secure his absolute authority. His philosophy was widely adopted by Qin Shi Huang, the first emperor of all China, and continued to influence following dynasties, though it was officially discarded after the Han Dynasty.

Han Fu

Han Fu, literally translated as Han costume, is a traditional style of clothing that can be traced back to the Han Dynasty. There seems to have been a revival of Han Fu in recent years in China. Unhappy about the traditional clothing of qi pao (for women) and changshan (for men), that are not actually the clothes of Han Chinese, the revivalists try to encourage people to wear Han Fu in everyday life or at least during traditional festivals and celebrations. The commonest styles are:

shenyi – a one-piece robe wrapped around the body (for both men and women);
ruqun – a top garment with a separate lower skirt (for women);
paofu – a closed full body robe (for government officials).

Han Gaozu, *a.k.a.* *Liu Bang*

Originally a minor official and not of royal blood, Emperor Gaozu (247-195BC) led a revolt against the Qin Dynasty (221-206BC) and successfully established the Han Dynasty (206BC-220AD). Following on from this he replaced his predecessor's harsh Legalist principles of governance with a more benign system based on Confucianism.

Having risen from poverty, Emperor Gaozu was poorly educated and despised impractical scholars to such an extent that he once even urinated in one of his advisor's hats. He was, however, intelligent, brave and generous. And as a result of his ability to listen to and evaluate the political advice he was given, he was able to lay the foundation stones for a dynasty that went on to rule China for more than four hundred years.

Han Guang Wudi

A descendant of Emperor Jingdi, Guang Wudi (5BC-57AD) rekindled the Han Dynasty (206BC-220AD) by declaring himself Emperor in 25AD. The period he ushered in moved the Han capital from Chang'an to Luoyang, and is therefore referred to as the Eastern Han Dynasty (25-220AD).

The initial years of Guang Wudi's reign were so plagued with bloodshed that he forbade people to use the word "war" in his presence. However, skilful economic management, the establishment of state monopolies, the reduction of poll taxes, the development of government examinations and a strategic use of political marriages helped him to establish some degree of stability.

Han Mingdi

Mingdi (28-75AD) was a hard-working and able ruler who, together with his son, the Emperor Zhang, created the golden age of the Eastern Han Dynasty (25-220AD). Conscript labour was used to build luxurious imperial residences throughout the country. But Mingdi was a believer in harsh punishment for officials who failed to show

integrity. And, when convinced that two of his brothers were plotting against him, he launched a mass execution, killing tens of thousands of people. During Mingdi's reign, Buddhism began to spread into China, and a group of missionaries was sent to Afghanistan, from where they returned with an image of Gautama Buddha, the Sutra Of Forty-Two Chapters and two eminent monks. The next year, Mingdi ordered the construction of China's first Buddhist temple, which was named White Horse Temple after the steed that had carried back the sutras.

Han Shizhong

Han Shizhong (1089-1151AD) was a famous general who lived through the turmoil of the transition between the Northern and Southern Song Dynasties. He started his military career as a common soldier and rose through the ranks to become a general. He won numerous victories in the wars against invaders from China's bordering states, mostly Xi Xia to the northwest and Jin to the northeast. One of his best-known victories was in the battle of Huangtiandang against the Jin forces that outnumbered Han's troops by about ten to one. It is said that his wife, Liang Hongyu, beat the drums to assist the attack. Han is regarded as a national hero who helped his country repel invaders. He is also regarded as an honourable man who dared to stand up and protest when Yue Fei, another top-rank general, was framed and persecuted.

Han Wendi

Chosen by his half-brothers because his mother did not have any powerful relatives who might endanger the continuation of the Han Dynasty (206BC-220AD), Emperor Wendi (202-157BC) is said to have been an ideal ruler. Under his leadership, the economy was stabilized, storehouses were filled with grain to secure against famine, and it became possible to dramatically reduce taxes on products. Perhaps Emperor Wendi's most significant contribution to Chinese history, however, was the introduction of recruitment to the civil service by examination (which later developed into the system of Imperial Civil Examinations).

Han Wudi

One of the longest reigning emperors in Chinese history, Emperor Wudi (141-87BC) of the Han Dynasty (206BC-220AD) was a well-read leader, but had a fearsome temper and refused to accept criticism of any sort. Under the restraining influence of Dowager Empress Dou, his initial years in power were extremely successful, with strict administration ensuring economic prosperity. However, the intensive military campaigns with which he later began to expand his empire brought the nation to its knees, weakened imperial control and led to hugely destructive power struggles amongst officials and consorts.

Han Xiandi

The last emperor of the Eastern Han Dynasty (25-220AD), Xiandi (181-220AD) found himself continuously running for his life as powerful warlords fought to take control of China. Eventually he was brought under the protection of Cao Cao, who orchestrated a marriage between the emperor and his daughter. Cao Cao's son usurped the throne after Cao Cao's death, and in doing so brought an end to the long-running Han Dynasty (206BC-220AD).

Han Xiaopeng

Chinese freestyle skier and Winter Olympic champion, Han Xiaopeng (1982-) entered Shenyang Sports Academy in 1995 to learn freestyle skiing. At the 2006 Winter Olympics in Turin he performed surprisingly well and won the freestyle gold medal. His overnight success brought China its first and only Winter Olympic victory in men's events.

Han Xin

Han Xin (?-196BC) is one of the greatest military commanders and strategists in Chinese history. He was invaluable to Liu Bang (also known as Han Gaozu) in setting up the Han Dynasty. During his early years, he wandered the land, poor and jobless.

A couple of anecdotes from this period: he once crawled between the legs of a local bully who challenged him, showing that he was ready to bear humiliation in order to achieve his ambitions. And he was fed by an old lady when almost dying of hunger. He rewarded both of these people after he became a famous general.

At the beginning of his service under Liu Bang he felt he was being sidelined and consequently tried to run off. Liu Bang's chief advisor, Xiao He, chased after him and persuaded him to return – this famous event is known as *Xiao He Chasing Han Xin in the Moonlight*. On Xiao's recommendation, Han Xin was promoted to the rank of commander-in-chief.

He masterminded a plan for Liu Bang to defeat his main adversary, Xiang Yu, and thus take over all of China. Han, a true master of the art of war, was never defeated in all his many battles. He made a famous remark on his own military ability. When Liu asked him how large a force he could command, he answered "the more the better". But Liu Bang, when he became emperor of the Han, saw the powerful generals, who had been made princes, as threats to his empire and started to have them removed. It was alleged that Han Xin was going to rebel. Empress Dowager Lü conspired with Xiao He, captured Han Xin and executed him while Liu was away.

Hence, there is an idiom, used a lot in modern Chinese, relating to Han Xin's life – Xiao He is the key to his success and also his undoing (cheng ye xiao he, bai ye xiao he). The idiom says that the success or failure of an undertaking can all be due to the same person or thing.

Han Yu

A prose stylist and poet in the Tang Dynasty, Han Yu (768-824AD) ranks first among the Eight Giants of Tang and Song Prose for his achievements in advocating a simple and direct style of writing in contrast to the popular, florid and fomalized styles. Han Yu, one of the leaders of the Confucian counterattack on Buddhism, is also considered a pioneer of a Confucian intellectual revival that climaxed in the 11th and 12th centuries with the rise of Neo-Confucianism. His influence was widespread in literary circles during his time and in the coming dynasties.

Hangzhou

AS THERE IS PARADISE IN HEAVEN, THERE ARE SUZHOU AND HANGZHOU ON EARTH

The capital city of Zhejiang Province, Hangzhou is one of the most charming and wealthy cities in eastern China. And old Chinese saying, still widely quoted, attests to its beauty: as there is paradise in Heaven, there are Suzhou and Hangzhou on earth. It was the capital of several kingdoms and dynasties and was much admired by Marco Polo. Today

©iStockphoto.com/Jonathan Larsen

West Lake at sunset, Hangzhou

Hangzhou is generally known as a tourist city with a rich cultural heritage, famous for the picturesque West Lake, Longjing Tea and silk.

Harbin → *Ha'erbin*

He Shen → *Qing Qianlong*

Heavenly Kingdom of Taiping → *Hong Xiuquan*

Henan

Henan Province was established in the Ming Dynasty (1368-1644). Its name means "south of the river", the Yellow River (though part of it is actually on the north side). Henan lies in the heart of China, and its capital Zhengzhou is a modern-day communications hub for the whole country. Henan is predominantly rural, producing a lot of wheat and, in the south, some rice. Winters are bitterly cold and the summers very hot. Although Henan Province is about half the size of Germany, its population is greater than Germany's: about ninety million.

The Yellow River flows out from the hills into the plain in Henan Province. Because its bed is higher than the surrounding countryside there have been terrible floods and famines. The legendary emperor Da Yu worked for thirteen years to control the river four thousand years ago. "If it weren't for Yu we would all be fish," it is said.

IF IT WEREN'T FOR YU WE WOULD ALL BE FISH

Henan is one of the oldest centres of Chinese civilization. Anyang in northeast Henan Province is where the earliest Chinese writing has been found, the oracle bone inscriptions.

Luoyang in the west was the capital of China for five hundred years during the Spring and Autumn Period, in the first millennium BC. Nearby is the oldest Buddhist temple in China, the White Horse Temple, and in the hills beyond is the Shaolin Temple, where the monks trained (and still do train) in martial arts. Kaifeng in the east, once visited by Marco Polo, was the capital of China during the Northern Song Dynasty until it fell to the Jurchen in 1127AD.

Heng'e → CHANG'E

Hong Kong

Hong Kong is called a Special Administrative Region of China and is one of the world's major financial and trade centres. After the First Opium War (1839-1842), Hong Kong Island was ceded to the British, and later in 1862 and 1898 the adjacent Kowloon and New Territories were successively leased to the British colonists for 99 years. The Chinese government carried out rounds of tough negotiations with the British government in 1982-84. Under the creative initiative of Deng Xiaoping's One

Hong Kong skyline and Victoria Harbour

©iStockphoto.com/Cheng Chang

Country Two Systems policy, Hong Kong's sovereignty was transferred back to China on 1st July 1997.

Most Chinese people regard the cession of Hong Kong to Britain as a stigma and a symbol of the adversities and humiliation that China experienced in the 19th and the early 20th centuries. Hong Kong, like Taiwan and Tibet, is regarded as an inalienable part of China. For the Chinese the return of Hong Kong is seen as proof of China's rapid rise and strength, though the transfer itself didn't have a direct impact on people's life in mainland China.

Hong Xiuquan

Hong Xiuquan (1814-1864), born in Guangdong in southern China, was the leader of the Taiping Rebellion against the Qing Dynasty and the founder of the Heavenly Kingdom of Taiping. Having on four separate occasions failed to pass the Imperial Civil Examinations (often as much a sign of the system's corruptness as of the individual's lack of ability), he determined, in 1843, to found his own brand of religion, known as the God Worshipper. This was based largely on copying the concept of equality from Christianity. The God Worshipper sect grew very quickly and gained a large following, mainly from among the Chinese poor, who rose up against the corrupt Qing regime. In 1851 Hong Xiuquan, who had started to call himself the Brother of Jesus Christ, plotted the Jintian Uprising and established the Heavenly Kindom of Taiping. Over the next 14 years Taiping troops pushed forward with overwhelming momentum and took control of more than 600 towns, becoming a serious threat to the Qing Dynasty. However the Kingdom of Taiping was troubled by internal power struggles among its top military leaders and gradually started to fall apart. In 1864 Hong Xiuquan died in Tianjing (now Nanjing) – the capital city of the kingdom. Some believe that

THE BROTHER OF JESUS CHRIST

he committed suicide rather than succumb to illness. One month after his death, his capital fell, marking the end of the Heavenly Kingdom of Taiping.

hot and sour soup

Chinese hot and sour soup originates in Sichuan cuisine. It can be either vegetarian or meat-based. Typical ingredients are day lily buds, mushrooms, bamboo shoots and tofu. The broth is flavoured with pieces of chicken and squid. White peppers account for the spiciness and vinegar for the sourness. Try this soup if you lose your appetite – the results are always good.

©iStockphoto.com/Ceneri

hot pot

Hot pot (or huo guo) is an extremely popular way of cooking and eating, especially in winter. A pot of stew sits simmering on the table. Diners choose whatever they like from the plates beside the pot (raw ingredients not pre-cooked) and dip them in the pot to cook, like a fondue. A great occasion for conviviality.

hot water shops

Hot water shops used to be a common feature of Chinese life. People would go to the shop to get their hot water. These days, at universities, students who live on campus still get hot water from hot water shops. And some big factories have them too.

Houyi

A great archer in ancient Chinese mythology who is said either to have lived during the reign of King Yao or to have been the leader of the Youqiong Tribe in the Xia Dynasty (c.2100-c.1600BC). Houyi's wife Chang'e is revered as the Goddess of the Moon. According to legends, there were once ten suns in the sky, scorching the world and burning everything. People had nothing left to eat. Houyi was sent to shoot down nine suns with his bow and arrows. But he got slightly carried away and was just on the point of shooting

down the tenth sun when King Yao stopped him, as the world would have sunk into total darkness without any sun.

Another heroic deed of Houyi's is to have killed the monsters that were roaming around and causing great destruction and loss of life. Among them were a chisel-toothed monster with teeth five feet long, a giant python that disturbed the peace of Dongting Lake, and a ferociously large bird that caused storms merely by flapping its wings. Houyi, a tragic hero, was finally killed by his student who was jealous of Houyi's incomparable skills as an archer.

Hu Bing

Male supermodel, actor and singer Hu Bing probably got his muscular physique from canoeing when he was young. His success as a fashion model opened up possibilities in other areas of the entertainment industry and he has starred in several hit TV series and has released a few albums.

Hu Jintao

Hu Jintao (1942-) is the General Secretary of the Chinese Communist Party (CCP), President of China and Chairman of the Central Military Commission. A graduate of Tsinghua University, Hu gradually rose to political power when he was elected General Secretary of the Chinese Communist Youth League in the mid 1980s. He succeeded Jiang Zemin as General Secretary of the CCP in 2002 and the following year was elected President. In 2004 he took control of the Central Military Commission after Jiang resigned. Most political commentators see Hu's rise as representative of China's transfer of power to a generation of younger, more pragmatically minded technocrats.

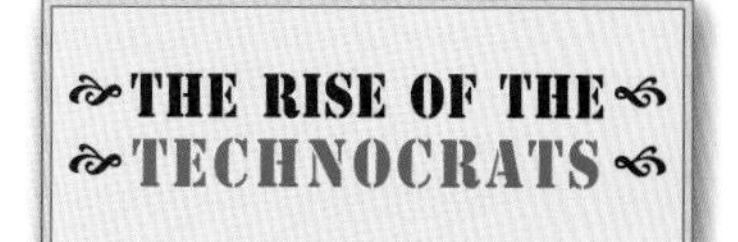

Hu Shi

FATHER OF CHINESE LITERARY REVOLUTION

An influential scholar and philosopher who made a major contribution to the reform of the Chinese literary style in the New Culture Movement in the early years of the 20th century. Well-educated in the traditional Chinese classics, Hu Shi (1891-1962), went to the United States in 1910 on a government scholarship to study at Cornell University and later Columbia. He studied philosophy under John Dewey. Returning to China with a PhD in 1917 he took up an appointment at Beijing University and soon started to attract attention and gain influence. He advocated a reform of Chinese literature and urged people to write using the spoken language instead of classical Chinese, thus making it easier for common people to read and write. New forms of literature, taking up his proposals, soon began to emerge. So great was the impact of this reform that Hu Shi was named the "Father of Chinese Literary Revolution". An ardent pragmatist all his life, Hu advocated reforms on social, political and intellectual issues, mostly through his writings. He remained a highly influential voice in discussions focusing on the re-evaluation of Chinese culture. He was ambassador of the Republic of China to the US from 1938 to 1942. Subsequently he was Chancellor of Beijing University. In 1949, he left China for the States and then Taiwan, where he spent the rest of his life.

Hu Yaobang

Hu Yaobang (1915-1989) was General Secretary of the Chinese Communist Party Central Committee from 1981-1987. Hu was honoured for his great efforts to ensure the rehabilitation of those who were persecuted during the Cultural Revolution. He advocated freedom of speech and freedom of the press. He was an important supporter of Deng Xiaoping's economic reforms and was Deng's designated successor. However, he was forced to resign in 1987, being castigated for his tolerance of the trend of "bourgeois liberalization" and his sympathetic

©AFP/Getty Images

Hu Yaobang (right) with Chinese Communist leader Deng Xiaoping in Beijing, September 1981

attitude towards the students' campaign for democratic reform. Hu died of a sudden heart attack in April of 1989.

When Hu died, students gathered in Tiananmen Square to mourn his death and to remember his contribution to the construction of modern China in the aftermath of the Cultural Revolution. This memorial gathering had been banned by the government. It thus became a demonstration calling for political and democratic reform and culminated in the Tiananmen Square protest.

Hua Guofeng

Hua Guofeng (1921-2008) was a passionate and unwaveringly loyal disciple of Mao Zedong. Mao chose him as his successor to the position of Chairman of the Communist Party of China, the supreme position in all China. Hua ended the Cultural Revolution after Mao's death in 1976. But he was deeply conservative and strongly opposed to political and economic reforms. Gradually he lost power to the stronger Deng Xiaoping and disappeared from the centre of China's political stage in the early 1980s.

Hua Yanjun → *A Bing*

Huang Gai

Huang Gai was a general in the service of the Kingdom of Wu during the Three Kingdoms era. The novel Romance of the Three Kingdoms is so popular that Chinese people tend to muddle up the historical facts about the Three Kingdoms era with fictional episodes from the novel. A very famous story is this.

Huang Gai showed great wisdom and loyalty in the Battle of Red Cliff. Under threat of invasion from Cao Cao's mighty fleet from the Kingdom of Wei, Huang suggested to Zhou Yu, the commander-in-chief of the Wu troops, that he use fire as a means of attack, since he had seen that Cao Cao had chained all his ships together in order to prevent his soldiers, mostly from the north, from being seasick. Huang came up with a trick which is told in the famous story called *Zhou Yu beating Huang Gai*. Huang allowed himself to receive a public beating from Zhou Yu, pretending that Zhou Yu had accused him of suggesting surrender to Cao Cao. Word of this beating reached Cao Cao through his spies. Cao Cao was fooled and believed Huang when he later pretended to want to defect to Cao Cao's side. Huang loaded his boats with straw and grease and headed for Cao's fleet. When his boats were close to Cao's fleet, he set them on fire and steered them at the enemy. Fire soon spread through the fleet causing enormous damage, finally forcing Cao Cao to retreat.

When talking about Huang Gai, Chinese people usually think of this story of *Zhou Yu beating Huang Gai*. The name of the story is the first part of an idiomatic double pun still used today. The second part is "one is willing to give a beating, and one is willing to take a beating". It is used to describe a situation in which both parties to a conflict agree of their own free will.

huangjiu

Huangjiu is any fermented liquor brewed from grains like glutinous rice, millet and wheat. Unlike baijiu, it has a much lower alcohol content and is yellow in colour (huang in Chinese). Huangjiu is also widely used in Chinese cooking.

Hui → *ISLAM*

hukou

The hukou, or residence permit, is one of the most precious documents that a Chinese person possesses. Registration of citizens has been in force in China for thousands of years. Under the command economy of the Communists in the middle of the 20th century this registration was tightened to restrict the movement of migrant workers around the country, in particular from countryside to cities. Working in an area not covered by your hukou, and without the relevant amendments

A MOST PRECIOUS POSSESSION

and official endorsements on the hukou, could land the worker in trouble with the authorities. Controls and restrictions are not as rigid now, but they are still there.

huli jing, *a.k.a.* ***fox spirits***

Huli jing are fox spirits in Chinese mythology that have magical powers. They can take on human form to cause mischief and seduce. Fox spirits in folk tales and legends usually appear as beautiful young women. Often they are described as evil and dangerous – but not those in Pu Songling's collection of tales *Strange Stories from a Chinese Studio*, most of whom are charming, kind and loving. The most notorious fox spirit in legends is probably Daji, whose story is told in The Investiture of the Gods. She was married to the cruel tyrant, King Zhou, of the Shang Dynasty. Daji, with her body possessed by a fox spirit, is said to be to blame for the fall of the kingdom, as she bewitched the king and invented many cruel instruments of torture to persecute good people. In modern Chinese slang, huli jing is a derogatory expression for a woman who seduces men.

Hundred Days of Reform → *LIANG QICHAO*

Hundred Flowers Award → *MEDIA AWARDS*

Huo Yuanjia

Huo Yuanjia (1868-1910), a master of Chinese martial arts, is regarded as a national hero for his patriotic passion in publicly challenging hostile foreign fighters in order to defend Chinese people's dignity. A true master of the kung fu style of Mizongyi, Huo founded the Jingwu Sports Association in Shanghai to promote Chinese martial arts and the idea of "building up health and mind". He believed that through learning traditional combat skills Chinese people would rebuild their confidence and get rid of the insulting nickname "the sick man of East Asia". Nowadays there are many movies and TV series based on his legendary life and suspicious death. One of the common conspiracy theories about his death is that he was poisoned by the Japanese who sought revenge for their defeat in a judo competition.

hutong

Hutongs are traditional narrow alleys and lanes in Beijing with a typical width of 9 metres. They were called "hottog" or "water wells" in Mongolian. Beijing hutongs date back 700 years, being originally built during the Yuan Dynasty and then continued through the Ming and Qing Dynasties – right up

Morning in a hutong in Beijing

to 1912. Hutongs were constructed as passageways which served the function of linking siheyuan (Chinese courtyards) – a traditional northern Chinese housing structure.

The design of both hutong and siheyuan follows the traditional rules of Chinese feng shui, with most hutong lying east-west and siheyuan running north-south.

A lot of hutong were bulldozed in the new build fury before the 1990s. But the authorities have recognized their value and according to recent statistics there are more than 1000 hutong extant in Beijing. It is said if all the hutong were connected together end to end they would be longer than the Great Wall. Nowadays the best preserved hutong attraction is in the Bell and Drum Tower area, close to Qianhai Lake and Houhai Lake.

I. M. Pei

A world-famous Chinese-born architect, Pei (1917-) emigrated to the US in 1935 and studied at the University of Pennsylvania, MIT and Harvard. In 1964, his innovative designs and talents grabbed the attention of the Kennedy family, who entrusted him with the design of the John. F. Kennedy Library. His East Wing of the National Gallery of Art, Washington DC, has been hailed as a classic of modern architecture. His works can be found in many metropolises all over the world, such as the Fragrance Hill Hotel in Beijing, the Bank of China Tower in Hong Kong, and, most importantly, the controversial Glass Pyramid in the courtyard of the Louvre in Paris. In 1983, he was awarded the Pritzker Architecture Prize – the "Nobel Prize of Architecture".

Ice Festival → *HA'ERBIN*

Imperial Civil Examination

The Imperial Civil Examination was a system used in imperial China for a period of 1300 years to recruit government officials from among the intellectuals. The system started in the Sui Dynasty (581-618AD) and it was fully developed in the Song (960-1279). The examinations included three levels: prefectural, provincial and the imperial examinations. The successful candidates at the final level would be granted official positions. With its very high failure rate, however, only a fraction of candidates would pass all the examinations and qualify. Take the Song Dynasty, for example. In a period of over 300 years, there were only some 20,000 candidates who were recruited. The system was widely criticized by historians for restricting intellectuals' minds. This was especially the case during the Ming and Qing dynasties when the content of the examinations was exclusively based on the Four Books and Five Classics, the Confucian classic texts chosen by the Song Neo-Confucian Zhu Xi. The system was abolished in 1905 shortly before the fall of the Qing Dynasty.

Investiture of the Gods → *Fengshen Yanyi*

Iron Man → *Wang Jinxi*

iron rice bowl

The concept of the iron rice bowl is used to symbolize the notion of a job for life with all the benefits and perks of full-time employment irrespective of the employee's actual performance. (Nothing like that in the West, of course). It followed the employment style of the former Soviet Union and was associated with a centrally planned economy. The iron rice bowl existed mainly in state-owned Chinese enterprises, government or public institutions, and brought a package of staff welfare such as free medical treatment and free housing in spite of low efficiency and poor productivity. The iron rice bowl started to crack during the labour reforms starting from the 1980s. But it hasn't entirely disappeared and some Chinese would say the iron rice bowl is still alive and well in some areas of government.

Islam

The introduction of Islam to China can be traced back to the 7th century, to the Tang Dynasty. Chinese Muslims have exerted a sound influence – mostly in trade and culture – over the course of Chinese history. The most famous Muslim in medieval China may be Zheng He, the pioneering explorer and diplomat in the Ming Dynasty, who commanded the fleets that made seven great voyages to the Indian Ocean from 1405 to 1433. Nowadays, Chinese Muslims can be found in every region of China, with big populations in such provinces as Xinjiang, Gansu and Ningxia in the northwest, Yunnan in the southwest, and Henan in central China. Traditionally the Han Chinese call Muslims Hui Hui or the Hui people, as almost half of Chinese Muslims belong to the Hui ethnic group. Another big Muslim minority group is the Uygur, which accounts for about 40% of the Muslim population.

J

Jackie Chan, *a.k.a.* *Cheng Long*

Jackie Chan, born in 1954 in Hong Kong, is a prominent figure in the Chinese motion picture industry. Best known to the Western world as a kung fu and action movie actor, he is also successful at film directing, producing, martial arts choreography and singing. As a child he went through rigorous martial arts and acrobatics training with a Peking Opera master of Wusheng (male warrior role). Starting out as a stuntman, he developed his own acting style, featuring visual gags and acrobatic fighting, in the so-called kung fu comedy films. He became a household name in East Asia. Jackie Chan performs most of his own stunts, many of which have nearly cost him his life. After several unsuccessful attempts to make an impact in the North American market, he made a breakthrough in 1980 with *Rumble in the Bronx*. He achieved the status of most popular Asian actor with box-office hit movies like *Rush Hour* and *Shanghai Noon*. Jackie Chan is actively engaged in charitable and philanthropic work around the world.

Jacky Cheung → *Zhang Xueyou*

jade

In China jade is more than just an ornamental stone: it carries special significance in Chinese culture and its use dates back to the New Stone Age. Chinese people believe that the rarity, hardness and pure colour of jade make it the embodiment of nobility, righteousness and flawlessness. It is also said

Lucky charms made from jade

that jade drives out evil. That's why Chinese people always like to wear jade. In ancient times, jade items were often used for ceremonial purposes from imperial seals to burial suits. More precious and more costly than gold, jade was only used by the royal family and the nobles. It has been a popular hobby, from the earliest dynasties down to the present day, for Chinese people, especially in the middle and upper classes, to collect different kinds of finely crafted jade. Kunlun jade from the Kunlun Mountains in northwest China was used to make one side of the Olympic medals for the 2008 Beijing Games.

Jade Emperor

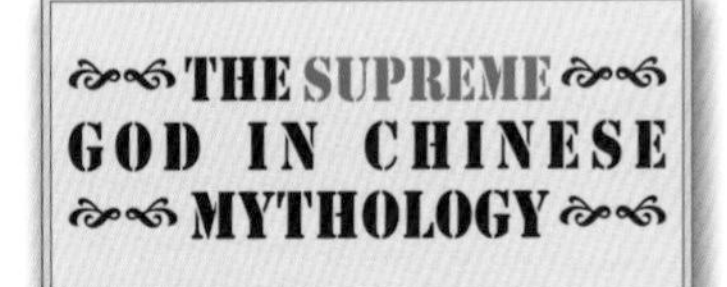

Not a real emperor but an emperor in Chinese mythology, the Jade Emperor is the supreme god who rules the Kingdom of Heaven. All mythical gods and goddesses answer to him. In Taoism, the Jade Emperor ranks directly beneath the Three Pure Ones, but acts as the de facto ruler of Heaven and Earth. As the head of the pantheon, he has a vast company of civil servants and bureaucrats at his beck and call. For example, the Town God and Tu Di Gong (the God of Land) look after the paperwork of the world of mortals, whilst Zao Jun (the God of Kitchens) files a report every year on the conduct of each family for him to evaluate. The Jade Emperor is supposed to make an annual inspection of every person on the earth, granting rewards and punishments according to merits or demerits. His birthday is said to be on the ninth day of the first lunar month. Taoist temples usually hold a Jade Emperor worshipping ritual on that day and people come to burn incense and make food offerings.

Jay Chou, *a.k.a.* ***Zhou Jielun***

Jay Chou (born 1979) is a talented Taiwanese musician, singer, actor and director. His music combines both Chinese and Western styles to produce a distinct and fresh sound with hints of R&B, rock and rap. His lyrics cover a variety of issues, such as domestic violence in *Dad I am Back*, the damage done by war in *Wounds of War* and a high regard for family values in *Listen to Your Mother*. Well trained in classical music, he was initially hired to write songs for other singers. He released his first album *Jay* in 2000 and soon established a reputation in the pop music industry as a gifted singer and songwriter who is also the producer of all his albums and a music video director. Since then, he has produced one album per year. As well as being commercially successful, he has been recognized with hundreds of awards. He had his acting début in *Initial D*, for which he won the Best Newcomer at the Golden Horse Awards in Taiwan in 2005. He starred in several hit movies including *The City of Golden Armour*, directed by Zhang Yimou, featuring international Chinese stars Chow Yun-Fat and Gong Li. He directed his first film *Secret* in 2007.

©Mike Clarke/Getty Images

Jet Li (right) with Taiwanese singer Jay Chou in Hong Kong, January 2006

Jet Li, *a.k.a.* ***Li Lianjie***

Li Lianjie (1963-) started out as a wushu (martial arts) champion, with 15 gold medals in the Chinese national championships to his credit. He became an action movie superstar after his successful debut in a Hong Kong-produced film *Shaolin Temple* (1982). This started a martial arts film boom in mainland China. From then on, he gradually shifted his attention from sport to film and made many films including the famous series about legendary martial arts hero Wong Fei Hung. He also became a Hollywood star with his box office hit movies like *Lethal Weapon 4* and *Romeo Must Die*. A Buddhist believer, he was named the "Philanthropic Ambassador" of the Red Cross Society of China. In the 21st century he became more active in charity work and founded the Jet Li One Foundation.

Ji Gong → *DAOJI*

Ji Mi, *a.k.a.* *Jimmy Liao*

Ji Mi, born in Taipei, Taiwan, is perhaps the most popular of Chinese illustrators. After working in advertising for 12 years, he switched his focus to illustration. He has published 18 well-received illustrated books since 1998. His books touch readers of all generations with their poetic text, paired with beautiful and haunting paintings. Ji's illustrations, rich in originality and imagination, tend to put sad things in a lighter way and invite readers to go on a journey full of fantasy and magic, always with hope at the end. Some of his books were made into films such as *Sound of Colours*, in which a young blind girl ventures on a subway trip while her imagination leads her to many wonderful places, and *A Chance of Sunshine* (also known as *Turn Left, Turn Right*), which is about two young people in search of true love.

Jia Nanfeng → *Empress Jia*

Jia Zhangke

A Chinese film director and independent filmmaker who is considered a leading figure of the "sixth generation" of directors in China, Jia Zhangke was born in 1970 in Fenyang, a small coalmining town in Shanxi Province. He constantly returns there for inspiration and used the place as the backdrop for his first two films. After graduating from Beijing Film Academy, he won international acclaim for his debut feature *Xiao Wu* (known as *The Pickpocket*). Most of his films have limited runs in China, but this doesn't stop them attracting world-wide attention. His latest film *Still Life* won the 2006 Golden Lion at the 63rd Venice International Film Festival. What is special about his films? His works are noted for their honest portrayal of the lives of ordinary people in a fast-changing China and deal with various themes from disorientation of young people to the pressure put on ordinary people by globalization. Jia Zhangke is obsessed with a documentary style of film making, insists on using long takes, works with non-professional actors who have strong accents and uses natural sound effects.

Jiang Jieshi

This is the standard Mandarin name for Chiang Kai-shek.

Jiang Qing

Jiang Qing was born in 1913 as Li Yunhe in Shandong Province and became the third wife of Mao Zedong in 1939.

Before her marriage she worked from 1934-1937 as a film actress in Shanghai under the stage name of Lan Ping. In 1938 she went to Yan'an, the Chinese Communist Party headquarters, where she changed her name to Jiang Qing. She played an active part in political propaganda in the fields of literature and art, attacking traditional Chinese culture and helping pave the way for the Cultural Revolution. During the course of the Cultural Revolution she became a powerful political figure.

I WAS A DOG OF CHAIRMAN MAO'S AND I BIT WHOEVER THE CHAIRMAN ASKED ME TO BITE

Joining up with Zhang Chunqiao, Yao Wenyuan and Wang Hongwen, Jiang Qing became the leader of the notorious Gang of Four which had as its objective the usurpation of greater power within the party by criticizing and bringing down the party patriarchs.

In October 1976, one month after Mao Zedong died, Jiang Qing and her allies were arrested on a charge of plotting against the state. And in 1981 she was sentenced to death. This sentence was later commuted to life imprisonment. Then, in the course of a period of release on bail for medical treatment in 1991, it was announced that she had committed suicide.

One of her famous sayings during her trial was "I was a dog of Chairman Mao's and I bit whoever the Chairman asked me to bite".

When she was a young girl Jiang would often see her father, a poor carpenter, get drunk and beat up her mother. For her, perhaps, the traditional past and traditional culture were full of fear and darkness and things to be overcome.

©Keystone/Getty Images

Jiang Zemin

Chinese Communists wrap up their 17th five-yearly Party Congress inside the Great Hall of the People in Beijing, 21 October 2007, as President Hu Jintao (left) and former President Jiang Zemin applaud

Former General Secretary of the Chinese Communist Party (1989-2002) and President of the People's Republic of China (1993-2003), Jiang Zemin (born 1926) rose to power in 1989 following the Tiananmen Square incident. This was a somewhat unexpected arrangement, for Jiang, though he had served as Secretary of the CCP Shanghai Committee, was not a member of the standing committee of the Politburo. Some critics think that Jiang was chosen partly because of his adept handling of the 1989 Shanghai crisis and partly out of a desire to avoid internal friction within the CCP. During his presidency, China continued to undergo rapid economic growth and steady reforms. In 2003 Hu Jintao succeeded Jiang as President and Jiang Zemin retired from the political scene.

His political ideology was called the "Three Represents" theory, and is written into the party and state constitution – alongside Marxist-Leninism, Maoism and Deng Xiaoping's Thoughts. During his presidency China witnessed the return of Hong Kong, joined the WTO and won the bid to host the 2008 Olympics. The strongest criticism against Jiang was his harsh treatment of the Falun Gong.

Jiangsu

The province of Jiangsu lies along the lower reaches of the Yangtze River, next to Anhui, Zhejiang and Shanghai and has its capital in Nanjing. One of China's most populous and wealthy provinces, Jiangsu had the third largest GDP in 2007. Culturally, the northern part of Jiangsu Province differs from the south. The former, including the historic city of

Xuzhou, is considered typical of northern virtues: people are bold, generous and big-hearted; the latter, with such opulent cities as Suzhou, Wuxi and Changzhou, belongs to a southern culture which is famous for delicate classical gardens, silk and embroidery.

Jianzhen

Jianzhen (688-763AD), who might well enjoy greater reverence in Japan than in China, was a learned Chinese monk in the Tang Dynasty (618-907AD). Taking up an invitation from two Japanese Buddhist envoys, he started his missionary expedition to Japan in 743. He failed five times to reach Japan, but at his sixth attempt, at the age of 65 and having lost his eyesight, Jianzhen finally arrived at Nara and was welcomed by the Emperor of Japan. He devoted the rest of his life to promoting Chinese culture and Buddhist teachings. Today the Japanese people are still indebted to Jianzhen's legacy in religion, architecture, calligraphy and medicine. A memorial museum was built in Yangzhou, Jianzhen's hometown, in 1974, designed by Liang Sicheng, to commemorate his great contributions to Sino-Japanese relationships.

jiaozi

Jiaozi, a traditional Chinese food, are crescent-shaped dumplings, usually filled with minced meat and vegetables, wrapped into a piece of thin, round dough. Jiaozi can be either boiled, steamed or fried. It has long been a tradition on Chinese New Year's Eve for family members to gather around a table making jiaozi together. The joyful atmosphere of the family reunion fits perfectly with the essence of the Chinese Spring Festival. Traditionally people eat jiaozi in the early morning of New Year's Day.

Jimmy Liao → *Ji Mi*

Jin Ping Mei

Jin Ping Mei, which translates both as *The Golden Lotus* and *The Plum in the Golden Vase*, is one of the most important classical novels written during the late Ming Dynasty. The real identity of the author, Lanling Xiaoxiao Sheng, remains a mystery. The title of the book is taken from the three leading female characters – Pan Jin-lian (literally Golden Lotus), Li Ping-er (Little Vase) and Pang Chun-mei (Spring Plum Blossoms). The opening chapter is based on an episode from the Water Margin where Pan Jinlian, a beautiful young girl married to an ugly dwarf, is seduced by Ximen Qing, a well-to-do young merchant and womanizer. After murdering her husband, Pan marries Ximen Qing and becomes one of his six wives, or rather, his fifth concubine. The plot follows her new life in this wealthy middle-class household, a life which is rife with competition, infidelity, corruption, domestic violence and eroticism. The book was officially banned for centuries on account of its sexual descriptions. It is seen as a microcosm of Chinese society in the 16th century.

Jin Wudi, *a.k.a.* *Sima Yan*

Originally a general serving under Wei Wendi, Jin Wudi (236-290AD) established the Western Jin Dynasty (265-317AD) by usurping the last Wei Dynasty Emperor, Yuandi, and defeating the Wu Kingdom.

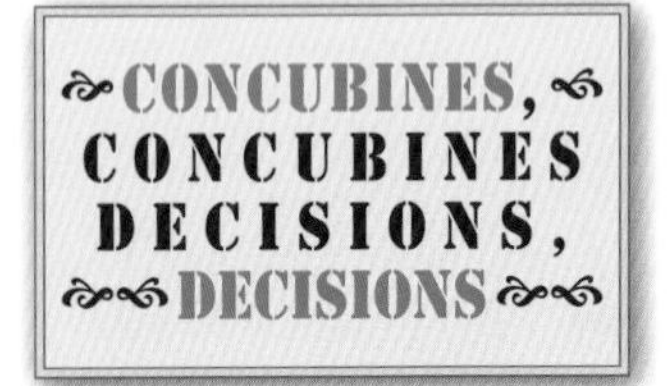

Like most of the men who established new dynasties in China, Jin Wudi was a strong and visionary leader who encouraged stability and scholarship. However, his efforts to build an empire were undermined by corruption, excessive rewards for loyal supporters of the imperial family and large-scale tax evasion.

Jin Wudi was known for his extravagance and sensuality and had over ten thousand concubines in his palace. However, it is said that, finding it difficult to decide who to sleep with every night, he would ride out on a goat-drawn cart and wherever the goats stopped, that was where he would spend the night. A lot of women would, therefore, put bamboo leaves in front of their doors to attract the old goat's goats.

Wudi left the empire to his retarded son, who was controlled by his cruel and ruthless wife, the Empress Jia. Her autocratic rule caused hugely destructive in-fighting, which brought the dynasty to an early end.

Jin Xing

A famous modern dancer and choreographer, Jin Xing was born – as a boy – in 1967 and received his dance training at the military's dance troupe in Shenyang at the age of nine. In 1987 he became the first Chinese dancer to be awarded an arts scholarship to study in the United States. He came back to China six years later with a major decision that would change his life forever. Often aware that he was a woman trapped in a man's body, he underwent a sex change operation in 1995, a daring move in a such a conservative society. Jin Xing then went to Shanghai to continue her career and establish the contemporary dance company *Shanghai Jin Xing Dance Theatre* to promote modern dance and train dancers. With her great courage and creativity, she is a tireless trail-blazer in modern dance.

HE UNDERWENT A SEX CHANGE OPERATION IN 1995, A DARING MOVE IN SUCH A CONSERVATIVE SOCIETY

Jin Yong

Jin Yong (born 1924) is the pen name of Louis Cha (Zha Liang Yong), one of the most influential Chinese novelists specializing in the wuxia genre (martial arts and heroism). He was also the co-founder of the Hong Kong daily *Ming Pao*. There is a saying that wherever there are Chinese people, there are readers of Jin Yong. He has sold over 100 million copies of his 14 books. Boys love Jin Yong's swash-buckling wuxia world where sword-bearing men and women (in the world of wuxia women also carry swords or daggers) embark on quests for honour, power and supreme skill in martial arts. Jin Yong is also a Chinese history scholar and his books are full of references to almost every aspect of traditional Chinese culture: such as traditional Chinese medicine, calligraphy, music, weiqi (a Chinese board game), tea and wine culture, the philosophies of Confucianism, Buddhism and Taoism. He likes to intertwine his stories with historical events and figures in an effort to create a realistic background and express his opinions about them in an indirect way. All his works have had numerous cinema and TV adaptations, making Jin Yong a household name throughout Chinese-speaking communities.

Jing Ke

Jing Ke is perhaps the most famous assassin in ancient China. His story is recorded in the chapter "Biographies of the Assassins" in *Records of the Grand Historian*, also called *Shiji*, written by Sima Qian. Jing Ke is best known for his failed assassination of Ying Zheng, the king of Qin, who later became Qin Shi Huang. The story is that, in the Warring States Period, the state of Qin had become the most powerful state of all and had started to gobble up the other six states. When Qin was about to attack the state of Yan, Dan the crown prince of Yan, in desperation, called on Jing Ke to assassinate Ying Zhang, the king of Qin. On the day Jing Ke was leaving for his mission, many people came to the border river of Yi to see him off. Jing Ke sang his famous song *The wind is howling, and the river of Yi freezing. The hero departs, and he will never return!* Ying Zheng called Jing Ke to his palace as Jing was to present him with a gift: a map of Yan and the head of a runaway Qin general. As Jing unrolled the map scroll in front of the king, he seized the poisoned dagger hidden inside and struck out at Ying Zheng. But Jing Ke missed and was killed by the palace guards.

A view of the 88 floor, 420 metre high Jingmao Tower, which houses offices and a hotel

Jinggang Mountains

This name is very significant for the Chinese. The Jinggang Mountains in Jiangxi Province are the cradle of the Chinese revolution. Mao established the first Soviet-style regime there.

Jingmao Tower

A colossal modern hotel in Shanghai. With its 88 storeys it symbolizes China's economic resurgence.

Jingwei

According to Chinese mythology, Jingwei was the daughter of the Yan Emperor, a legendary ruler of China some 5000 years ago. She went to swim in the East Sea when she was a little girl and drowned. Her spirit turned into a black bird with a white beak and red claws. Filled with hatred for the dangerous waves, she started to pick twigs and pebbles and drop them to the sea in an effort to fill it up. Legend says that she claimed that she would not abandon this endeavour, even if it took a hundred million years. "Jingwei filling the sea" (Jingwei tian hai) is a Chinese idiom derived from this story and is used to denote great perseverance and untiring effort in the achievement of one's goal.

jobs

There was a time when Chinese people, mostly college graduates, did not have the option of choosing a job. The government assigned them jobs. This regime faded away in the late 1980s.

John Woo, *a.k.a.* ***Wu Yusen***

A world-famous film director and producer, John Woo (born 1946) started out as an assistant director in Hong Kong and directed his first feature film in 1974. He worked in a variety of genres before making the sensational action movie *A Better Tomorrow* (1986), a masterwork of John Woo's "Heroic Bloodshed" genre featuring beautifully fashioned gunplay and emotional conflicts and tension between his tragic heroes. His successful collaboration with the leading actor Chow Yun-Fat in a series of ultra-violent gangster films marked a new era of Hong Kong action cinema. John Woo was offered a Hollywood contract in 1993 and went to the United States to seek further career development. Disoriented in the strange new culture and completely different working environment, Woo hardly had any opportunities to do what he was good at. After several unsuccessful movies he came up with *Face Off*, an action thriller bearing his trademark style that was widely acclaimed. Among his later Hollywood works, though *Mission Impossible II* was a huge success at the box office, the other two were considered disappointments by critics. His latest project was *Red Cliff*, an epic film based on a famous historical battle from Romance of the Three Kingdoms.

Journey to the West

Journey to the West is one of the Four Great Classical Novels of Chinese literature composed during the Ming Dynasty (1368-1644). Based on real events from the life of the great Buddhist monk Xuanzang in the Tang Dynasty and related folktales, it is the story of how Xuanzang, also known as the Monk Tang in folk culture, travels from China to the West – which here means India – to collect true Buddhist sutras from the Buddha, in order to bring enlightenment to his people. On his travels he is accompanied by his three disciples appointed by Guanyin: Sun Wukong (a powerful and mischievous monkey), Zhu Bajie (a lazy and greedy pig) and Sha Wujing or Friar Sand (a loyal and steadfast immortal). The white horse that Xuanzang rides on is a transformed Dragon Prince. His pilgrimage is long and arduous. Numerous demons and spirits attempt to ambush him, so as to take him captive and eat him, it having been said that whoever should eat the monk's flesh would become immortal. Their adventures are full of miraculous happenings and humour, pranks and practical jokes, set against a background of Chinese folk culture, mythology and popular religions. The story is such a favourite of the Chinese that it has been adapted into operas, television series, movies and cartoons many times over.

Kang Youwei → *Liang Qichao*

Kangxi → *Qing Kangxi*

Kazakh

An ethnic group living mostly in Xinjiang although there are some in the provinces of Gansu and Qinhai. The Kazakh number over 1.2 million people and generally lead a nomadic lifestyle. Their language is Kazakh.

Kenneth Hsien-yung Pai → *Bai Xianyong*

kites

Kites are a part of China's folk culture. They are traditionally made in the shape of birds, animals, insects and fish. Giant centipede kites may be eighty metres long.

In olden days aspiring scholars would fly kites on the ninth day of the ninth month. The higher the kite flew, the higher their career would be. There were military uses too. One emperor sent his soldiers home to till their fields but told them that, if there was an emergency, kites would fly and they must return to the ranks.

These days kites are flown for fun, especially in the spring. At the Qing Ming Festival there is a tradition of flying kites after a visit to the family graves. Sometimes the string is cut and the kite flies off, taking away worldly cares. At weekends kites drift almost out of sight up above the parks. The town of Weifang in Shandong is especially famous for kites, and hosts an annual international kite festival.

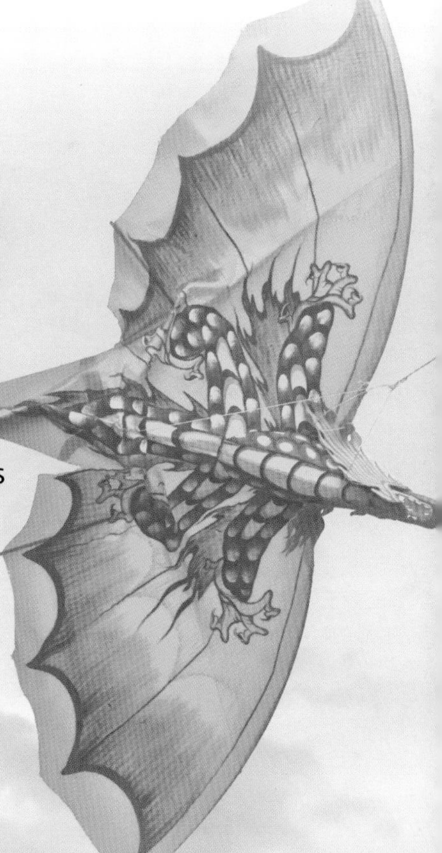

KMT → *Kuomintang*

Kong Qiu → *Confucius*

Kong Zhongni → Confucius

Korean

An ethnic group mostly living in the provinces of Jilin, Liaoning and Heilongjiang. They originated from immigrant communities from the Korean Peninsula. The language they use is similar to the Korean spoken in the two Korean nations.

Kua Fu

Kua Fu is a giant in Chinese mythology, best known from the story *Kua Fu Chasing the Sun*. He was said to be the leader of a clan of giants that lived in the mountains in prehistoric times. One day Kua Fu decided to capture the sun so that he could ensure that the world would always be warm and bright. The closer he got to the sun the thirstier he became.

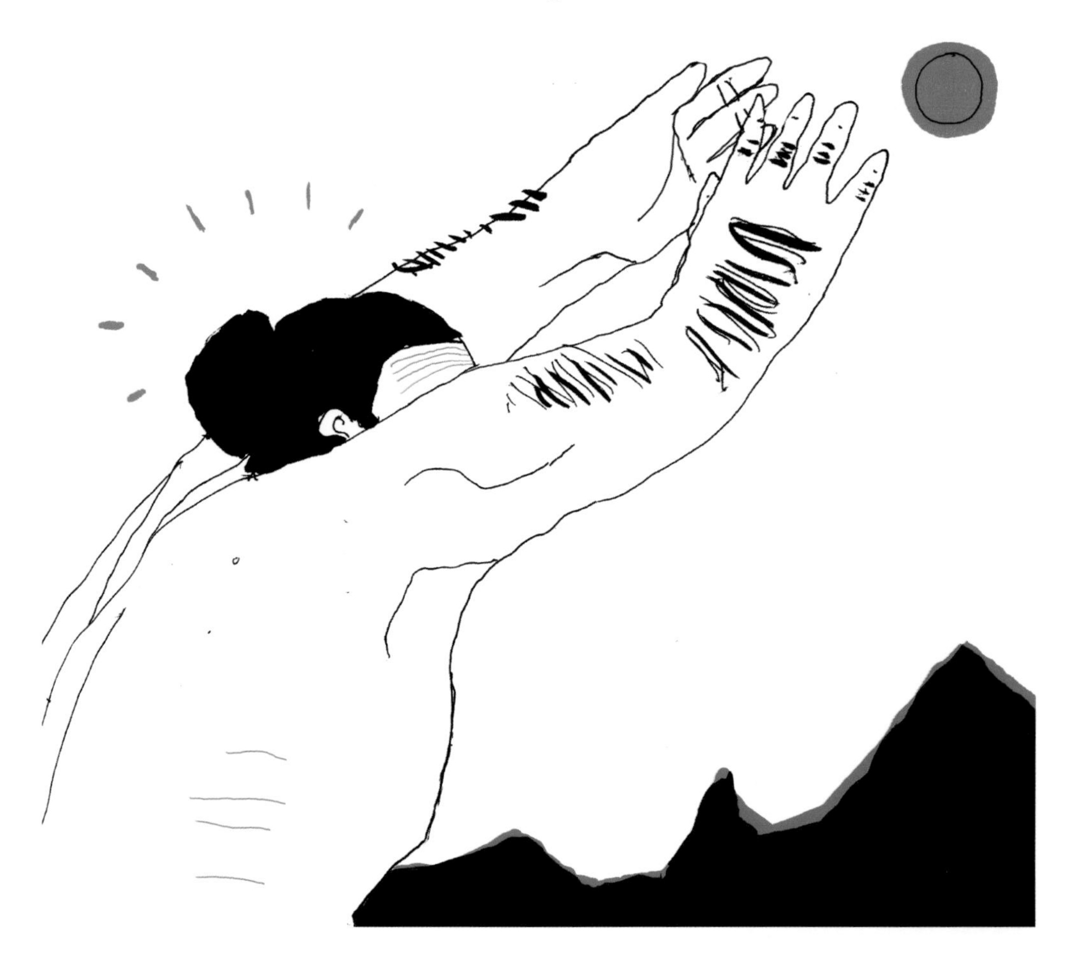

He drank the Yellow River and the Wei River dry, but was still consumed by a raging thirst. Exhausted and parched, he died on his way to a big lake in the north. His body turned into a mountain and the wooden club he was carrying turned into a forest. In modern Chinese, the idiom "Kua Fu chasing the sun" is used to describe someone who overestimates his abilities and cannot achieve what he sets out to do.

Kublai Khan → *YUAN SHIZU*

Kuan Yin → *GUANYIN*

kung pao chicken → *GONG BAO JIDING*

Kuomintang

The Kuomintang (KMT), also known as the Chinese Nationalist Party, was the ruling party of the Republic of China on the mainland from 1928 to 1949. The KMT was founded in 1912 by Sun Yat-sen and Song Jiaoren. With the support of the Soviet Union and in alliance with the Chinese Communist Party, the KMT gradually developed into a powerful political party. It adopted Sun Yat-sen's political philosophy of the Three Principles of the People as its creed: the Principles of Nationalism, Democracy and People's Livelihood.

When Chiang Kai-shek rose to power, he started to purge the Communists in the organization. In 1928 Chiang established the central government in Nanjing under single-party rule. When the Japanese army invaded the heartland of China in 1937, the KMT government was forced to move its capital from Nanjing to Chongqing, leaving the wealthy coastal regions exposed to Japanese outrages. Although severely threatened by the Japanese, the KMT continued to attack the Communists. It was not until the famous Xi'an Incident in 1937 when General Zhang Xueliang arrested Chiang Kai-shek that Chiang agreed to form an alliance with the Communist Party. However, the conflicts between the two parties continued during the war and escalated to a full-scale civil war after Japan's surrender in 1945. The Communist Party gradually took control of the country. Chiang Kai-shek and the remnants of his armies retreated to Taiwan in 1949.

Chiang held office until his death in 1975. The Kuomintang's position of political dominance began to fade after a split in the party in 1994 and, some years later, the KMT was put out of office after losing the 2000 Taiwanese presidential election to the Democratic Progressive Party (DPP). In the 2008 elections, however, the KMT made a comeback and won an overwhelming victory over the DPP. The former KMT chairman Ma Ying-jeou is the current President of Taiwan.

Laba Festival

The Laba Festival falls on the eighth day (ba = 8) of the twelfth month in the Chinese Lunar Calendar. It is a Buddhist festival to commemorate Gautama Buddha who attained enlightenment and founded Buddhism on that day. Monks are supposed to cook congee, usually made of mixed grains, nuts and fruits, as an offering to the Buddha, and hand it out to Buddhist believers. Gradually this practice has spread to the whole nation and congee has become an indispensable part of the celebration. So Laba is also known as the Congee Festival.

land ownership

People can own the house they live in but not the land on which the house is built. All Chinese land belongs to the Chinese state.

landscape painting

Landscape painting, or shan (mountain) shui (water) hua (painting), is an important genre of traditional Chinese ink-wash painting, which, to some extent, illustrates the essence of Chinese man-nature philosophy. Chinese landscape painting does not take a realistic approach to depicting mountains, rivers and trees. It lacks nuances of light and shade or any sense of meticulous geometrical composition. Instead of setting out to duplicate a natural scene, it is more like an embodiment of the painter's meditation about nature, reflecting influences of Taoist cosmology, the integration of spirituality and naturalism and the interaction between human beings and nature in order to achieve harmonious unity.

Lang Lang

A gifted concert pianist. Lang Lang (1982-), is already well established as one of the world's top pianists. He won his first international prize at the Tchaikovsky International Young Musicians Competition in 1995. He was awarded the Leonard Bernstein Award in 2002. Lang has played with almost all the leading orchestras in the world and is regarded by many critics as a rare prodigy.

Lang Xianping

Born in Taiwan in 1956, Lang Xianping received his PhD in finance from the University of Pennsylvania in 1986. He worked for the World Bank and some well-known universities. He is now based in Hong Kong working as finance professor in the Chinese University of Hong Kong and Cheung Kong Graduate School of Business. Professor Lang was given the nickname "supervisor Lang" by the Chinese media on account of his fierce criticism of irregularities in the Chinese stock market. He argued in particular that regulation of the Chinese stock market should focus on protecting the interests of smaller investors. Professor Lang also strongly criticized the loss of national assets during the ownership reform of state-owned enterprises (privatization) in China, launched in the 1980s, and he proposed the introduction of a professional manager system to support the reform.

Lantern Festival

The Lantern Festival falls on the fifteenth day of the first month in the Chinese Lunar Calendar and officially ends the Spring Festival celebrations. People go out onto the streets to watch the lantern parade, sometimes carrying their own lanterns. The most common designs are rabbit and lotus. Another popular activity is to solve riddles written on the lanterns. It is a day for the whole family to gather together and share the traditional food tangyuan – glutinous rice balls of different sizes with or without fillings, boiled in water.

Lanzhou

Lanzhou, on the upper Yellow River, is the capital of Gansu Province in west-central China and used to be an important trade centre on the Silk Road. Its advantageous geographical position has made it a traffic hub linking central China to the western regions since as far back as the Sui Dynasty (581-618AD). From 1949 on it has developed into an industrial and cultural centre, as well as into one of the most heavily polluted cities in China.

©iStockphoto.com/William Perry

Factory and apartments in Lanzhou

Lao She

A notable novelist and playwright, Lao She (1899-1966) is the pseudonym of Shu Qingchun who was born of Manchu descent in Beijing. His writings give a true flavour of old Beijing in the early 20th century. He is perhaps best known for his novel *Rickshaw Boy* in which he portrays a hardworking rickshaw puller, who struggles at the bottom of the social ladder, gradually sinks into a degenerate lifestyle and finally dies one snowy night. The English version became a bestseller in the US in 1945. Lao She's most frequently staged play is *Teahouse*, written in 1957. The story is set in a Beijing teahouse from 1898 to 1945 while various major world events, such as the fall of the Chinese empire, the chaos under the rule of warlords and the Second World War, unfold. These days the Lao She Teahouse, featuring performances of traditional art forms, is a popular tourist attraction in Beijing.

Lao Zi

An important philosopher in ancient China who is traditionally regarded as the founder of Taoism. Originally named Li Er or Lao Dan, Lao Zi is an honorific title meaning "Old Master". He probably lived during the sixth century BC and was about 20 years older than Confucius. It is said that there was a meeting between these two remarkable men. Confucius admired Lao Zi, saying his wisdom was unfathomable.

Misfortune might be a blessing in disguise.

Knowing others is wisdom; knowing the self is enlightenment.

Lao Zi is credited with writing the major Taoist scripture *Daodejing*, literally *The Classic of the Way and Virtue*. It concerns Dao or "the Way" which is the essential cosmic principle through which one can achieve eternal harmony. He uses Dao to explain his idea of cosmology – "In Dao the only motion is returning, the only useful quality is weakness. For though all creatures under heaven are the products of Being, Being itself is the product of Not-being." Consisting of only 5000 Chinese characters, the text covers various themes from political propositions to a system of values. Some words of wisdom are still frequently quoted: "Misfortune might be a blessing in disguise." "Knowing others is wisdom; knowing the self is enlightenment."

Sixth century sage, Lao Zi, riding an ox

Though himself the earliest known atheist in Chinese history, Lao Zi is regarded as a god in the Taoist religion and is still worshipped in Taoist temples. For the non-religious he is an ancient philosopher.

Last Emperor → *Puyi*

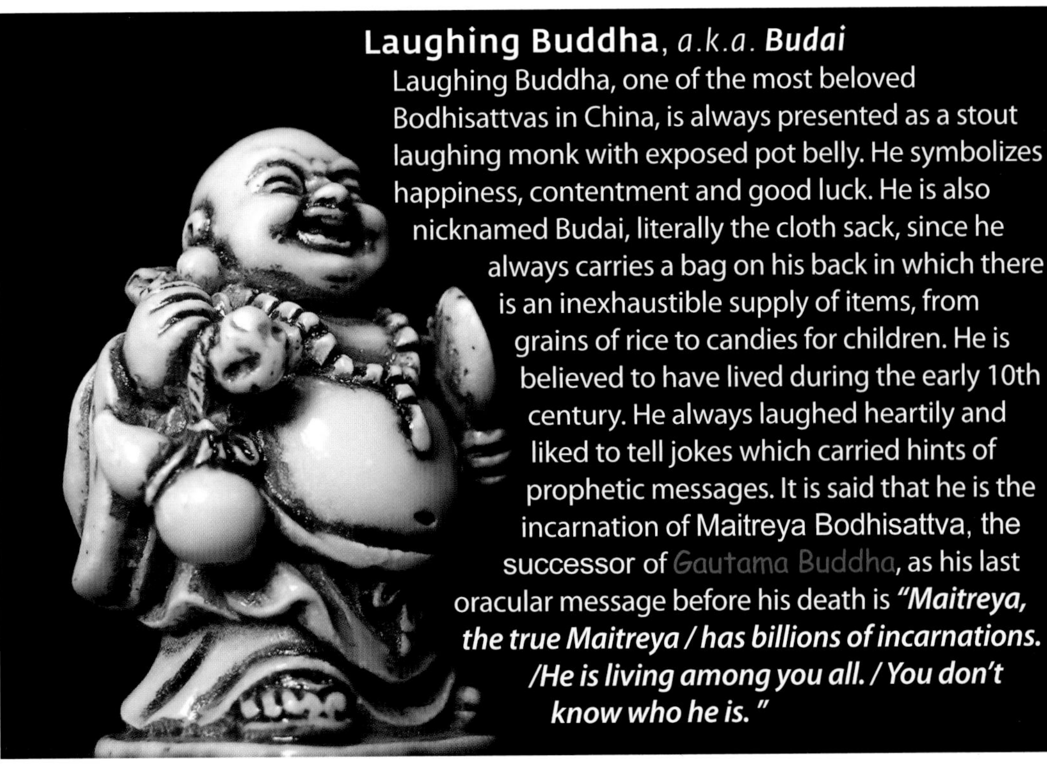

Laughing Buddha, *a.k.a.* ***Budai***

Laughing Buddha, one of the most beloved Bodhisattvas in China, is always presented as a stout laughing monk with exposed pot belly. He symbolizes happiness, contentment and good luck. He is also nicknamed Budai, literally the cloth sack, since he always carries a bag on his back in which there is an inexhaustible supply of items, from grains of rice to candies for children. He is believed to have lived during the early 10th century. He always laughed heartily and liked to tell jokes which carried hints of prophetic messages. It is said that he is the incarnation of Maitreya Bodhisattva, the successor of Gautama Buddha, as his last oracular message before his death is ***"Maitreya, the true Maitreya / has billions of incarnations. /He is living among you all. / You don't know who he is. "***

©iStockphoto.com/Steven Perry

Legalism → *Han Fei*

Lei Feng

Lei Feng (1940-1962) is the model young Chinese Communist whose life is celebrated on Learn from Lei Feng Day (March 5th). Lei Feng had a life filled with hardship and tragedy. His father was killed by the Japanese, his mother committed suicide after being raped by their landlord, one of his two brothers died young and the other lost an arm in an industrial accident. Lei Feng devoted his life to serving the Party and became a true, self-sacrificing worker hero. He died in an accident at the age of just 22.

Lenovo Group

The largest PC manufacturer in China, Lenovo, originally named New Technology Developer Co. Ltd and Legend Group Ltd, was founded in 1984 in Beijing. In 1988, it became a listed company on the Hong Kong Stock Exchange and has dominated the Chinese domestic PC market since then. In 2005 Lenovo bought IBM's PC division and overnight became the fourth largest PC manufacturer in the world.

Leslie Cheung → *Zhang Guorong*

Li An → *Ang Lee*

Li Bai

Li Bai (701-762AD), along with his friend Du Fu, is regarded as one of the two giants of ancient Chinese poetry. If Du Fu's work represents the zenith of realist poetry, Li Bai's certainly marks the high point of romanticism. He is famous for extravagant imagination, spontaneity and defiance of poetic convention. He was known as the God of Poetry and excels in touching his readers at a personal level through communicating his true feelings directly. He was a court poet for a short period during the reign of the Emperor Tang Xuanzong but spent most of his life travelling through China, indulging in wine and revelling in the beauty of nature. Many of his famous poems are associated with wine. For example, from *Drinking Alone by Moonlight*:

> *A cup of wine, under the flowering trees;*
> *I drink alone, for no friend is near.*
> *Raising my cup I beckon the bright moon,*
> *For her, with my shadow, will make three people.*

Or, from *Bringing in the Wine*:

> *Oh, let a man of spirit venture where he pleases*
> *And never tip his golden cup empty towards the moon!*
> *Since heaven gave the talent, let it be employed!*
> *Spin a thousand pieces of silver, all of them come back!*

Legend has it that Li Bai drowned in a river while drunkenly trying to embrace the reflection of the moon.

Li Fuguo

A powerful eunuch official during the reign of the Emperor Suzong (Li Heng) of the Tang Dynasty, Li Fuguo (704-762AD) was a servant of Gao Lishi and was then later appointed to serve the crown prince Li Heng. He gradually rose to power as he helped Li Heng seize the throne during the Anshi

Rebellion. Li Fuguo became the commander of the imperial guards and the real decision-maker in the empire. An era where eunuchs ruled began. Li Fuguo continued to control the court after Suzong's death and was eventually killed by Suzong's son, the Emperor Daizong. But the tradition of eunuchs wielding power carried on till the end of the Tang.

Li Houzhu

Li Houzhu (937-978AD), personal name Li Yu, and also known as Nan Tang Li Houzhu, was the last ruler of the Southern Tang Kingdom during the Five Dynasties and Ten Kingdoms Period. Though an incompetent ruler, Li Houzhu showed great artistic talents in calligraphy, painting, music and literature, and was particularly gifted in ci – a type of Chinese poetry with a fluid form and normally used as lyrics by folk singers. Li Houzhu expanded the range of ci from popular topics (like love) to more serious matters (like history and philosophy) and had a great influence on the development of ci writing. In 978, three years after being taken captive by the Song Dynasty, Li Houzhu was poisoned by the emperor Song Taizong because of a poem he wrote in which he lamented the fall of his kingdom.

POISONED BY THE EMPEROR SONG BECAUSE OF A POEM IN WHICH HE LAMENTED THE FALL OF HIS HIS KINGDOM

Li Lianjie → *Jet Li*

Li Lianying

A despotic eunuch of the late Qing Dynasty, Li Lianying (1848-1911) started as a low-ranking eunuch in charge of combing hair for the Empress Dowager Cixi. He became a favourite of Cixi and was appointed Head Eunuch after An Dehai, another favourite of Cixi, died. Supporting Cixi in her rise to become the power behind the throne, he began to form a clique of important government officials and take control of court

Portrait of Li Lianying, Empress Cixi's Head Eunuch

affairs. He is notorious for amassing a great personal fortune through taking bribes and selling official imperial positions.

Li Longji → *TANG XUANZONG*

Li Ning

Li Ning (1963-) is a world-famous gymnast, Olympic champion and entrepreneur. He took up gymnastics at the age of eight. His most stunning performance came at the 1982 World Cup when he went home with six gold medals out of a possible seven for individual events, a record unlikely to be challenged in the near future. At the 1984 Los Angeles Olympics, he won six medals (including three golds). He has become known as the "Prince of Gymnastics" in China. However, because of ankle injuries, the 1988 Seoul Olympics turned out to be a fiasco and a nightmare for Li and prompted him to retire. His business career took off in 2000 when he founded Li-Ning Ltd, a company which has now developed into a top-ranking sportswear and sporting equipment producer in China and has sponsored many major sports events. It was Li Ning that lit the Olympic flame at the opening ceremony of the 2008 Beijing Olympic Games.

PRINCE OF
OF GYMNASTICS
LIGHTS OLYMPIC
FLAME

Li Shimin → *TANG TAIZONG*

Li Shizhen

One of the greatest physicians and pharmacologists in Chinese history, Li Shizhen (1518-1593), was born into a family with a strong medical background. He worked as a senior doctor at the Imperial Medical Institute where he read a wide range of medical works. Finding many errors and obscurities, he decided to compile a comprehensive and more accurate medical book himself and set about writing a work, later to be known as *Bencao Gangmu (Compendium of Materia Medica)*. But before it was finished he went off on his travels. He travelled extensively, carrying out fieldwork and collecting samples of plants, animals and minerals. He then took up his writing again and, after 27 years of effort, he eventually completed his monumental work on pharmacy at the age of 60. The book, well-illustrated, includes details of over 1800 kinds of herbal medicine and more than 10,000 prescriptions. Its taxonomy of plants was the most advanced in the world at the time. Regarded as an encyclopedic work, *Bencao Gangmu* remains to this day a significant reference book for herbal medicine.

Li Shuxian

The fifth and last wife of China's last emperor, Puyi, who had abdicated as a boy in 1912, Li Shuxian (1926?-1997) worked as a nurse in a Beijing hospital, married Puyi when he was released from prison and took up a life as an ordinary citizen. She stayed with him until his death in 1967. She then withdrew from the public gaze.

Li Siguang

A Chinese geologist and founder of geomechanics, Li Siguang (1889-1971) was sent to study in Japan when a young man and there joined Sun Yat-sen's political group, the United League. His most outstanding achievement was the foundation of geomechanics, which provided the theoretical basis for the prediction that northern China was an oil-bearing region. Under his direction huge oil fields were discovered in Daqing, Shengli and Dagang. These strikes relieved China from its heavy dependence on oil imports. He once served as Minister of Geology of the People's Republic of China and was Deputy President of the Chinese Academy of Sciences.

Li Tie

Li Tie (1977-) is a Chinese professional football player, a midfielder, who started his career in 1993 when he was selected to take part in a five-year youth training programme in Brazil. He returned to become the mainstay of both Liaoning Football Club, the Chinese Olympic Youth Team and the national team. He was voted China's Soccer Player of the Year in 2001. The next year he joined Premier League club, Everton, in England, where he spent a successful season. Unfortunately injuries kept him out of the starting line-up. In 2006, he was transferred to Sheffield United and in 2008 he came back to play for Sheffield United's sister club Chengdu Blades in China.

Li Yu → *Li Houzhu*

Li Yu → *Li Houzhu*

Liang Chaowei, *a.k.a.* *Tony Leung Chiu-wai*

A famous Hong Kong actor who has won the Best Actor Award at the Cannes Film Festival and the same title at the Hong Kong Film Awards five times. He started out as a TV star and later focused on movies. He has become a familiar figure at many film festivals since his successful collaboration with the internationally noted director Wong Kar-wai in a series of films, among which the most notable ones are *Happy Together*

Tony Leung as Chow and Maggie Cheung as Li-zhen in the Wong Kar-wai film, In The Mood For Love

(1997), a disturbing story about love between two men with Leslie Cheung in the cast, and *In the Mood for Love* (2000), Wong's stylistic masterpiece, also starring Maggie Cheung, depicting the struggle between repression and indulgence of a man and woman who find out that their spouses are having an affair. Liang is a versatile actor, capable of different types of roles in various film genres, ranging from drama to comedy, action to martial arts epics. His latest successful role is as a sadistic and violent national traitor in *Lust, Caution* (2007), a thriller based on Eileen Chang's short story and directed by Ang Lee.

Liang Qichao

A prominent figure at the turn of 20th century in Chinese politics and literature, Liang Qichao (1873-1929) was well-versed in traditional Chinese classics. He studied at the age of 18 with Kang Youwei, a political thinker and reformist whose ideas were considered unorthodox at the time. Kang's teachings about Western ideologies strengthened the young man's resolution to reform China. They led the Gongche Shangshu Movement in 1895 while taking the Imperial Civil Examination in Beijing. More than a thousand candidates signed the petition to the emperor requesting reform and expressing opposition to the humiliating Treaty of Shimonoseki. In 1898, Kang and Liang again led the famous Hundred Days of Reform, calling for political and economic reforms in accordance with patterns existing in Western countries and advocating that China be restructured as a constitutional monarchy. The conservative party led by Empress Dowager Cixi put an end to the campaign. Liang was exiled to Japan. He started to focus more on journalism and became an influential figure. Credited with founding two widely read newspapers, he wrote to express his political ideas and patriotism.

After the fall of the Qing Dynasty, Liang served as Minister of Justice in the republic's government. In the 1920s he quit politics and concentrated on academic research. He was a versatile scholar and a prolific writer. His works are assembled in the *Collected Works of Yinbingshi* (the room of coldness), which runs to 148 volumes.

Liang Shiqiu

SCHOLAR TRANSLATES COMPLETE WORKS OF SHAKESPEARE, HAS LATE LIFE ROMANCE WITH YOUNGER WOMAN

Essayist, literary critic and translator, Liang Shiqiu (1903-1987) was educated at Tsinghua University and later studied at Harvard and Columbia Universities. He concentrated on teaching and writing after returning to China. Liang stresses the aesthetic value over and above the propaganda purpose of literary creation. In the 1920s he started a critical polemic with Lu Xun, the famous leftwing writer and favourite of the Communist Party. This might explain why his literary achievements have been denied for many years in communist China. In 1949, concerned at political developments, he moved to Taiwan and continued teaching till his retirement. He is known to most Chinese young people for his monumental work, the translation of Shakespeare's complete works into Chinese – and for his romance with Han Jingqing (30 years his junior) at the age of 71.

Liang Sicheng

Liang Sicheng (1901-1972), the son of Liang Qichao, is generally recognized as the founder of modern Chinese architecture. After finishing his studies at the University of Pennsylvania and Harvard, he returned to China in 1928 and founded the Architecture Department at the Northeast University in Shenyang. He also founded the Architecture Department of Tsinghua University. Focusing on the study of ancient Chinese architecture, he engaged in extensive fieldwork throughout China with his wife Lin Huiyin. Their research and Liang's milestone work *The History of Chinese Architecture* laid the foundations for the discipline of the history of Chinese architecture. Liang Sicheng also initiated a campaign to restore valuable Chinese historic buildings. As an architect, he was the chief designer of China's National Emblem and the Monument to People's Heroes in Tiananmen Square. He insisted on preserving the old inner city of Beijing during the period of post-war urban planning in the 1950s.

The Monument to the Heroes of the People in Tiananmen Square, Beijing

Unfortunately his protests were ignored. The city walls and many old buildings were torn down, an irreparable loss to Chinese architecture.

Lie Yukou, *a.k.a.* ***Lie Zi***

A Taoist philosopher who is held to be the author of the Taoist classic *Liezi*. There is little to be found about Lie Yukou's life in historical records. It is said that he lived during the Warring States Period. Most of his stories have more in common with legend than true stories. The book *Liezi*, starting from the creation of the universe, discusses various aspects of life with the focus on his philosophy of yielding to one's fate and indulging in physical and temporary pleasures. Lie Yukou is similar to Zhuang Zi in his style of writing. Both of them like to express their ideas through fables. Some stories are still popular today, for example, *The man of Qi worried that the sky might fall down*, and *The Foolish Old Man removes the mountains.*

Lijiang

Lijiang inYunnan Province in southwestern China is a popular tourist destination inhabited by 12 ethnic minorities such as the Naxi, Yi, Bai, and Mosuo. Naxi culture used to dominate the Lijiang area and nowadays a hybrid of Naxi and Han culture is dominant. Lijiang lies next to Tibet and Sichuan Province and is a country of mountains, rivers and lakes with a natural abundance of flowers and herbs. It is also known for its Old Town, one of the best preserved old towns in China and the only old Chinese town without city walls. The Old Town still offers the original taste and flavour of the local culture and lifestyle, music and food and was listed as a World Cultural Heritage site in 1997.

Lin Biao

A prominent military leader who plotted an abortive coup in 1971, Lin Biao (1907-71) joined the Chinese Communist Party when studying at the Huangpu Military Academy. Later he joined up with Mao

Zedong in the Jinggang Mountains and started his military career. Throughout the next 20 years, from the Second Chinese Civil Revolutionary War (1927-37) to the Sino-Japanese War (1937-45) and the Liberation War (1945-49), Lin proved to be a brilliant military tactician and his army was a formidable force for any rival on the battlefield. He was made Marshal in 1952 in honour of his military feats. During the Cultural Revolution Lin quickly rose to power and was named as Mao's successor in the constitution. It was said that, probably due to his poor health, Lin was too impatient to wait for an orderly transition of power upon Mao's death. His first attempt to take power away from Mao at the second plenum of the CCP's Ninth Congress in 1970 failed. Lin, fearing that he was about to be purged, started to plan a coup against Mao. When the plot was exposed, Lin attempted to flee to the Soviet Union. In September 1971 he died in a plane crash in Mongolia. He was later posthumously stripped of all ranks and honours and was expelled from the CCP.

Lin Huiyin

The writer and architect, Lin Huiyin (1904-1955), educated at the University of Pennsylvania and Yale, was regarded by Hu Shi as "the most accomplished lady of her generation". Stunningly beautiful, she had great talents as a writer and student of architecture. She was involved with her husband Liang Sicheng in the study and preservation of traditional Chinese architecture. She was said to have been emotionally involved with the famous poet Xu Zhimo.

Lin Moniang → *MATSU*

Lin Yutang

A Chinese writer whose works are well-received in the West, Lin Yutang (1895-1976) was fluent in both English and Chinese. He was seen as a messenger between Western and Eastern cultures. His works on Chinese history and philosophy and his translations of Chinese literary masterpieces opened windows for a better understanding of Chinese culture in the West. His first two English books *My Country and My People* (1935) and *The Importance of Living* (1937), published in the US, brought him international fame. He also has two popular English novels to his credit: *Moment in Peking* (1939) and *The Vermillion Gate* (1953). His witty essays express the Chinese way of thinking and living, promoting a leisured and enjoyable lifestyle (typical of the élite classes in old China).

Little Red Book

Officially known as the *Quotations from Chairman Mao Zedong*, the Little Red Book was an item of required reading and study for Chinese citizens in the mid 1960s during the time of the Cultural Revolution. It went through a couple of editions, the most popular edition being bound in red and produced in pocket format. Hence the nickname "Little Red Book" in the West. It has 33 chapters, a total of 427 excerpts from Mao Zedong's speeches or articles, covering most aspects of Maoism such as the Communist Party, class struggle, serving the people, youth and study. More than 40 billion copies of the Little Red Book are said to have been printed during its period of popularity from 1964 to 1976, making it arguably the second most printed book on the planet, coming in second only to the Bible. Huge numbers of the book were given away to certain groups of Chinese society: soldiers, students and workers. When the Little Red Book was popular, passages would be read out at all sorts of public gatherings. It was common for meetings, films, theatrical performances, concerts to be started off with a quotation from the Little Red Book. Older Chinese people can still remember and quote passages. The significance of the book faded with the disappearance of the personality cult for Mao Zedong after the end of the Cultural Revolution.

All reactionaries are paper tigers.

Every Communist must grasp this truth: political power grows out of the barrel of a gun.

All ideological questions can only be resolved by democratic means, by discussion, criticism, persuasion and education.

Liu Bang → *Han Gaozu*

Liu Bowen → *Liu Ji*

Liu Dehua → *Andy Lau*

Liu Huan

A famous pop singer and composer, Liu Huan (1963-), though without any formal training in music, is considered one of China's trailblazers in pop music. People came to know him mostly through the theme songs of various TV serials. His music is characterized by an elaborate combination of different elements, whether modern or traditional, folksong or rock and roll. In 1994 his performance at New York's Carnegie Hall was a big success. Liu's high-pitched and emotionally exuberant singing is spellbinding. He was selected to sing the theme song at the opening ceremony of the two grandest sport events ever held by China – the 1990 Asian Games and the 2008 Olympic Games.

Liu Huaqing

Born in 1916, Liu Huaqing joined the Chinese Communist Party in 1935. He was member of the Standing Committee of the Political Bureau of the Central Committee of the CCP and Vice-Chairman of the Central Military Commission from 1987 to 1998. He is known for overseeing the technological development and modernization of China's armed forces since the 1980s.

Liu Ji, *a.k.a.* ***Liu Bowen***

Liu Ji (1311-1376) was a famous military strategist and statesman who helped Zhu Yuanzhang found the Ming Dynasty. Liu started his political career as an official for the Mongol government of the Yuan Dynasty (1271-1368). He was disenchanted with the fatuous and corrupt imperial court and, although he had already retired, he accepted an invitation from Zhu Yuanzhang to serve as chief advisor in Zhu's rebel army. He devised major plans and strategies which enabled Zhu to defeat his rivals and take over the whole country. He continued to assist Zhu in establishing the new order of Ming China.

Liu Shaoqi

Chairman of the People's Republic of China (1959-68), statesman and communist theoretician, Liu Shaoqi (1898-1969) was born into a relatively wealthy family. At the start of the 1920s Liu became a political activist – he and Mao Zedong organized the Socialist Youth Corps in 1920 and the following year he joined the Chinese Communist Party (CCP) while studying in Moscow. A firm supporter of Mao and an able theoretician, he helped to establish Mao's authority in the CCP and disseminate Maoism during the 1930s and the 1940s. In 1959, after he succeeded Mao as Chairman, he adopted a series of pragmatic and progressive reforms, contrasting with Mao's radicalism, to revitalize the devastated economy in the Great Leap Forward Movement (1958-60). However, his reformative ideology, which was labelled a "capitalist road", met with strong opposition and he was removed from power and expelled from the CCP in 1968. He died a year later in Kaifeng, but his death was kept a secret from the public until 1974. Posthumous political rehabilitation came in 1980.

Liu Xiang celebrates his gold medal for the men's 110m hurdles final at the Good Luck Beijing China Athletics Open in May 2008

Liu Xiang

Liu Xiang (born 1983) became a hero and Chinese superstar after he won the men's 110m hurdles final in the 2004 Olympic Games in Athens, equalling the world record. It was the first gold medal that a Chinese male athlete had ever won in Olympic track and field. Then at the Super Grand Prix in Lausanne in July 2006 Liu set a new world record for the 110m hurdles with a time of 12.88 seconds. In August 2007 at the World Athletics Championships in Osaka, Japan, he won gold in the same event and so became the first Chinese athlete to hold the three supreme athletic titles – world record holder, world champion and Olympic champion. Liu Xiang is held in great affection in his native

China because of his very natural personality and the way in which he openly displays such joy at his own sporting triumphs.

The fact that injury prevented him from taking part in the 2008 Beijing Olympics was tantamount to a natural disaster in China.

Liu Xiaoqing

A famous actress during the 1980s and 1990s, Liu Xiaoqing (born 1951) shot to stardom after starring in the hit film *Little Flower* (1980). She won awards for her superb performances in such films as *Hibiscus Town* (1984) and *Chun Tao* (1988). From the 1990s, she began to shift her attention to real estate investment and soon made a fortune. She published her autobiography *My Road* and a book about her success in business *From a Movie Star to a Billionairess*, which were both bestsellers. In 2002 she was found guilty of tax-evasion and was imprisoned for more than a year. Now she is active again in movies and TV shows.

Liu Zongyuan

A Chinese scholar in the Tang Dynasty who was one of the Eight Giants of Tang and Song Prose. Liu Zongyuan (773-819AD) was a keen promoter, along with Han Yu, of literary reform especially in prose. Following the spirit of classical prose as it was before the Han Dynasty, he suggested people write essays in a simple and direct way so as to express their ideas freely. He excelled in prose and poetry, with prominent achievements in travel literature, which started at that time to become a major form of prose writing. The Chinese are writing travel literature and reforming prose styles over 200 years before the Norman conquest of Britain in1066.

CHINESE WRITE TRAVEL LITERATURE OVER 200 YEARS BEFORE NORMAN CONQUEST OF BRITAIN

Liusong Houfei Di, *a.k.a.* ***Cang Wu Wang***

Ascending the throne during the Liu Song Dynasty (420-479AD) as a mere child, Emperor Houfei (463-477AD) soon developed a reputation as a bloodthirsty ruler.

He was famed for his random killing sprees, during which he and his guards would venture out of the imperial palace and kill all of the humans and animals that had the misfortune of encountering them.

Eventually, Houfei brought about his own downfall by painting a target on the belly of a general named Xiao Daocheng while he slept and shooting at him with blunt arrows. Desperate for revenge, the general persuaded Houfei's attendant, Yang Yufu, to cut off the Emperor's head while the Emperor was asleep. Xiao Daocheng later became Emperor Qi Gaodi of the Qi Dynasty (479-501AD).

Liusong Mingdi

A famously fat Liu Song Dynasty (420-479AD) Emperor known as "The Pig", Mingdi (449-477AD) was an avid Buddhist and commissioned many magnificent projects in the name of his faith. However, his religious beliefs did not deter him from poisoning his wife, three of his brothers, 28 of his nephews, and his brother-in-law in order to protect his position of power.

Liusong Wudi

Originally a fisherman, Song Wudi (355-422AD) became a Jin Dynasty soldier and quickly rose to the rank of general. For many years he faithfully served the Jin. However, over time it became apparent that the dynasty was incapable of maintaining effective control, and Song Wudi usurped the throne and declared the start of the Liu Song Dynasty (420-479AD). Under his rule, order was reasserted and potential invaders north of China were successfully kept at bay.

Long March

The Long March was the great military retreat of the Red Armies led by the Chinese Communist Party during 1934-1936 in order to escape from the Kuomintang troops. There were several routes of the Long March undertaken by different Communist armies. The most famous one is the march started in 1934 from Jiangxi Province to Shaanxi Province covering a distance of some 7800 miles and passing through some formidable terrain, including snow-covered mountains and torrential rivers. The Communist soldiers had to keep up a constant action against the Kuomintang troops, local warlords and hostile ethnic minorities. Out of an initial 80,000 or so marchers only a few thousand survived. The Red Armies finally united in 1936 at their new revolutionary base in Shaanxi where they had a chance to recuperate and regroup for their future victory over the Kuomintang. The Long

March also marks the rise of Mao Zedong who secured his leadership in the Communist Party with his great military talents.

long pao → *photograph at Qing Qianlong*

Long pao, literally dragon robes, is a type of robe embroidered with dragon patterns, made exclusively for emperors. Since the time of the Tang Dynasty, the colour bright yellow had been reserved for imperial use. So long pao is sometimes called huang pao (yellow robe). The dragon patterns embroidered on the robe varied in different dynasties.

lotus

The lotus is an auspicious symbol in Buddhism, representing purity, peace, enlightenment and rebirth. It appears in all kinds of Buddhist art, such as Buddhist textiles, ceramics and architecture. Every depiction of an important Buddhist deity is in some way associated with the lotus. The deity will either be sitting on a lotus seat or holding a lotus in his hands. In Chinese culture, the lotus is regarded as the "gentleman of virtues" among all flowers, as its blossoms remain pure and clean though rooted in the mud. Countless works pay tribute to the lotus in Chinese literature. Widely cultivated in China, the lotus is also a favourite subject of traditional painters and porcelain craftsmen.

There are many idioms and sayings related to the lotus:

twin lotus sharing one stem
love between a man and a woman

the lotus root snaps but its fibres stay connected
people (lovers) stay in touch though separated

Lu Xun

Lu Xun (1881-1936), the pseudonym of Zhou Shuren, is one of the greatest Chinese writers of the 20th century. He became one of the leading figures in the New Culture Movement with the publication of his short story *Diary of a Mad Man*, the first literary work written in vernacular Chinese and an acrid criticism of the dominant but outdated Confucian culture. Another famous novel of his is *The True Story of Ah Q,* in which Lu Xun creates a classic character of modern Chinese literature. Ah Q is known for his so-called "spiritual victory", namely an act of self-deception in the face of humiliation and defeat. Today the term "the spirit of Ah Q" is still used to describe someone who does not face up to reality but indulges himself in purely imaginary success. His works are full of acute satire and harsh criticism of social problems. He is regarded as the most influential figure in modern literature and was praised by Mao Zedong as a "hero unparalleled in our history". Though a sympathizer of the Communist Party and tagged a "freedom fighter", he remains in essence a humanist.

Lunar Calendar

The traditional Chinese Lunar Calendar is a unique time measurement system dating back to the Xia Dynasty (2100-1600BC). Unlike the Western Gregorian calendar, it adopts the synodic month for timing, i.e. the length of a month is determined by the time that elapses between one new moon and the next (29.5306 days). Therefore, the 12 months of a year are alternatively 29 or 30 days long, adding up to 354 days. Then 7 intercalary months are almost evenly inserted into each 19 year span so as to round off the remaining days. Animal star signs from the zodiac are used by the calendar to represent a cycle of 12 years. The year 2008 was the year of the rat, the first animal star sign, and is followed by the ox, tiger, rabbit, dragon, snake, horse, goat, monkey, rooster, dog and pig. The year represented by the animal star sign starts from the Spring Festival, instead of from New Year's Day as in the Western Gregorian calendar.

Luo Guanzhong → ***Romance of the Three Kingdoms***

Ma Chao

Ma Chao was a general who lived at the end of the Han Dynasty and the Three Kingdoms Period and who was known as one of the Five Tiger Generals of the Kingdom of Shu. His courage and might were compared to that of Han Xin and Ying Bu, two famous generals during the early Han. Ma Chao (176-222AD) is best known for the Battle of Tong Pass described in the Romance of the Three Kingdoms. Ma Chao led an uprising against Cao Cao who had just executed Ma's father. They met at the Tong Pass where Ma defeated many of Cao's top generals in duels. Then Ma launched an attack and ordered his soldiers to capture Cao Cao, who was wearing a red robe and had a long beard. Cao's army suffered a severe defeat. In order to escape, Cao Cao cut off his beard and threw away his robe and was finally rescued by his men.

Ma Junren

Ma Junren (born 1944) was hailed as a miracle track coach in the early 1990s. He trained several superb middle and long-distance female runners and world record holders. His female track team almost swept the board in major domestic and international events in 1993. However, Ma also courted controversy on account of his extremely rigorous and tyrannical training methods. Some of his athletes even sued Ma after his retirement, alleging that he illegally withheld part of bonuses and allowances due them. Some people also charged him with using drugs to enhance the performance of his athletes, but although this was never confirmed, neither was he cleared.

After he and his team broke up he gradually faded from the spotlight. A great loss to Chinese track and field.

Ma Yanli, *a.k.a.* ***Mary Ma***

Supermodel Ma Yanli, a former rower, hit the catwalk in 1994 and became China's top model four years later. She retired from the runway and started her career as a fashion designer in 1999. In 2006, she established MaryMa Couture Company, a fashion studio tailored to the needs of local celebrities, especially élite athletes. She is also very involved in charity work with projects to bring help to mothers in poverty-stricken regions of China.

Supermodel Mary Ma

Maggie Cheung, *a.k.a.* ***Zhang Manyu***

→ *photograph at Liang Chaowei*

A great Hong Kong actress who has won more acting awards than any other woman in China, Maggie Cheung (born 1964 in Hong Kong) was raised in England and shot to stardom in television and films when she won second place in the 1983 Miss Hong Kong beauty contest. After a series of roles in which she played both comic and tough-guy characters, the most notable of which was that of the girlfriend of Jackie Chan in the *Police Stories* movies, she proved herself to be a talented actress capable of portraying complicated and nuanced parts in films like *As Tears Go By* (1988), the first of her long-term collaborations with filmmaker Wong Kar-wai, and *Centre Stage* (1992), for which she won the Berlin Silver Bear award for Best Actress. In the mid 1990s, she started to work with the French director Olivier Assayas, whom she married in 1998 and divorced three years later. The role of a drug-addicted singer in Assayas' film *Clean* won her a Cannes Best Actress award in 2004. She starred in seven movies with Tony Leung Chiu-wai, who is considered her perfect partner on the silver screen. The most famous film in this partnership is probably *In the Mood for Love* (2000).

magpie

Magpies are a symbol of good luck in Chinese culture and are a favourite subject of painters. Legend has it that at the Qi Xi festival magpies formed a bridge over the Milky Way so that the separated Cowherd and Weaver Girl could have a one-night reunion. The Bridge of Magpies, therefore, sometimes refers to anything that brings a man and a woman together.

BRIDGE OF MAGPIES

Magpie Festival → *Qi Xi*

mah-jong

This is a game usually played by four individuals. The objective is to win sets of tiles. The winner is the first player to hold four sets and a pair of like tiles. It is also known as a "game of encirclement", as legend says that mah-jong was invented by an ancient Chinese military strategist who used tiles to mock up battle formations. In the olden days people gambled at mah-jong and this does still happen, although gambling is forbidden in China. The government has made strenuous efforts to change the game into a wholesome, non-gambling-based activity by introducing a set of rules for the national competition.

Manchu

An ethnic group living mostly in northeastern China, the Manchu rose to power in the 17th century when they ended the rule of the Ming Dynasty and founded the Qing Dynasty. The term Manchu came into being when Huang Taiji (1592-1643), the first Qing emperor, changed the name of their ancestral tribe (Jurchen) to Manchu. They had their own language. However, with intermarriage and cultural assimilation with the Han Chinese, most Manchu people gradually adopted Chinese customs and started to speak Chinese. Only a small number of people nowadays can speak Manchu.

Mandarin

Mandarin, or modern standard Chinese, is the official spoken language of mainland China and Taiwan, and is largely based on the dialect used in and around Beijing. It is the most widely spoken form of Chinese and is the native language of more than two-thirds of the Chinese population. Mandarin has four tones (or pitches of pronunciation), and one neutral tone, which are used to distinguish between words which would otherwise sound the same. Mandarin is the world's most spoken language.

mantou

A steamed bread roll, common in the north, sometimes eaten instead of rice.

Mao Dun

The famous Chinese writer, Mao Dun (1896-1981), pseudonym of Shen Yanbing, was the co-founder of the Literary Research Association, one of the most important societies in the New Culture Movement. He also created an influential literary journal the *Short Story Monthly*. His main novels include *Midnight* (1932), *The Shop of the Lin Family* and a trilogy entitled *Eclipse, Corruption, Rainbow*. After 1949 he was appointed China's first Minister of Culture and held the post until the outbreak of the Cultural Revolution. He did not return to public life until 1978 when he was elected Chairman of the Chinese Writers' Association. After his death the Mao Dun Literature Prize, the highest award for writers in China, was set up in honour of his achievements.

MAO DUN
LITERATURE
PRIZE

Mao Geping

Mao Geping is one of China's top makeup artists and owes his reputation largely to his working relationship with Liu Xiaoqing, a famous actress during the 1980s and 1990s. With Mao's brilliant skills, Liu Xiaoqing successfully portrayed Wu Zetian from the age of 16 to over 80 in the TV series of the same name. He founded his own cosmetics brand MGPIN in 2001 and has won many awards for makeup. Currently he runs the Mao Geping Image Design Art School with schools in four major cities in China.

Mao suit → *ZHONGSHAN ZHUANG*

Mao Zedong

The law of the unity of opposites is the fundamental law of nature, society and thought.

Mao (1893-1976) was supreme leader of the Chinese Communist Party (CCP) and of Chinese military forces for over four decades, co-founder and leader of the People's Republic of China and one of the greatest Marxist theorists and statesmen the world has known. As one of the earliest members of the CCP, he held that the key to the success of Chinese revolution lay in the hands of the peasantry and not the proletariat, an idea quite contrary to that of his colleagues who were followers of the Russian model of revolution. This belief was to become a cornerstone of Maoism. In 1927, he led the Autumn Harvest Uprising in Changsha, Hunan Province. Later, together with Zhu De, he established the first Soviet-style regime in the Jinggang Mountains of Jiangxi Province and created the Red Army. However, Mao's successful guerrilla tactics were rejected by the CCP and he lost his leading position as the result of a political struggle within the CCP. Coming under siege from the Kuomintang government, the Red Army was forced to start the Long March during 1934-1936, a strategic retreat. During the expedition, his leadership and military talents helped the army survive in bitter struggles and build new revolutionary bases in the province of Shaanxi. Gaining great prestige and wide support in the party, he secured his position as party leader and commander-in-chief in the 1940s. During the Civil War (1946-1950), Mao led the CCP to victory against the Kuomintang and founded the People's Republic of China in 1949. Mao was Chairman of the CCP until his death and was acting head of state until his resignation in 1959. However, Mao's ambition

The Tiananmen Gate of Heavenly Peace, Beijing

©iStockphoto.com/Tor Lindqvist

and personality cult severely impaired his judgment of Chinese economic conditions. The Great Leap Forward Movement (1958-1960), initiated by him and aimed at bringing about a drastic change in China's fortunes, transforming it into a modern, industrialized country seriously devastated the economy and caused a severe famine, killing millions of people. It was followed by a more disastrous humanitarian havoc – the Cultural Revolution (1966-1976). Critics generally remain silent or puzzled about the causes behind the outbreak of the Cultural Revolution, though officially it has been recognized as a serious mistake on Mao's part. The aftermath of the 10-year turmoil did not die away until Deng Xiaoping rose to power as the leader of the CCP and introduced political and economic reforms in the 1980s.

The people, and the people alone, are the motive force in the making of world history.

Revolution is not a dinner party.

What do the Chinese think of Mao?

The official appraisal

Generally positive. His achievements are indisputably great, blemished only by some serious mistakes committed in his old age (mostly the Cultural Revolution).

What do ordinary people think nowadays?

Since younger generations don't have any personal experience of the turmoil of the 1960s and 1970s, what they learn about Mao comes only from books or what their parents tell them. So most young people treat him more as a cultural icon (a bit like Che Guevara) than a great politician. For instance, Mao's boldness in challenging established institutions, his strong nationalistic stance – such things still have a resonance for young people. They don't normally have any personality cult towards him.

What do older generations think?

Older generations might have rather an ambivalent attitude to Mao. They suffered a lot during the Cultural Revolution. Their passion and youth were wasted, destroyed even. They felt betrayed. But what would happen to them without Mao? No one could tell. Some older people tend to choose forgiveness rather than hatred. Negative opinions (including the view that he was a necessary evil) are not expressed in public.

maotai

A unique, clear spirit made from fermented sorghum, maotai is to China what whisky is to Scotland.

mapo doufu

Mapo doufu is a popular Sichuan dish made of doufu and minced meat (beef or pork) dipped in a spicy sauce of chilli, garlic, ginger and pepper oil.

Marco Fu

A professional snooker player from Hong Kong, Marco Fu (1978-) was Asia's number one until superseded by Ding Junhui. His miraculous performance in 1998 when he came second in the Grand Prix stunned the whole world. Nine years later in 2007, Fu won his first major championship at the Royal London Watches Grand Prix.

marriage

Technically, the form of marriage practised in China has always been monogamy – a man can only have one wife. However, throughout the long history of China, it was common for Chinese men, especially the rich or privileged, to have a wife and several or even dozens of concubines. One of the reasons is that people believed the principal purpose of a marriage was to produce sons, the more the better, to carry on the name of the father's family. It was not exactly like polygamy, since the wife (qi) was regarded as the man's lawful spouse who should be wedded through a proper ceremony and had the right to join the ritual of ancestor worship, while the concubines (qie) had a very low status in the family and were treated more or less as the man's servants. Furthermore, sons born of a concubine were inferior to sons born of the wife and had fewer rights. The wife was also the mistress of the concubines and technically had the right to sell them off to another family. It was not until the establishment of the People's Republic of China in 1949 that the law clearly stated a man can only be married to one woman.

Arranged marriages were common in the old days. But after 1949, the Communist government advocated the so-called "free marriage"– a marriage entered into out of a couple's own free will. However, there were still many traditional arranged marriages, because a marriage could not be completely "free" if, as was the case, a couple still had to get approval from their employer if they wanted to marry.

From the 1980s, or even later, arranged marriages became less common. But it seems that some people today, with the rise in the divorce rate, are calling for a return to this tradition.

In today's China, the traditional "big family" where three generations live together has been replaced by the nuclear family, especially after the practice of population control policy known as the One Child Policy. There is a trend of late marriage and late pregnancy among young people. Nowadays it's getting common for people to stay single well into their thirties.

Mary Ma → *Ma Yanli*

Matsu, *a.k.a.* ***Lin Moniang***

Matsu, the goddess of the sea in popular belief, is revered as the patron saint of sailors, fishermen and those who travel on the sea. It is said that her mortal name was Lin Moniang, that she was born on a small island in Putian, Fujian Province and that she devoted all her life to helping people in need, especially guiding fishing boats out of danger. Legend says that Lin Moniang, after she passed away, was seen flying across the sea, dressed in red garments and rescuing the victims of shipwrecks. So people started to build temples in her honour and to pray to her to grant a safe journey. Matsu is still widely worshipped in the southeastern coastal areas of China where there is a strong sea-faring tradition as well as in most southeastern Asian countries which have large numbers of Chinese immigrants.

May Fourth Movement → *New Culture Movement*

media awards

The two most famous Chinese film awards are the Hundred Flowers Award (started in 1962) and the Golden Rooster Award (started in 1981). The Golden Eagle Award started in 1983 for TV programmes. But it is not unknown for there to be a kind of impartiality/criteria issue, because some awards go to those films/TV programmes that are propaganda-oriented and not actually well-received in the market. Things are changing though in recent years.

©Sam Yeh/Getty Images

Mei Yanfang listens to questions from journalists, November 2002, the year before her death

Mei Yanfang, *a.k.a. Anita Mui Yim-fong*

Mei Yanfang (1963-2003) was a superstar in Cantopop and a gifted actress. Starting her show business career in early childhood, she was generally regarded as a Hong Kong pop diva and won numerous music awards. She had a large fan base in Asia. Dubbed the "Madonna of Asia", she was renowned for her extravagant stage performances and her sensational and exotic costumes. She also had a very successful acting career, being capable of playing a range of roles, both comic and tragic. Her best part may be the spirit of a tragic courtesan who returns to the world to search for her lover in the film *Rouge* (1987), which won her Best Actress at the Golden Horse Awards in Taiwan and at the Hong Kong Film Awards. She half retired from singing in the early 1990s, but never faded from the limelight until she was suddenly diagnosed with cancer in 2003 and passed away at the early age of 40.

Mencius

Mencius was a Chinese philosopher during the Warring States Period and the most important Confucian thinker, second only to Confucius himself. Very little is known about his early life apart from a few stories about how his widowed mother raised him. For example, his mother moved home three times in order to find a better studying and living environment for her son. The stories, though without solid foundation, are often quoted these days as an example of good parenting. Mencius (c.372-289BC) was an extreme idealist who viewed human nature as basically good although at times darkened by evil. He urged people to recover their innate goodness through learning. Mencius had a high regard for the ordinary man and advocated benevolent rule of a country. He believed that if the ruler failed to bring peace and order, and abused people, the citizens in this case could be absolved of loyalty and could justifiably revolt. That is probably why Mencius has sometimes been regarded as a potentially "dangerous" author throughout Chinese history. His ideas have been preserved in a book titled *The Mencius*.

DISCOVER YOUR INATE GOODNESS THROUGH LEARNING

Meng Po

Meng Po, literally the Old Lady Meng, is an underworld deity of forgetfulness in Chinese mythology. She guards the Bridge of No Return (or the Naihe Bridge) leading to the Reincarnation Door. Her task is to ensure that the souls of the dead passing by lose all memory of their previous life and of what they have experienced in hell. She prepares for them a potion made out of herbs collected from ponds and streams. One sip of her five-flavoured brew and you will completely forget who you were. And thus you can start your life afresh when you are reborn.

mianren, miansu → DOUGH FLOWERS

Miao

One of the oldest ethnic groups in China, the Miao people live mostly in the south, in the provinces of Guizhou, Hunan, Yunnan, Hubei and Guangxi. The Miao are famous for their singing and dancing. The womenfolk like to wear silver ornaments and the jewellery worn by a woman in full traditional dress can weigh several kilos. The Miao have their own Miao language, but most of them can speak and write Chinese.

©iStockphoto.com/Rami Ben Ami

Miao Shan → *Guanyin*

Mid-Autumn Festival

The Mid-Autumn Festival falls on the fifteenth day of the eighth month in the Chinese Lunar Calendar when the moon is at its fullest – the reason why it is also known as the Moon Festival. Like Chinese New Year, the Mid-Autumn Festival is an important occasion for family reunion. Family members are supposed to gather together to offer sacrifice to ancestors, and to eat mooncakes while admiring the moon. The story of the moon goddess, Chang'e, is said to be closely associated with this festival. In 2007 it was made a public holiday.

Middle Kingdom

A name for China, literally translated from the Chinese for China, Zhongguo, a term which manifests the world view of the Chinese during imperial times – that China was the centre of the world.

migrant workers

Until fairly recently, before the 1980s, most people in China would work for their entire lives in the place where they were born and grew up. Before the economic reforms of the 1980s were fully underway, every citizen was registered in a certain place (recorded on their hukou), and they were not allowed to leave their place of residence to work elsewhere without permission – and even when permission was granted, it was extremely difficult for someone who had moved away to become a registered city resident or enjoy any form of social security in the new place, including the right to schooling for the next generation.

However, as the economies of the richer parts of China grew, and the demands for cheap labour with them, the rules gradually relaxed, allowing increasing numbers of people to travel from poor countryside areas to find work in the big cities. Migrant workers often do the work city people do not want to do, such as construction, sanitation, factory work or work as domestic servants, and their pay and living conditions are pretty poor by city standards. However, because incomes and prices in the countryside are so low, a meagre wage by city standards becomes an enviable salary to someone from a poor rural area – enough, for example, to put a younger sibling through school. As a result, migrant workers, though not always a visible group, are a large one, and city life would be very different without them.

The public profile of migrant workers has risen and there is a growing awareness of their service to the community and their needs. At the same time, migrant workers have brought an awareness of what life is like in the outside world to those back at home in their isolated villages.

In the past, young people would go to the city for a few years, earn enough to get married and settle down, then return to village life. But in recent years, growing numbers of people have been moving to the cities, showing no signs of wishing to return.

Min dialect

The Min dialect is one of the major dialects spoken in Fujian Province, Taiwan and among overseas Chinese communities. It retains the pronunciation of ancient Chinese, dating back to the Han Dynasty (206BC-220AD). As the Chinese classics and Buddhist scripture were first interpreted in ancient Chinese, it is much easier for Min speakers to understand the concepts behind the words.

HEAR HOW PEOPLE SPOKE 2000 YEARS AGO

Ming Chengzu

Ming Chengzu (1360-1424), whose personal name was Zhudi, was the fourth son of Ming Taizu and the third emperor of the Ming Dynasty. He was also known as Emperor Yongle.

The uncle of the second emperor, Jianwen, he usurped the throne in 1399 and proclaimed himself emperor after defeating Jianwen's army. Ming Chengzu changed the title of reign to Yongle and later decided to move the capital to Beijing in order to enhance the defence of the northern border against constant invasions by Mongolian tribes like Tartary and Wala. In the early period of Yongle, Ming Chengzu slaughtered many supporters of the Emperor Jianwen so as to consolidate his own position. He ordered the most severe punishment in Chinese history – the killing of the famous scholar Fang Xiaoru, killing in total 873 people including Fang's family, relatives and even students and peers. The crime? Loyalty to Jianwen.

Like his father the Emperor Ming Taizu before him, Ming Chengzu also furthered agriculture and had the Grand Canal repaired. He put in hand the compilation of the Yongle Encyclopedia, the biggest and most comprehensive encyclopedia in Chinese history. Another of Ming Chengzu's notable accomplishments was to expand Chinese influence overseas by sending the eunuch Zheng He, who was made admiral of a huge fleet, to explore the Indian Ocean and the South Pacific. But Ming Chengzu's successors thought such voyages a waste of money and manpower and gradually wound them down.

Ming Taizu, *a.k.a.* ***Zhu Yuanzhang***

Born Zhu Chongba and later renamed Zhu Yuanzhang, Ming Taizu was the founder of the Ming Dynasty and one of only two Chinese dynasty founders who were of plebeian origin (the other being Han Gaozu, founder of the Han Dynasty). Ming Taizu had a legendary life. He rose from Buddhist monk, cowherd and beggar to be general of a rebel army then national leader in the fight against the Yuan Dynasty. In 1368 Taizu proclaimed himself emperor of the Ming Dynasty and set up his capital in Nanjing. Conscious of the needs of the class from which he sprang, Ming Taizu

ONE OF ONLY TWO CHINESE DYNASTY FOUNDERS WHO WERE OF PLEBEIAN ORIGIN

distributed land to small farmers and had irrigation systems constructed. Through a series of successful reforms, agriculture became the main source of government revenue for the Ming Dynasty and general living standards among the Chinese people improved. He punished corrupt officials and had them put to death if they embezzled more than 60 taels of silver.

Ming Taizu saw to it that power was centralized and took more authority into his own hands by abolishing the Imperial Secretariat and the post of prime minister. But as well as being known for benevolent reforms, he was also notorious for his brutality. Suspicious of every high-ranking official or military leader, he was responsible for the deaths of more than 30,000 people when crushing his grand chancellor Hu Weiyong's plot against his reign.

EMBEZZLING MORE THAN 60 TAELS OF SILVER CARRIES DEATH PENALTY

AND EMBEZZLING LARGE SUMS OF MONEY STILL DOES CARRY THE DEATH PENALTY IN MODERN CHINA

Mo Yan

An outstanding modern novelist, Mo Yan (1955-) was born in Gaomi, Shandong Province, where many of his stories are set. He did not receive much schooling during the years of the Cultural Revolution. After a spell working in a factory he joined the army at the age of 20. His novel *Red Sorghum* (1986) won him overnight fame when the story was adapted into a film directed by Zhang Yimou. Known as a "root-seeking" writer, he uses powerful, evocative language to write about the brutal unrest in rural China where superstitious customs still linger on, where ballads and stories about ghosts and spirits are still constantly recounted. His other important works include *The Republic of Wine* (1992), *Big Breasts and Wide Hips* (1995) and *The Sandalwood Torture* (2001).

Mo Zi

A Chinese philosopher who lived after the time of Confucius and before that of Mencius, Mo Zi, originally a Confucian, founded the school of Mohism which advocated the doctrine of universal love and condemned offensive wars. A precursor of utilitarianism, he proposed utility as the appropriate measurement of all actions. Unlike Confucians, he believed in the existence of ghosts and spirits and the fact that they can reward virtue as well as punish vice. In this sense, the Mohist group was more disciplined and religious than any other philosophical organizations at the time. They were regarded as "warriors" who were willing to sacrifice their lives to serve their ultimate goals. At first a rival of Confucianism, Mohism died out after the 2nd century BC.

Mogao Caves → *Dunhuang*

Mohism → *Mo Zi*

Mongols

An ethnic group that live mostly in the Inner Mongolia Autonomous Region in northern China. The Mongols are originally from the Mongolian Plateau and have a splendid past. Their ancestors, under the leadership of Genghis Khan, swept across the vast regions of central Asia and created a powerful empire in the 13th and 14th centuries. A lot of Mongols still preserve their ancestral nomadic tradition of ranching and herding. Their written language, which is still in use, was created by Genghis Khan. The dominant religion among the Mongols is Tibetan Buddhism.

Monk Tang → *Xuanzang*

Monkey King → *Sun Wukong*

Moon Festival → *Mid-Autumn Festival*

mooncake

Mooncakes are traditional pastries made for the Mid-Autumn Festival. They are usually round with a soft, thin crust and various kinds of filling. In Chinese culture, mooncakes represent harmony, reunion or perfection – the symbolic meanings of their rounded shape. Words of blessing are sometimes imprinted on the top of the crust. Mooncake production is a complicated process and it is very rare these days for people to make them at home. They can be elaborate and expensive and make a good gift at Mid-Autumn Festival time.

©iStockphoto.com/Kit Sen Chin

Mooncake with red bean paste and melon seed filling

moxibustion

Moxibustion is used in traditional Chinese medicine. A herb called mugwort is ground up and the resulting substance is burnt over or on the patient's skin, causing a beneficial stimulation to the flow of blood.

Mudan Ting or The Peony Pavilion

This is one of China's greatest love stories, written by Tang Xianzu, perhaps the finest dramatist in the Ming Dynasty. The play, traditionally written for Kunqu opera performance, revolves around the love between Du Liniang, the daughter of a high-ranking official, and Liu Mengmei, a young scholar. While taking a walk in the garden, Du Liniang falls asleep. In her dream she has an affair in the Peony Pavilion with Liu Mengmei whom she has never met before. On awaking she becomes lovesick and gradually pines away. She buries a portrait of herself under a stone in the garden before she dies. Shortly afterwards, her family move to another town. Liu comes to stay in their old house where he finds Du's portrait and resumes their relationship in a dream in which Du reveals to him where her body lies. At Du's request, Liu digs out her coffin and he finds her lying there – alive.

Du's father, however, instead of recognizing Liu as his son-in-law, accuses him of grave robbing and treats his resurrected daughter as an impostor. In the end, Liu proves his innocence and the whole family reunites. The play, listed in the repertoire of all Kunqu opera troupes, is still wildly popular today.

Naihe Bridge → *Meng Po*

names

The order of Chinese names is

1. family name
2. given name.

So, for example, in Mao Zedong, Mao is the family name and Zedong the given name.
Quite often when Chinese people go overseas they invert the sequence of their names so as to match Western conventions. So, if Mao had gone to London University's SOAS to study, he might well have called himself Zedong Mao.
When a woman marries, she does not change her name (although most women in Hong Kong and Taiwan may do this, putting their husband's family name in front of their own name).
Chinese people when talking to each other as friends or work colleagues will use the given name preceded by xiao (=little) or lao (=old).
Tongzhi is Chinese for comrade and was standardly used to address people in the old Communist days. It is still used by some government workers as well as by ordinary people in a tongue-in-cheek sort of way. Interestingly, though inexplicably, it has also acquired a modern slang meaning of gay.

Nan Qi Gaodi, *a.k.a.* ***Xiao Daocheng***

A member of the powerful Xiao family, Qi Gaodi usurped Emperor Shundi of the Liu Song Dynasty (420-479AD) and established the short-lived Southern Qi Dynasty (479-502AD). An avid Buddhist, he lived with many monks in his palace. He invested a great deal of time and effort tracing his lineage back more than 600 years to a Han Dynasty commander in the hope of validating his position as emperor.

Nanjing

A city in eastern China, on the Yangtze River, Nanjing is known as the former capital of six dynasties, which had their day from the third to sixth century AD and again from 1368 to 1421. It was also the capital of the Republic of China from 1912 to 1949. Nanjing was occupied by the Japanese (1937-1945) during the Sino-Japanese War and witnessed the outrageous Nanjing Massacre in which some 300,000 people were slaughtered. Now it is the capital of Jiangsu Province. The most famous places of interest are the mausoleum of Sun Yat-sen and the tomb of the first Ming emperor. The well-preserved city wall, which encircles most of the modern city, was built some 600 years ago and it is the longest city wall in the world. Nanjing is the location of many institutions of higher learning, notably Nanjing University.

Nanjing Bridge

The construction of the Nanjing Bridge was a great achievement of the young Communist Party and the completion of the work in 1968 was, and remains, a cause of great celebration and national pride.

Nanjing Road in Shanghai

Nanjing Road

The busiest street in Shanghai, this is China's Fifth Avenue, China's Champs Elysées. Running from the famous Bund to the ancient Jing'an Temple, Nanjing Road is lined with shopping centres, restaurants, theatres and night clubs. As of the early 20th century Nanjing Road has been *the* area where foreigners and trendy young people flock to have fun or make it big.

Naxi or Nakhi

The Nakhi are an ethnic group living mostly in Yunnan and Sichuan Provinces, with a concentrated group in Lijiang and a small number in Tibet. They number over 308,000. The traditional religion of Nakhi people is Dongba, an aboriginal religion with a trace of Tibetan influence. Others believe in Tibetan Buddhism and Taoism. The ethnic group is known for its unique form of music, Nakhi music, performed on ancient, traditional musical instruments. This music has a history of 500 years and is regarded as a "living music fossil". Today it is constantly performed in Lijiang, mostly for tourists.

Ne Zha

Ne Zha is a god in Chinese mythology who is usually represented in the form of a child. His stories can be found in folklore and such literary works as Journey to the West and Investiture of the Gods. Ne Zha, a naughty boy possessed of magic powers, was said to have killed the son of Ao Guang, the East Sea Dragon King. He committed suicide in order to save his parents and the town people from Ao Guang's vengeance. But he was then brought back to life by his master, who gave him greater powers. It was said that he could transform himself into a figure with three heads and six arms holding six different magic weapons in each hand and riding on wheels of fire – a popular image of him in paintings or cartoons. Later he conquered the sea and overpowered Ao Guang, a very popular story which has given rise to a large number of paintings, animated cartoons etc, called *Ne Zha Conquering the Sea*.

Neo-Confucianism

Neo-Confucianism refers to the developments in Confucian thought starting from the 9th century and becoming fully developed during the Song Dynasty (960-1279AD). Based on the core of Confucian concerns with social order and benevolent rule, it is a philosophy that synthesizes Taoist cosmology and Buddhist spirituality to meet the new intellectual and spiritual expectations of the time.

One of the most important early Neo-Confucian thinkers is Zhu Xi (1130-1200) who combined the achievements of former Neo-Confucian scholars into a coherent metaphysical framework, which was subsequently developed into the School of Principle (Lixue). He believed that there is one universal li (principle) which describes why things are. Li itself is good and pure, a statement adapted from Mencius' assertion that original human nature is good, and evil arises not from li but from qi (energy). The bad qi can only be purified through education and self-cultivation. The knowledge of li can be acquired through "investigation of things" (gewu).

By the 14th century Zhu's version of Confucian thought was set as the standard curriculum for the Imperial Civil Examination system. And its dominance continued till the whole system was abolished in 1905.

Zhu Xi's rationalist approach was strenuously challenged by Wang Yangming (1472-1529), another influential Neo-Confucian thinker in the Ming Dynasty who represents the School of the Mind (Xinxue). He claimed that li lies in the mind (xin), because all people have the "innate knowledge of goodness", and there is no better place to seek this than in oneself. His doctrine of the "unity of knowledge and action" exerted a profound influence both at home and abroad. Neo-Confucianism was in fact an international movement which predominated in the intellectual and spiritual life of China, Korea, and Japan prior to the modern era.

New Culture Movement

This was an influential intellectual and sociopolitical movement in modern Chinese history. Chen Duxiu's creation of the *New Youth* journal in 1915, advocating democracy and science, marked the beginning of the New Culture Movement. Intellectuals called for a re-evaluation of traditional Chinese culture and blamed it for preventing China from developing into a modern country. The movement reached a climax in a mass demonstration on 4th May 1919, which is remembered as the May Fourth Movement. An angry crowd, mostly students, held a large-scale protest against the Versailles Peace Conference's decision to transfer the former German leasehold of Jiaozhou, Shandong Province to Japan. Later it developed into a nationwide patriotic campaign against imperialists and local warlords. It awakened Chinese of all social levels, particularly in the big cities, to a consciousness of the new ideas that were sweeping the country. Chen Duxiu and his colleague at Beijing University, Li Dazhao, introduced Marxism. Hu Shi promoted the use of vernacular Chinese. Many Western concepts such as democracy and women's participation in politics were becoming popular. The movement was at its peak between 1917 and 1923 but then its influence faded away.

New Year pictures

There is a Chinese custom of pinning up pictures of scenes of prosperity and happiness as part of the Spring Festival celebrations. The tradition is particularly strong in rural areas. New Year pictures appear on walls and doors and windows. They'll be put up on furniture and the kitchen stove. Typical themes are harvests, landscapes with birds and flowers, contented babies, all boding well for the year to come.

Nian

Nian, which is also a word for "year" in Chinese, is a beast in Chinese mythology who would appear on every Chinese New Year's Eve to eat people, especially children. People believed that the monster

©iStockphoto.com/Ho Yeow Hui

New Year decorations

was afraid of loud noises and the colour red. So they would decorate their houses and front doors in red, and set off firecrackers around Chinese New Year in order to scare the beast away. And so this became part of the tradition of celebrating the New Year. The Chinese phrase for the New Year celebration is guo nian which literally means the passing of Nian, the beast.

Nian Gengyao

A famous military commander in the Qing Dynasty, Nian Gengyao (1679-1726) was greatly favoured by the Emperor Yongzheng for having successfully defeated the revolutionary forces in Qinhai and put this region completely under the control of the Qing government. He was granted many honours and privileges after his victories and became one of the most powerful figures at the imperial court. But he gradually grew arrogant and greedy, thus incurring his emperor's wrath. He was finally forced to commit suicide. There are many TV series today based on Nian's dramatic life.

Nie Er

A famous composer whose work *March of the Volunteers*, composed in 1935, was chosen as the national anthem of the People's Republic of China in 1952, with words by Tian Han. He also wrote some so-called revolutionary songs, which are not so popular these days although his national anthem lives on. Nie Er himself died very young, in 1935 at the age of 23.

Nie Rongzhen

A prominent commander of the Communist military forces, Nie Rongzhen (1899-1992), trained at a military academy in the old USSR and held important positions in the Communist military during the Sino-Japanese War (1937-1945) and the Civil War (1946-1950). In 1955 he was made one of the ten Marshals in the People's Liberation Army.

Night of Sevens → *Qi Xi*

noodles

A generic term for any paste or dough often made of flour, eggs and water and shaped into thin, long, flat strips which are commonly boiled in water and served with sauces or eaten in soup. Noodles are widely found in Chinese cuisine all around the nation with many regional flavours and variations in shape. It is generally believed that the Chinese were the first to make noodles, a theory which gained some support from recent archaeological excavations. The oldest noodle remains found in China are said to be nearly 4000 years old.

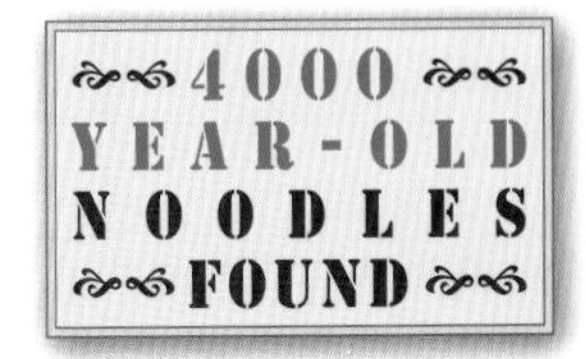

numbers

Chinese people usually prefer even numbers to odd numbers because the latter are associated with loneliness or "the absence of a pair".

Numbers like 6 (often associated with smoothness) and 8 (pronounced fa in Cantonese, also meaning "prosperity and well-being"), or numbers consisting of a succession of 6s or 8s (such as 666 or 888), are greatly favoured.

Businessmen particularly like the number 8 because it is seen as bringing good luck.

The even number 4, however, is considered ominous, because it is pronounced si – which is close in sound to the Chinese for "death".

Some number-sensitive people choose their car number plates and mobile numbers very carefully in order to avoid such unlucky numbers.

9 is a traditionally auspicious number representing immensity and supremacy. It is also used as a sign of eternity as it sounds like the word jiu meaning "ever-lasting". 9 roses (not the Western dozen) are the thing to send on Valentine's Day, 9 here meaning "eternal love".

Traditionally the number 7 was associated with funeral rites. A complete funeral lasts at least 7 days, some very formal ones even last forty-nine days (7x7). The 7th month of the Chinese Lunar Calendar is known as the Ghost month.

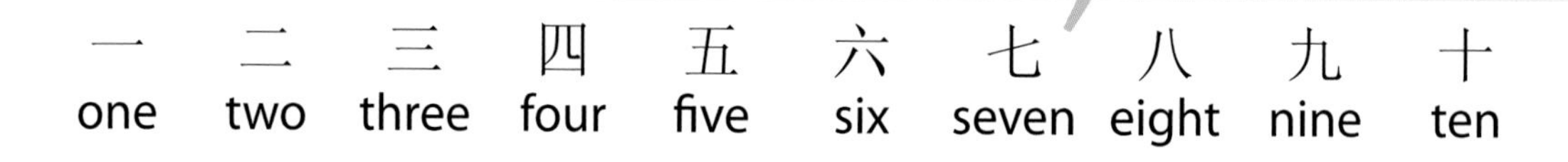

The Chinese have a fascination for using numbers in names. For example:

One *Country Two Systems*

Three *Sovereign Ones*

Three *Kingdoms Period*

Three *August Ones*

Three *Pure Ones*

Four *Kings (of Hong Kong pop)*

Four *Treasures of the Study*

Four *Emperors*

Four *Heavenly Kings*

Four *Heavenly Kings or the* ***Four*** *Great Jin Gang*

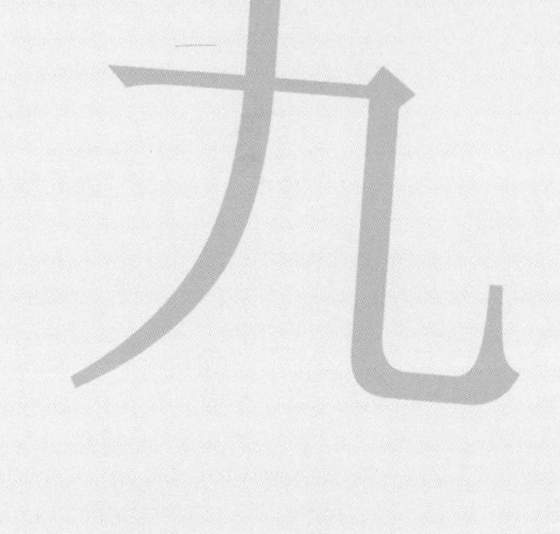

Four *Great Classical Novels*

Gang of ***Four***

Four *Beauties of ancient China*

Five *Emperors*

Five*-flavoured brew*

Five *Tiger Generals*

Five *Principles of Peaceful Coexistence*

Seven *Masters of Quanzhen*

The Night of ***Sevens***

Eight *Immortals*

Eight *Giants of Tang and Song Prose*

一	二	三	四	五	六	七	八	九	十
one	two	three	four	five	six	seven	eight	nine	ten

Nüwa

A goddess in Chinese mythology who is known as the creator of mankind. Legend says that Nüwa lived at the beginning of the world, when there were no human beings. Feeling lonely, she made a figure out of yellow clay in her likeness. The figure came alive and became the first human being. Nüwa was so pleased that she continued to make more figures in the shapes of men and women.

Another legend says that she married her brother Fu Xi, one of the Three August Ones, and started to have children, the offspring being humans. They are usually depicted as half human, half serpent with their tails intertwined.

Nüwa is also known for mending the sky. It is said that once the pillar holding up the sky collapsed because of a war between two gods. The sky was broken and the earth started to tilt, causing great catastrophes, floods and fires and letting loose man-eating monsters that roamed the earth. Nüwa patched up the broken sky with stones of five different colours and cut the foot off a giant tortoise to replace the fallen pillar, so saving people from hideous misery.

O

One Child Policy

The One Child Policy has been implemented by the Chinese government since 1979 in an attempt to control the growth of the Chinese population in a way that matches social and economic development. The essence of the policy is to limit Chinese urban couples to one child by imposing fines and abortions in the event of second or subsequent pregnancies. An exception is made for citizens from rural areas and ethnic minorities.

Normally the option of either a fine or an abortion is given to "offenders".

Compulsory abortions are not official policy but have happened in some areas. The level of fines is set by local governments and will vary according to local economic conditions and standards of living. The fines tend to be high, and can be in excess of a person's annual income.

A WHOLE NEW GENERATION OF LITTLE EMPERORS

The One Child Policy is claimed by the government to have contributed to a prevention of 400 million births since its inception, as well as having brought some other benefits like reduced pressure on resources, increased savings rates and improved social services. It is nonetheless criticized by many people as being inhumane and for having caused negative social and economic effects such as infanticide in the case of female babies (due to the traditional Chinese attitude of preferring boys to girls), a reduced amount of youth labour and the challenge of an ageing population.

Despite the controversy this policy is set to remain in place throughout the modernization of Chinese society. One recent revision of the policy was made in 2007 (by most provincial authorities except Henan Province), stipulating that an urban couple with both parties having no siblings may seek government permission to have a second child.

One negative consequence for Chinese society in general is that the only child is normally (but naturally) pampered and spoiled by both parents and grandparents. The only children become the centre of the family and are known as "little emperor" or "little sun" of the family. A whole new generation of little emperors is on the make.

One Country Two Systems

One China, two political systems (communism together with capitalism in Hong Kong), a slogan created by Deng Xiaoping on the return of Hong Kong to China, signifying the conscious and planned accommodation within a single state of radically divergent economic principles.

Open Door Policy

There are two definitions of the Open Door Policy. The first refers to the historic article in the treaties signed between the Qing Dynasty and Western powers such as Britain and France from the 1880s to 1900s, whereby the foreign powers forced the

Chinese government to open its ports to foreign trade, the ambition being access to China's vast market and abundant resources.

Nowadays the Open Door Policy refers to the concept put forward by Deng Xiaoping (the general designer of China's reform) from 1978 onwards to promote foreign trade and international investment in China with the aim of driving up Chinese economic development and putting an end to the international isolation that China had experienced under Mao Zedong.

Subsequent tactical measures to implement the Open Door Policy included the creation of Special Economic Zones (SEZs) in south China, the establishment of coastal economic and trading zones and the opening up of city ports along the eastern coastline, all of these linking together to form one open zone for foreign trade and boosting the economy within that vast area. The Open Door Policy has been recognized by China as one of the most influential polices in increasing trade with the outside world and as being a major contributing factor to the rapid rise of the Chinese economy.

opera

Opera in China, unlike its counterpart in the West, is a form of drama that integrates many different art forms such as music, dance, singing, martial arts, acrobatics and some regional art forms. The origin of Chinese opera may be traced back to the pre-Qin period (before the 2nd century BC). Emperor Tang Xuanzong of the Tang Dynasty (618-907AD) is generally credited with the foundation of the first royal opera troupe. During the Yuan Dynasty (1271-1368) Chinese

opera developed into a complete form, especially with the introduction of the specialized roles like sheng (male), dan (female), jing (painted face) and chou (clown). The Ming and early Qing Dynasties witnessed an opera boom in which Kunqu, an opera genre which came from the Wu-speaking area, took the dominant position. The 19th century saw the rise of Beijing opera – still a popular form of opera that is regarded as a national treasure. Some surveys show that today there are hundreds of regional opera types nationwide. The most popular and influential ones include Beijing Opera, Kunqu, Shaoxing Opera, Huangmei Opera, Sichuan Opera and Cantonese Opera.

oracle bone inscriptions

Oracle bone inscriptions are ancient Chinese characters found on tortoise shells and animal bones and presumed to have been carved by the ancient Chinese in the Shang Dynasty (1600-1046BC). They are the earliest known examples of Chinese script. The oracle bone inscriptions were mainly used to record the results of divinations for rulers in the Shang Dynasty, and involve references to such diverse subjects as ancient politics, economy, military matters, Chinese culture, customs, astronomy and medicine.

When farmers dug up these bones, they thought that they were dragon bones, and sold them for medicine.

The discoverer of the inscriptions is thought to have been a scholar in the Qing Dynasty, over a thousand years later, called Wang Yirong. It is said that Wang Yirong, an official at the Imperial Academy, once fell sick and his servant bought some Chinese medicine for him. One day when Wang happened to see the ingredients of his medicine, he noticed some pieces of bone, which the doctor called "dragon bone" were actually carved with strange symbols. Being an enquiring sort of man, he started to study and decipher these strange symbols. He made the link tracing the bones to Anyang (in Henan Province) which proved to be the origin of the oracle bone inscriptions. Up to the present day a total of more than 150,000 pieces of oracle bone inscriptions have been discovered with about 4500 characters of which more than 2000 have been deciphered.

origami

There's a special type of origami called Chinese money folding. It's used to make boats, animals or models of buildings out of paper notes, one connected to another, all folded in the same shape. Thousands of notes could be used for just one work. The Chinese 1 Fen note is often used since its gold colour symbolizes prosperity. A gift made from these could convey a wish of good fortune.

ornamental archway

Archway in the Summer Palace, Beijing

The ornamental archway is a traditional form of Chinese architecture used as a gateway at entrances to gardens, temples, mausoleums or main streets. It usually consists of four decorated columns supporting a lintel with eaves added on top. Some archways are purely ornamental. But many are built to commemorate a significant event or pay tribute to a person's moral integrity. For example an archway might be inscribed in commemoration of a widow's chastity or a son's filial piety (hardly likely to be causes for architectural endeavour in the West).

Outlaws of the Marsh → *WATER MARGIN*

Ouyang Xiu

A prominent scholar, poet, historian and statesman in the Song Dynasty, Ouyang Xiu's influence in ancient Chinese literature is often compared to that of Han Yu in terms of their accomplishments in the reform of the prose genre. Included as one of the Eight Giants of Tang and Song Prose, Ouyang Xiu (1007-1072AD) led a traditionalist movement away from a florid prose style to a simpler form of writing. His best known prose work *Zuiweng Tingji* (literally *Regarding the Pavilion of the Old Drunkard*) is a standard feature in Chinese middle school textbooks, and contains a line which is still widely quoted today.

> *the old drunkard's intention is not in the wine, but lies between the mountains and streams*

The first part of this piece of inscrutability is usually quoted by itself, meaning that a person's intentions are probably not what, at first sight, they may appear to be. Ouyang Xiu is also credited with the *New Tang History* and a *New History of the Five Dynasties*.

Ox Head and Horse Face

In Chinese mythology, Ox Head and Horse Face are two jailers in the service of Yanluo, the Ruler of the Underworld. Their duty is to bring the souls of the deceased to the underworld. In folk literature they are usually represented as human-shaped monsters, one with the head of an ox, the other the face of a horse.

pagodas

Pagodas are tiered towers with multiple eaves typical of traditional Chinese architecture. They can be made of wood, brick, iron, coloured glaze or even gold and silver, and can be constructed in square, hexagonal or octagonal shapes. They are mostly found near or in Buddhist temples, as Buddhists belief that pagodas can ward off evil.

©iStockphoto.com/Robert Churchill

Third-century AD pagoda, the Ruiguang Ta, in Suzhou

Pan Yue

Pan Yue has worked as an environmentalist since 2003. As a high-ranking government official, Pan Yue has put enormous effort into monitoring and supervising the environmental situation in China. He adopted the "environmental impact evolution" approach to assess whether a construction project will negatively impact on the local environment. This means that badly performing plants are fined. Pan's activities led to a "storm of environmental protection" across the country and he has been nicknamed "whirlwind Pan". Pan is also at the forefront of work on the formulation of an environment tax to further reduce pollution and protect the ravaged environment.

Peaceful Rise

Peaceful Rise is a recently created concept to describe China's foreign policy and its influential involvement in world affairs, a diplomatic and strategic response from the Chinese government to the "China threat" argument initiated by the Western powers. It was first used by the Chinese scholar Zheng Bijian at the Bo'ao Forum for

Asia in 2003 and was then restated by top-level Chinese leaders like Premier Wen Jiabao and President Hu Jintao at international meetings and important speeches within the Communist Party of China. The essence of this approach derives from the traditional Confucian value of "harmony" which argues in favour of harmonious relations among human beings and between human beings and nature. Essentially "Peaceful Rise" is viewed by the Chinese government as a new path for development in today's new world, which emphasizes that China will develop peacefully without presenting a challenge to the established world order and that in turn its development will help maintain world peace.

However this strategy seemed too controversial to some Chinese scholars and politicians, too full of unclear connotations. For example, they argued that it is too early to talk about China's rise when China still faces so many social and economic problems; also that it leads to a contradictory treatment of the Taiwan issue, clashing with previous Chinese policy. In 2004 at the Bo'ao Forum President Hu Jintao accordingly adopted a less controversial phrase "peaceful development".

peach wood sword

A weapon made from peach wood used for Taoist exorcism. The peach wood sword is believed to ward off demons and evils. People usually hang it on a wall to protect the household and wish for happiness.

Pei Xiu

A Minister of Works under Jin Wudi, Pei Xiu (224-271AD) invented the grid map. Using one inch to represent the equivalent of 125 miles, he was responsible for accurately mapping much of China's territory during the Western Jin Dynasty (265-317AD).

GRID MAP INVENTED IN 3RD CENTURY AD

Peking roast duck

Peking roast duck, a trademark dish of Beijing cuisine, is said to have a history of about 800 years. Ducks are either roasted in ovens or hung over the fire until the skin turns brown with oozing grease and a pleasant fragrance. Roast duck is served in thin slices together with pancakes, spring onions and sweet noodle sauce. Quan Jü De and Bian Yi Fang are two restaurants in Beijing which are famous for their first-rate duck.

peng

A giant mythological bird first described in Zhuang Zi's essay *A Happy Excursion* (Xiao Yao You). According to Zhuang Zi, the peng is a gigantic bird that has grown out of a kind of giant fish called the kun, that lives in the northern sea. When it flies, its wings are like clouds in the sky. It can travel three thousand li (a Chinese mile – equivalent to half a kilometre) with one beat of its wings. But it flaps its wings slowly, taking six months to fly to the southern sea, where it can finally rest. The Chinese word peng is a popular given name meaning ambition and a promising future.

peony

The peony, in Chinese culture, is known as the "fugui flower" – a flower symbolizing wealth (fu) and nobility (gui). Down the centuries it has been a popular subject in all forms of artistic creation. In recent years there has been a strong move to designate the peony as China's national flower, though it is not yet officially endorsed. The city of Luoyang in Henan Province, famous for its peony growing, is also called the City of Peonies.

Peony Pavilion → *MUDAN TING*

Phoenix → *FENGHUANG*

pickled vegetables

Pickled vegetables are vegetables processed and preserved in brine. They taste salty or sour. In Chinese cuisine there are a variety of pickled vegetables, including cucumber, Chinese cabbage, ginger, radish and kohlrabi. They are usually served with congee. In many places pickled vegetables are synonymous with salted vegetables (xian cai).

Ping An Insurance

Ping An Insurance (Group), founded in 1988, is a holding company listed both on the Hong Kong and Shanghai Stock Exchanges with its headquarters in Shenzhen. Ping An started out as just a property insurer, but when it achieved a monopoly in the life insurance business, its greater expansion and growth was simply a matter of time. In the mid 1990s Ping An diversified into financial services and overseas investment. Nowadays Ping An is one of China's biggest companies in the fields of insurance and finance.

pinyin

Pinyin, also known as the Chinese phonetic alphabet, refers to a system of transliterating Chinese ideograms into the roman alphabet. The pronunciation and intonation of the romanized spelling is based on the Beijing dialect of Mandarin. It was developed in the 1950s and officially accepted as an international standard in 1979. It replaced the older and less accurate system, Wade-Giles, which was used in the West, especially in terms of the spelling of Chinese geographical or personal names. These days pinyin is taught in Chinese schools, even in kindergartens in some big cities. It is of great help for foreigners to learn the standard Mandarin pronunciation (although you will have to learn certain special pronunciations like, for example, ou which is pronounced as in go or c, which is pronounced as ts). Pinyin also facilitates the input of Chinese characters into computers.

pipa

A type of lute with four strings, the pipa originally came to China from Central Asia via the Silk Road in the Middle Ages. Held upright on the lap, the pipa is a very expressive instrument and is often used in folk music.

©iStockphoto.com/Peter Nguyen

Pixiu, *a.k.a.* ***Pixie***

A mythical beast said to be the ninth son of the dragon, Pixiu has a dragon's head, a horse's body, a qilin's feet and roughly resembles a lion. Powerful and fierce, it is seen as a guardian beast, as its second name Pixie (warding off evil) suggests. It feeds on gold, silver and jewellery. It never defecates because it has no anus. To Chinese people the Pixiu is an auspicious sign, since it can swallow wealth and never let it out. The Pixiu is commonly used as a mascot in feng shui. People are encouraged to wear a jade Pixiu to ward off evil or to put a Pixiu in their homes to attract wealth.

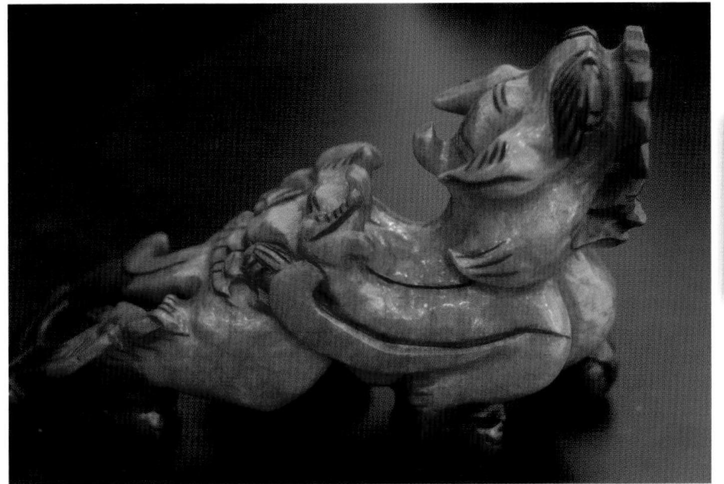

©iStockphoto.com/Jiaxi Shen

THE GOLD-EATING BEAST THAT NEVER DEFECATES

placenta → *EATING*

planchette writing

A variant of "automatic writing" used in divination for the purpose of communicating with spirits. It usually involves two people. One writes, presumably under spirit control, with a stick on a wooden board covered with sand or incense ashes, the other records everything the first person has written. The records are sometimes compiled into books under the names of Taoist gods or deities. Planchette writing was very popular among the upper classes in the Song Dynasty.

Pu Songlin → *STRANGE STORIES FROM A CHINESE STUDIO*

Puyi

Puyi, or the Emperor Qing Xuantong (1906-1967), was the last emperor of the Qing Dynasty and is widely known as the Last Emperor. At the age of two he was chosen by Cixi to be the next in line when his uncle, the Emperor Guangxu died. His father, the second Prince Chun, was appointed regent to deal with imperial affairs until 1911, when the Xinhai Revolution erupted.

Puyi was enthroned three times and abdicated three times. The first abdication was in 1912 and was forced on him by the capitalist campaign known as the Xinhai Revolution although he still retained his imperial title and the royal family was allowed to stay in the Forbidden City.

In 1917 the warlord Zhang Xun restored Puyi to his throne, but this was to last but a brief 12 days given the massive nationwide opposition and intervention from other warlords. After being expelled from the Forbidden City in 1924, Puyi managed to get to Tianjin and stayed in the Japanese Concession until 1932 when the Japanese made him the puppet ruler of Manchukuo with the title of reign of Datong. In 1934 Puyi was crowned Emperor of Manchukuo with a new title of reign:

Kangde. In 1945 he was captured by the Soviet army in northeastern China and was later repatriated to the Chinese Communists in 1950. He was declared "reformed" after a ten year government re-education programme and became a member of the Chinese Political Consultative Conference in 1964.

Puyi wrote his autobiography *From Emperor to Citizen* in the 1960s and died in 1967 during the Cultural Revolution. The Last Emperor, the last in the whole history of Chinese emperors, died of cancer.

The Last Emperor, 28th February 1934

pyjamas

You may be surprised to see people, usually housewives, busying themselves about the market place, bargaining with the traders, and still dressed in their pyjamas.

Qi Baishi

A great master of traditional Chinese painting in the 20th century, Qi Baishi (1864-1957) worked as a carpenter in his early years and taught himself to paint. He settled down in Beijing in the early 1920s and started to acquire nationwide recognition. His theory of art was that "painting must be something between likeness and unlikeness" and his paintings are known for their unconventional, playful style. His range covers a huge variety of subjects: landscapes, animals, figures, flowers etc. He was a prolific painter and didn't stop working until he died at the age of 93.

Qi Gaodi → *NAN QI GAODI*

qi pao

The qi pao, also known as the changshan, is a close-fitting, one-piece dress, usually high-necked and sleeveless, derived from the style of Manchu costumes. The original Manchu qi pao was a very long, loose-fitting gown that hung boringly straight down to the feet and had no claims at all to stylishness. Then around the 1900s the qi pao was re-tailored to cater to the modern taste for highlighting the feminine form. Before the Communist takeover in 1949, the qi pao, made from a variety of fabrics, was everyday women's wear, both for formal and informal occasions. These days the qi pao is still sometimes used as a party dress. But most people now consider it just a uniform for waitresses at fancy restaurants or something worn as a special kind of ceremonial costume.

Qi Xi

Qi Xi, literally The Night of Sevens, falls on the seventh day of the seventh month of the Chinese Lunar Calendar. It is associated with the well-known folk story of *The Cowherd and Weaver Girl*. The story is this: one day Zhinü (the weaver girl), daughter of the Goddess of Heaven (the wife of the Jade Emperor), sneaked away from the heavenly court with her fairy sisters. A young cowherd named Niulang happened to see Zhinü bathing in a lake and it was love at first sight. They married and their marriage sent the Goddess of Heaven into a fury: Niulang was a mere mortal! She forced Zhinü to return to Heaven and leave her husband and children behind. But Niulang, with the help of his magic cow, managed to go up to Heaven to search for his wife. The angry goddess took out her hairpin and drew a river to separate them forever, thus forming the Milky Way. It is said that once a year the couple were blessed with a one-night reunion when the magpies formed a bridge (called Que Qiao, the Bridge of Magpies) over the river on the seventh night of the seventh month.

Qi Xi is also known as Chinese Valentine's Day. In olden days, young girls would make an offering to Zhinü and pray for blessings to perfect their embroidery skills on the night of Qi Xi, a custom known as qi qiao (pleading for skills). It is also a day when unmarried girls pray for love and a happy marriage.

Qian Qichen

Qian Qichen was born in 1928 and joined the Communist Party of China in 1942. He gained extensive experience in foreign affairs, having worked for the Chinese Embassy in Moscow and in Guinea and at the Ministry of Foreign Affairs. He served as the Vice Premier of the State Council from 1993 to 2003. He was also directly involved in the preparations for the handover of Hong Kong and Macao. He was awarded the highest Mongolian national award – the Polaris medal – by the Mongolian government in 2005 for his long-term contribution to developing relations between Mongolia and China.

Qian Xuesen → *Tsien Hsue-shen*

Qian Zhongshu

A scholar and writer in modern China, Qian Zhongshu (1910-1998) is best known for his novel *Fortress Besieged*, which was also well-received in the Western world. A graduate of Tsinghua University, he studied literature at the University of Oxford and at the Sorbonne in Paris. He was appointed professor at Tsinghua after the People's Republic of China was founded in1949. During the Cultural Revolution he was persecuted, but survived and soon secured a niche for himself in the academic world on publication of his important monograph *Guan Zhui Bian*. This is translated into English as *Limited Views* and is a massive four-volume collection of essays and reading notes on the classics of early Chinese literature. His novel *Fortress Besieged* was adapted into a hit TV series, making him a household name. Qian continued to lead a secluded life until his death in 1998.

Qigong → *Falun Gong*

qilin

The qilin is an auspicious creature in Chinese mythology. It's described as a deer-like animal with a horn and an ox's tail and with scales all over its body. People believe that it brings peace and prosperity. During the Ming Dynasty, the giraffe brought to Beijing by the great explorer Zheng He after his voyage in 1414 was referred to as a qilin. The emperor proclaimed it a sign of his powerful reign. In folk culture it is believed that the qilin is capable of granting children. Legend says that Confucius was granted to his family by a qilin. To this day it remains a popular Chinese mascot.

This statue of a qilin, stands in the Emperor's Garden in the Forbidden City, Beijing

Qin Er Shi

As the second Emperor of the Qin Dynasty (221-206BC), Er Shi (230-207BC) inherited a state on the verge of disaster. The ordinary people had been worked to death on Emperor Qin Shi Huang's elaborate state projects, and those that had survived found themselves eating food fit for swine whilst corrupt officials grew fat with feasting. Failing to recognize the threat that such an enormous disparity between rich and poor presented, Er Shi allowed his eunuch tutor, Zhao Gao, to further increase the burdens of the poor with yet more taxes and the introduction of military conscription.

When Er Shi eventually tried to limit Zhao Gao's power, however, the eunuch took control of the palace, forced the emperor to commit suicide and installed his nephew Ziying on the throne. However, the reign of this puppet emperor was brought to an immediate end with the founding of the Western Han Dynasty (206-9AD).

Qin Shi Huang

Recognized as the first emperor to unite China, Emperor Qin Shi Huang (259-210BC) was a man of megalomaniacal genius. Through his use of a ruthlessly efficient army, he defeated all of his neighbouring states, established a centrally administered sovereignty based on Legalist governing principles and declared himself "The First August Emperor" of the Qin Dynasty (221-206BC). Thereafter he cemented his power by confiscating all weapons and melting them down into colossal bronze bells; joined together previously built defensive structures to produce the Great Wall Of China, standardized everything from money and writing through to weights and axle measurements, burned all books that might be used to undermine his authority and buried his outspoken critics alive.

THOUSANDS BURIED ALIVE IN EMPEROR'S TOMB

Obsessed with death, Emperor Qin Shi Huang is also said to have sent thousands of male and female virgins across the Eastern Sea to find an elixir of eternal life. Ironically, however, it was this very obsession with immortality that led to his untimely death. Drinking huge quantities of mercury in the belief that this would enable him to live forever, he unwittingly ended up slowly poisoning himself to death. What followed thereafter must have been one of the most elaborate funerals that the world has ever seen. Thousands of men, women and exotic animals were buried alive in the emperor's tomb because it was thought that they would then be able to accompany him into the afterlife. Thousands of life-sized Terracotta Warriors were buried in pits around his grave in the hope that they would go on to help him establish a new heavenly empire.

Qing Guangxu

Qing Guangxu (1871-1908) was the nephew of Empress Dowager Cixi and the successor of Emperor Tongzhi, who died of a sudden illness. Guangxu was specially chosen as the new emperor at the age of four by Cixi who wanted a young heir in order to continue her own domination of imperial power. When he reached the age of sixteen, Guangxu began to rule by himself but Cixi still remained a powerful influence. During Guangxu's reign the Qing army was heavily defeated by Japan in the Sino-Japanese War (1894). This led many people to call for capitalist reform to strengthen China's power. Guangxu himself was in favour of this and was pro Western ideas, modernization and capitalism. In 1898, with help from progressive scholars like Kang Youwei and Liang Qichao, he set in motion reforms in the fields of politics, the military, the economy and education, all with the aim of rehabilitating the decadent Qing government along the lines of the Japanese Meiji Reformation. The reform activity lasted just 103 days and became known as the Hundred Days of Reform. It was suppressed by Cixi who started a coup with support from the military. Emperor Guangxu was then placed under house arrest and many of his supporters fled or were persecuted. After years of captivity, Guangxu, the would-be reformer, died at the age of 38, poisoned, it is said, by Cixi.

Qing Kangxi

Qing Kangxi was the third emperor of the Qing Dynasty, son of Emperor Shunzhi, and ruled from 1661-1722, the longest reign in Chinese history. When he ascended the throne Kangxi was only 8 years old and the imperial court was dominated by four regents appointed by his father. For a long time the young emperor had no control. With help from his grandmother, the Grand Empress Dowager Xiaozhuang, and after years' of endurance and careful planning, Kangxi, at the age of 16, defeated the most powerful regent, Aobai, and his faction and began to govern the country himself. He later successfully put down the Revolt of the Three Warlords in southern China that was launched by three surrendered Ming Dynasty military leaders. During the 1680s, Kangxi won a series of battles against the Mongolian tribe Dzungar and against Russia and regained Taiwan from the Zheng family. This consolidated the empire and unified the whole country.

Qing Kangxi was also particularly interested in agricultural development and toured southern China six times to inspect the building and repair of dam and irrigation projects. He also ordered the compilation of a series of cultural and literary works, including the most complete ancient Chinese dictionary, the Kangxi Dictionary. As a diligent Manchu emperor, he studied not only Confucian culture but also algebra, geometry and astronomy, learning from Jesuit missionaries. Kangxi began an era called the "Kang Qian Golden Age" – the apogee of economic prosperity and culture of the Qing Dynasty.

During his 61-year reign the Qing Empire became one of the most powerful and prosperous countries in the world covering a vast territory. In the later years of his reign problems with border defences against ethnic minorities and civil war in Tibet caused great financial losses to the state treasury.

Qing Long, *a.k.a.* ***Azure Dragon***

Qing Long, literally Azure Dragon, is one of the four symbols of the Chinese constellations, representing the East and the season of spring.

Qing Ming Festival

Qing Ming Festival, literally Clear and Bright Festival, is a movable feast that usually falls around 5th April. Qing Ming is an occasion to commemorate and honour the dead. Traditionally people make a visit to the cemetery, sweep the graves, burn joss paper and make offerings of food and glasses of wine to their ancestors. It is sometimes also known as the Tomb Sweeping Festival. It is also a day for people to go outside and enjoy the arrival of spring, to fly kites and have rides on swings. The Qing Ming Festival was made an official public holiday in 2007.

©iStockphoto.com/Hulton Archive/Getty Images

Qing Qianlong

Qing Qianlong, the fourth son of Emperor Qing Yongzheng, was a capable and talented emperor who ruled from 1735 to 1795. Having inherited stable institutions and a prosperous empire from his predecessors, Qianlong continued the "Kang Qian Golden Age" for several more decades. He consolidated his position by launching a series of military campaigns against Chinese Turkestan, the Zungars, the Gurkhas and Tibet. He expanded the empire's territory with the inclusion of non-Han Chinese groups like the Mongols, Uygurs and Tibetans. Qianlong was an expert calligrapher, a painter, poet and art collector. He also built, or reconstructed, many royal gardens and palaces such as the Summer Palace and the Hall of Prayer for Good Harvests in the Temple of Heaven. Qianlong initiated the compilation of important classics of Chinese culture. The *Si Ku Quan Shu*, literally the Complete Library in the Four Branches of Literature, is the most comprehensive collection of Chinese literature up to the 18th century, containing more than 3460 works and contributed greatly to the preservation of China's cultural heritage.

A painting of Emperor Qianlong in the Forbidden City

However, he has also been severely criticized by historians for destroying or banning writings that were seen as anti-Manchu or rebellious against his own personage – many valuable books were lost, including the Yongle Encyclopedia published in the Ming Dynasty. He took his literary persecution to extremes, having many writers beheaded simply because the Chinese character Ming appeared in their writing.

In the later years of his reign the Qing Dynasty suffered from Emperor Qianlong's misplaced trust in a deceitful official, He Shen. He Shen was Qianlong's principal chancellor and had amassed a personal fortune of over 900 million taels of silver. This was equivalent to no less than 12 years of imperial tax revenue (without taking into account the money that he had spent). He Shen was the most corrupt official in Chinese history. In addition to these huge losses there were the costs of various military campaigns and Qianlong's own extravagant lifestyle – all contributing to the beginning of the end for the Qing Dynasty.

USE OF THE CHARACTER MING NOW CARRIES DEATH PENALTY

In 1795, in the 60th year of his rule, Qianlong decided to abdicate and passed the throne to his son, the Emperor Jiaqing, not thinking it right that he should reign for a longer period than his grandfather, the Emperor Qing Kangxi. Qianlong died at the age of 89, the greatest age reached by any Chinese emperor.

Qing Shunzhi

Shunzhi (1638-1661), the first emperor of the Qing Dynasty, was placed on the throne at the tender age of six. At first he was very studious and attentive to matters of state. But he was temperamental. Once, when his mother, the Empress Dowager Xiangzhuang, criticized him, he is said to have become furious and attacked his own throne with a sword. When his favourite concubine died, he went completely off the rails, gradually pined away and attempted suicide. A supporter of the Jesuits and a follower of Buddhism, he died aged just twenty-four.

Qing Xuantong → *Puyi*

Qing Yongzheng

Qing Yongzheng, the fourth son of Emperor Kangxi, ruled from 1722-1735 and was known as the most industrious of all Chinese emperors. He came to the the throne at the age of 45. Although he reigned for only 13 years – a much shorter reign than either his father or his son enjoyed – Yongzheng was a more prolific reformer and implemented reforms in bureaucracy and administration, agriculture, land and the law and thus played a major role in the maintenance of the "Kang Qian Golden Age". He

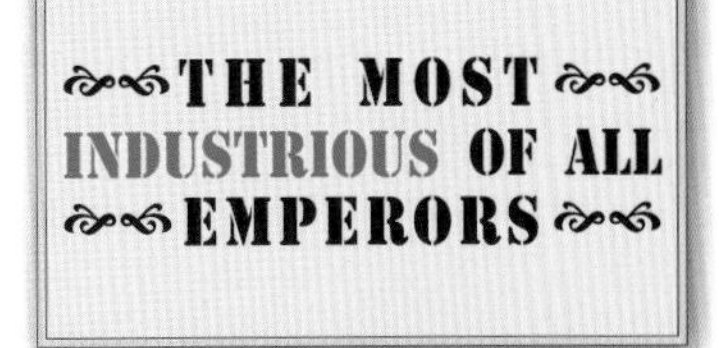

further centralized imperial authority by weakening the power of the princes and creating the "office of Military Secrets" as his secretariat to assist with government affairs. His iron fist was felt by the corrupt and he carried out nationwide investigations into property held by his officials. Government revenue grew. Qing Yongzheng was criticized by later historians for his "literary persecution" in suppressing writers and scholars who were seen as anti-Manchu or anti-Yongzheng's regime. But he remains the great workhorse of Chinese emperors. He would always be seen working well after midnight, poring over his officials' reports. Only on his birthday did he take a day off.

Qingdao

Qingdao is a coastal city and popular summer resort in Shandong Province. The city was under German and then Japanese occupation from 1897 to 1922 before the Republic of China took it back, although the government lost it to Japan again during the Sino-Japanese War. Well-preserved foreign styles of architecture lend Qingdao a unique atmosphere. It has been constantly listed as one of the most beautiful cities in China and one of the best places to live. A centre for water sports, Qingdao was one of the host cities for the 2008 Summer Olympics. It is also famous for its Qingdao Brewery.

Qingdao Beer

Qingdao is one of the most popular beers in China, brewed in Qingdao in Shandong Province. It is estimated that Qingdao, being exported to more than 50 countries, makes up about 50% of China's beer exports. The Qingdao Brewery was founded in 1903 by German settlers and is now the biggest brewery in China.

Qu Yuan → *Dragon Boat Festival*

Qufu

The birthplace of Confucius.

R

red envelopes

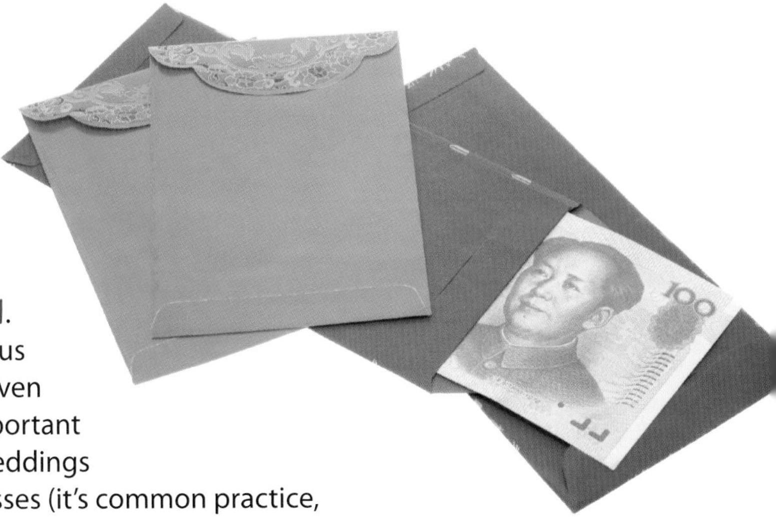

Traditionally, the concept of red envelopes refers to the lucky money sealed in red envelopes given to children or unmarried young adults by their elders at Spring Festival. Nowadays it is synonymous with any monetary gift given during holidays or on important occasions, for instance weddings or the opening of businesses (it's common practice, especially in the south of China, for entrepreneurs to give small sums of money to the people who come to the opening party for their new business). Red envelopes is also a euphemism for bribes given to surgeons, officials or lawyers in expectation of preferential treatment – a tacitly understood rule in China for a way of getting things done the way you want.

©iStockphoto.com/Yiap See Fat

Red Flag Fleet → *CHING SHIH*

Red Guards

The Red Guards were a large group of Chinese civilians composed mainly of militant school kids and college students and mobilized by Mao Zedong from 1966 to 1968. They were the main factor that caused nationwide unrest during that period and one of the most important forces in driving the Cultural Revolution movement across China. The Red Guards were viewed by Mao as the cultural shock troops to combat opponents (mainly those of a capitalist disposition) within Chinese society. The Red Guards enjoyed privileges such as free travel and free accommodation when sent out on their missions around China or when on a pilgrimage to the Jinggang Mountains. As with any large-scale movement, some members were more active than others. Some merely enjoyed the privileges. But others put the ideology into practice in a ferocious way. With most of their number being just teenagers, the Red Guards struck in schools and committed many acts of violence such as breaking into people's houses and confiscating possessions, attacking intellectuals and officials, and destroying museums, religious places and various types of government unit. The most symbolic image of a Red Guard is a person wearing green military uniform and red armband and holding the Little Red Book. After causing massive turmoil throughout the country, the Red Guard movement was eventually replaced by the activity of "educated youth to go and work in the countryside and mountain areas" as instructed by Mao Zedong in December of 1968. It was Mao himself who finally disbanded the Red Guards.

red paper strips

You'll see red paper strips hanging from buildings or hung up in rooms. They are there to bring good luck.

Ren Bonian

The famous 19th century painter Ren Bonian (1840-1896) learned to paint at an early age. He was an important figure in the Shanghai School which integrated traditional and popular elements in painting. Ren is best known as a portrait artist.

rock

Chinese rock started in the 1980s with Cui Jian's hit song *I Have Nothing*, which was heavily influenced by the folk songs of northwestern China (as well as Western rock). Following Cui Jian, a number of rock bands were formed, such as *Black Panther* fronted by Dou Wei, the first heavy metal band

Tang Dynasty, and the all-female group *Cobra*. Their music was popular among young Chinese who went in for black leather coats, jeans, silver metal ornaments and long hair for men. The Chinese government, however, tried to suppress rock music, banned it on television and placed restrictions on rock concerts. After a short period of popularity in the early 90s, Chinese rock had receded and went underground soon after. In the new millennium the underground rock scene grew maturer with the emergence of new subgenres such as New Metal, Post Punk and Extreme Metal. Rock festivals started to spring up under a more tolerant regime.

Romance of the Three Kingdoms

A martial epic written by Luo Guanzhong (1330-1400), it tells the tale, part history and part legend, of the fall of the late Han Dynasty and the beginning of the Three Kingdoms era. It is classed as one of the Four Great Classical Novels of Chinese literature. Hundreds of characters figure in the work, but the focus is on the three clans who eventually carve out the three kingdoms, namely the Kingdom of Shu led by Liu Bei, the Kingdom of Wei led by Cao Cao, and the Kingdom of Wu led by the Sun clan. It tells of political plots and intrigues, military tactics and warfare, heroism and treason, and the efforts the three clans made to achieve dominance over a period of 100 years. Combining history with fiction, the novel reflects Confucian values as well as the way in which the Chinese view history, which can be illustrated by the first and last lines of the book – "The empire long united must divide..." and "The empire long divided must unite..." The story holds a tremendous grip on the Chinese imagination and has been told and retold in numerous forms. TV series, comics and video games abound.

THE EMPIRE LONG UNITED MUST DIVIDE

THE EMPIRE LONG DIVIDED MUST UNITE

Romance of the West Chamber → *Xi Xiang Ji*

Rulin Waishi, *a.k.a.* ***The Scholars***

A classic novel written by Wu Jingzi (1701-1754), set in the Ming Dynasty, it is an acute satire of the hypocrisy and decadence of the Confucian intellectuals produced by the Imperial Civil Examination system, the disastrous influence of this institution and the darkness of society. Lacking a main character and a linear narrative, the novel is more like a group of short stories loosely connected one to another. With his concise and humorous vernacular language, Wu Jingzi vividly portrays various characters of different classes – arrogant officials, the mean landlord, the snobbish butcher…

Sakyamuni Buddha → *GAUTAMA BUDDHA*

Scholars → *RULIN WAISHI*

self-criticism

Self-criticism is a common form of education and self-improvement among Communist Party members. The practice originated with Mao and was very common when he was in power. It's a way of disciplining party members and of correcting their wrongdoing and misguided thinking. Nowadays people may still be required to write pieces of self-criticsm at Communist Party meetings and self-criticism is part of the Communist Party constitution.

Shaanxi & Shanxi

These are two different provinces in northern China, not spelling variants of one place. The aa and the a represent different tones in spoken Chinese.

Shanghai

One of the four municipalities in China and one of the largest cities in the world, Shanghai is the centre of Chinese finance and business and one of the busiest ports in the whole world. Originally a small fishing town near the mouth of the Yangtze River, Shanghai rapidly grew into the hub of international commerce in the first half of the 19th

The Pudong district of Shanghai in the late afternoon sun

century after opening its port to foreign trade at the end of the first Opium War (1839-1842). It developed its unique "modern" popular culture, later labelled Shanghai culture, during that time when its people were eager to experience anything that was modern or foreign. Its writers, like Eileen Chang, wrote about the city with a deep sense of cosmopolitanism. For almost a century, and in spite of the Communist takeover when all the foreign investment was withdrawn, Shanghai has remained in the minds of Chinese people as the city of fashion and material pleasure. Since the economic reforms of the 1990s, Shanghai has witnessed what is perhaps the fastest economic development for a city that the world has ever known. Symbolized by the modern landmarks that make up the new skyline of the financial district, Shanghai attracts people from all over the world to come and seek their fortune.

Shaolin Temple

Situated in the Songshan Mountain region in Henan Province , the Shaolin Temple, the cradle of Chinese Zen Buddhism, is honoured as "the Number One Temple under Heaven". It is also famous for its long tradition of martial arts. This Chinese kung fu mecca attracts thousands of people from all over the world who travel there to learn martial arts. Thanks to many Wuxia writers (martial arts and heroism), and in particular to Jin Yong, who repeatedly refers to the leading position of the Shaolin Temple in the world of Wuxia, the temple has become a household name resonant with mystery and legend.

Shaoshan

Shaoshan in Hunan Province is famous for being Mao's birthplace.

Shen Congwen

An important modern Chinese writer and historian, Shen Congwen (1902-1988) was born in Fenghuang, Hunan Province, a place which was the source of his inspiration. He is known as a regional writer who depicts in his novels the primitive yet charming world of Xiangxi (West Hunan) where the natives live in harmony with nature, no matter how painful and disappointing their lives might be. He was a great humanist and wrote of the beauty to be found in the souls of the native people and of the power of human nature, albeit contaminated by modern civilization. His most famous novels are *The Frontier City (Biancheng)* and *The Long River (Changhe)*, which were all written before the Communist Party came to power in 1949. After that social upheaval, he focused on non-fiction and published a groundbreaking monograph based on his study of Chinese costume and dress in history.

Shen Kuo

Shen Kuo (1031-1095AD) was a great Chinese scientist and statesman of the Song Dynasty, a true universal genius. He was a gifted mathematician, astronomer, geologist and poet. He produced work in the fields of medicine, biology and botany. He held government posts as diplomat, finance minister and state inspector. He was ahead of his time in many ways. For instance, he was the first to discover that the compass does not point directly to the north, but to the magnetic north pole, a discovery of great significance for navigation. In astronomy, Shen Kuo proposed the theory that heavenly bodies were spheres, basing this on his observations of the waxing and waning of the moon. His scientific work *Dream Pool Essays* (*Mengxi Bitan*), an encyclopedic account and description of many of the advances and inventions of the period, is a milestone in the history of Chinese science.

sheng

Also called the Chinese mouth organ, the sheng has as its base a wind chest, traditionally made from a gourd but which can also be of wood or metal. The player blows and sucks through the mouthpiece on the base and the sound comes from reed pipes attached to the wind chest.

Shenzhen

Shenzhen is a city in Guangdong Province, bordering on Hong Kong. Once a small fishing village, it has developed into a metropolis of about 8.6 million people (2007) and a GDP of RMB 670 billion (2007) within 30 years. The miracle of Shenzhen is due to large influxes of foreign investment. In 1980 Shenzhen was singled out by the late leader Deng Xiaoping as the first Special Economic Zone serving as the base for experiments in economic reform. It is now the manufacturing centre, financial hub and economic powerhouse of southern China.

Shi Nai'an → *Water Margin*

Sichuan

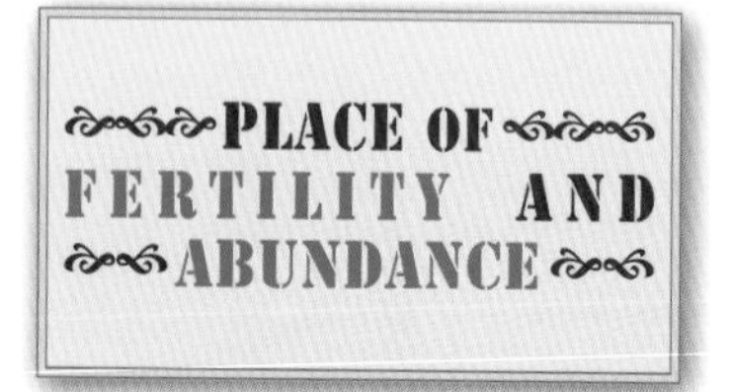

In the southwest of China, Sichuan Province shares a border with Tibet, Yunnan, Qinghai, Gansu, Shaanxi, Guizhou and Chongqing. It was the original site of the State of Shu during the Three Kingdoms Period. Sichuan is one of the most densely populated provinces in China and is currently the home of people of the Han and many ethnic groups. With its mountain-girded Sichuan Basin, Sichuan boasts breathtakingly beautiful landscapes, with the Himalayas to the west and the torrents of the upper Yangtze River running through. Historically known as the "Place of Fertility

A snow-capped mountain in Yading Nature Park in Daocheng, Sichuan

©iStockphoto.com/tcp

and Abundance", Sichuan was traditionally a major agricultural centre. It is now also an important industrial base with strength in such heavy industries as energy, iron and steel. Sichuan is also famous for its delicious food. It is the province where the famous Three Gorges Dam is to be found. As one of the Eight Great Traditions of Chinese cuisine, Sichuan cuisine is now popular all over the world.

Silk Road

Something of a misnomer, this road or route is not a single road and not only for trading in silk. Rather it is a network of routes linking China with the West, as far as the Mediterranean and has, since ancient times, been the route for trade and some cultural exchange between East and West.

Sima Qian

Sima Qian was a great historian in the Han Dynasty and is best known for his monumental work *Records of the Grand Historian (Shiji)*. This tells the history of a period of over two thousand years, from the Yellow Emperor, one of the Three August Ones and Five Emperors, to Emperor Han Wudi. Sima Qian (c.145BC-?) took the office of a Prefect of the Grand Scribes and started to compile *Shiji* during Han Wudi's reign. He made a big political mistake in defending a general who had lost a battle against a greatly outnumbered force of nomads from the north. Han Wudi took offence at this and sentenced Sima Qian to be castrated. Instead of committing suicide, as honour would have dictated, Sima Qian accepted the humiliation of castration in order to be able finish his great work. Later generations are indebted to him for most of the history of early China. His style of writing set a standard for Chinese historiography.

HISTORIAN STEPS OUT OF LINE AND IS SENTENCED TO CASTRATION

Sima Yan → *Jin Wudi*

Sima Yi

An outstanding politician and general in the Kingdom of Wei in the Three Kingdoms Period (184-280AD), Sima Yi (179-251AD) defended his homeland against the

Kingdom of Shu's Northern Expedition, led by the great strategist, Zhuge Liang. Sima Yi's victory in the year 234AD ended the life of Zhuge Liang and also brought to an end the military confrontation between the Kingdoms of Wei and Shu. In 249, while his Emperor, Cao Fang, was out of the capital, Sima Yi started a coup which brought the family of Sima to power. When Sima Yi died in 251 his grandson Sima Yan (236-290AD) founded the Jin Dynasty (265-420AD).

simplified characters

Simplified characters are the set of Chinese characters used in Mainland China, Singapore, Malaysia and the UN. The official process of simplifying the traditional or classical characters started in the 1950s in an attempt to promote literacy. The new system of writing went through several rounds of revisions and was finalized in the 1980s. They might not look very simplified to you or me or your average Westerner. For example,

traditional	*simplified*	
毛澤東	毛泽东	Mao Zedong
中國	中国	China
麵包	面包	bread
辭典	辞典	dictionary

Song Gaozong, *a.k.a.* ***Zhao Gou***

Song Gaozong was the first emperor of the Southern Song Dynasty. He was also a noted calligrapher and painter. In 1127 when his father, the Emperor Song Huizong, and his brother, the Emperor Song Qinzong, were both captured by nomadic troops from the Jurchen tribe, Gaozong ascended the throne but soon fled to Hangzhou in southern China to escape the Jurchen. It was in southern China that he re-established the Southern Song Dynasty. Under the leadership of generals like Li Gang, Yue Fei and Han Shizhong the Southern Song army defeated a series of invasions from the Jurchen and regained some lost territories. But Song Gaozong and his principal chancellor, Qin Hui, only set out to subdue, rather than conquer, the Jurchen because they feared that Gaozong's brother,

Song Qinzong, would return and claim the throne if the Jurchen were defeated outright. They eventually signed a treaty with the Jurchen in 1141, conceding a large amount of territory. In Chinese history, Song Gaozong and Qin Hui have been widely condemned for executing the great general Yue Fei and his supporters for the sole reason that Yue's reputation had grown during his battles against the Jurchen and he was consequently seen as a threat to Gaozong's power.

Song Lian

One of the most famous scholars in the early Ming Dynasty, Song Lian (1310-1381) was active in helping Zhu Yuanzhang (1328-1398) found the Ming Dynasty. He was appointed editor-in-chief of the *History of the Yuan Dynasty* and is best known for his work on this. He had a reputation as a book lover and started the fashion for private book collecting in the Ming Dynasty.

Song Taizu, *a.k.a.* ***Zhao Kuangyin***

Song Taizu was the founder of Northern Song Dynasty and ruled from 960-976AD. As Commander-in-Chief of the imperial army of the Later Zhou Dynasty (951-960AD), he was made the new emperor after the Chenqiao Mutiny in 960 which was launched mainly by his brother, Zhao Guangyi, and his supporters. When he became emperor, his first great achievement was to reunite a China fragmented by more than half a century's strife. He created the open social environment in which scholars and educated people were encouraged to discuss and participate in state affairs and scientific innovation. This engendered significant growth in the economy, technology, culture, literature and art of the Northern Song Dynasty. Song Taizu was also well known for his political astuteness in weakening the warlords' powers without force or bloodshed. He held a great banquet, invited these

Taizu, a painting on silk by an artist of the Song

warlords, and told them of his worries about mutinies (as he had himself experienced). A word to the wise. The governors understood his concerns and showed themselves willing to give up their power. Song Taizu died in 976 at the age of 49. He had laid the solid foundation of a strong empire, politically united and economically prosperous, and one seen as another golden age after the glorious Tang Dynasty.

The text on this spring couplet reads:

With the house filled with good fortune, the whole family are happy together;
With the new year coming, all the family members prosper.

(across the top)

May a river of gold flow into everyone's pocket.

soy milk

Soy milk is a drink made from soy beans. The Chinese like to drink it at breakfast together with youtiao. It is gaining popularity around the world as more and more people come to realize its health benefits.

Spirit Festival → *GHOST FESTIVAL*

spirit tablet

Usually a piece of board (sometimes a stone tablet) with the name of a deity or ancestor written on it. People put spirit tablets in shrines at home or in temples to designate the seat of a deity or ancestor. Incense sticks are usually burned at the tablet. Sometimes people put fruit and food in front of the tablet as offerings to the spirit.

spiritual money

Spiritual money, also called ghost money or joss paper, is sheets of paper resembling banknotes. Modern variants have the image of the Jade Emperor printed on the front. Spiritual money is usually burned at ancestor worship ceremonies or on other occasions, like the Qing Ming Festival, when the dead are commemorated. Burning spiritual money enables the deceased to enjoy a happy and rich life in the afterworld.

spring couplets

Traditionally Chinese people put spring couplets around the doorway of their homes at Chinese New Year. These little poems are normally written on two vertical strips of red paper. The couplets generally express people's wishes for prosperity, peace, longevity and good fortune in the coming year. The first verse is placed on the right side of the door and the second on the left. Usually a third line (generally a four-character-idiom) written on a horizontal strip will be placed above the couplets on the door.

Spring Festival, *a.k.a.* ***Chinese New Year***

Spring Festival is the most important traditional holiday in China. It is celebrated on the first day of the first month of the Chinese Lunar Calendar. The exact date may vary from late January to early February in the Gregorian calendar. The celebrations generally last a fortnight and officially end with the Lantern Festival. Preparations for the holiday start at least a week before New Year's Day. People busy themselves with shopping and housework. Every household will be decorated with spring couplets and New Year pictures, red Chinese knots and red paper cuts. Those working away from home in other cities make often heroic efforts to return to their hometown before Chinese New Year's Eve. On New Year's Day, people put on new clothes – symbolizing a new start in life. Red envelopes of lucky money are given to children as ya sui qian, money to ward off evil. The most popular activity is simply to pay a visit to relatives and friends and to wish each other a happy new year. In some places there are lion dances and New Year parades on the streets. There will be firecrackers and fireworks throughout the celebrations, which reach a climax on New Year's Eve.

Head of a dancing lion at the Spring Festival

steelyard

The steelyard is a straight beam balance consisting of an arm, a hook, lifting cords and a weight. Anything to be weighed is picked up by the hook, while the seller lifts up the whole steelyard, holding one of the cords. He then slides the weight left or right until he finds the perfect balancing point of the beam. The weight can be read from the gradation mark on which the weight-string rests. The steelyard is in widespread use by sellers at markets because it can be carried around quite easily without taking a whole set of weights.

©iStockphoto.com/liangpv

Stephen Chow → *ZHOU XINGCHI*

stinky tofu

Stinky tofu is a very popular snack. It's a kind of fermented doufu that has a strong odour. In spite of its unusual smell, it tastes surprisingly delicious. It can be steamed or stewed but is most commonly fried and served with chilli sauce.

stone lions

Traditionally, a pair of stone lions can often be seen as guardians standing in front of imperial palaces, temples, government offices, mansions and emperor's tombs. In Chinese myth they are believed to offer protection. For the same reason, along the oldest stone bridge in southwest Beijing, 501 stone lions, with different expressions and poses, are used to decorate the railings and protect pedestrians. These days stone lions are still common decorative and symbolic elements and will be found at the entrances to restaurants, hotels, supermarkets and other buildings, one sitting lion at each side of the entrance.

©iStockphoto.com/Hector Joseph Lumang

Two Chinese lions guard the entrance to a temple in Shenzhen

Story of a Marital Fate to Awaken the World → *XINGSHI YINYUAN ZHUAN*

Story of the Stone → *DREAM OF THE RED CHAMBER*

Strange Stories from a Chinese Studio

Written by Pu Songlin (1640-1715) during the early Qing Dynasty, *Strange Stories from a Chinese Studio* is a collection of 491 short stories with a wide range of subjects. The book abounds with supernatural tales about ghosts and fox spirits, where the boundary between reality and fiction becomes blurred. Sarcastic in tone, these stories invert traditional values and heap praise on ghosts and fox spirits, saying they are often more trustworthy than human beings. It is said that Pu Songlin opened a teahouse to collect stories. If anyone told an unusual story, he would not be charged for his tea.

©iStockphoto.com/Yanfei Sun

Tibetan Buddhist stupas in Yunnan Province

stupas

Stupas are reliquaries for keeping the holy relics of Buddha. The holy relics here refer to the bead-like crystals found among the ashes after Buddha's cremation.

Su Buqing

Su Buqing (1902-2003), a renowned mathematician, devoted all his life to mathematical research and teaching. His main achievements lay in the fields of differential geometry and computational geometry.

Su Dongpo → *Su Shi*

Su Shi

Su Shi (1037-1101AD), also known as Su Dongpo, was a gifted poet, essayist, calligrapher and artist. His father, Su Xun, and younger brother, Su Zhe, were also literati of the Northern Song Dynasty (960-1127AD). As a statesman, Su Shi voiced his opposition to Wang Anshi's reforms, which were, in his view, not in the interests of ordinary people. As a consequence of this opposition Su Shi was banished by the reformists who held power and who maliciously misinterpreted one of his poems as a criticism of the emperor. Su Shi then wrote many of his poetry and prose masterpieces from exile. As a poet, Su Shi's greatest contribution was in ci, a popular style of poetry in the Song Dynasty. Before Su Shi, the usual function of ci was to give poetic expression to small details of inner emotions. Su Shi's works in ci, however, explore wider social and historical subjects and produce an attitude of heroic abandon, which helped to develop a new style of ci called the Haofang (literally bold and unconstrained) School. A famous Chinese dish "Dongpo Pork" is also named after him.

Su Tong

A top novelist based in Nanjing. Su Tong (born 1963) shot to fame when his novel *Wives and Concubines* was adapted into the Oscar-nominated feature film *Raise the Red Lantern*, directed by Zhang Yimou. His delicate use of language is perfectly suited for depicting women and capturing the true flavour of the traditionally culture-rich region Jiangnan – to the south of the Yangtze River.

Sui Wendi

Born into a noble family, Emperor Sui Wendi (541-604AD) held important civil and military posts at the Northern Zhou court from the age of fourteen onwards. When his daughter married into the ruling family of the Northern Zhou Dynasty and her son was appointed emperor, Sui Wendi seized the opportunity and usurped his grandson's throne.

Founding the Sui Dynasty (581-618AD), Emperor Wendi then defeated the last Chen Emperor in southern China, and became the first person to reunite the whole of China in more than 300 years.

As the founder of the Sui Dynasty, Emperor Wendi was an excellent administrator, and upheld the law so stringently that he even refused to pardon his dying son for having stolen money from the royal treasury. He, however, felt himself to be above the law and even beat one of his own officials to death in a violent fit of rage.

Sui Yangdi

Emperor Yangdi (569-618AD) of the Sui Dynasty (581-618AD) was a talented poet and scholar. However, his love of luxury led to him commissioning several large construction projects that would eventually turn his people against him. The building of the Grand Canal, for instance, demanded the backbreaking labour of at least two million men. Similarly, his extension of the Great Wall cost nearly six million men their lives.

In addition to his exorbitant public projects, Yangdi spent vast amounts of time, labour and money on futile attempts at defeating neighbouring Korea. This led to a series of peasant uprisings and he was eventually strangled to death by the son of an official that he had disgraced.

Summer Palace

The Summer Palace, located northwest of Beijing, is the best preserved and biggest example of royal garden architecture in China. It was built in 1750 during the Qing Dynasty under the reign of Emperor Qianlong who wanted to construct a beautiful royal garden as a refuge from heatwaves and a place of entertainment to celebrate his mother's 60th birthday.

The design concept of the Summer Palace imitated the classical garden and architectural style of places like Suzhou and Hangzhou in southern China. It contains an abundance of ancient Chinese classical architectural features: pavilions, corridors, towers, hills and bridges. The Summer Palace has a total area of just under 1.25 square miles and consists of two main parts – the Kunming Lake, shaped like a peach, which covers 75 percent of the surface area, and Longevity

Hill, shaped like a bat. In traditional Chinese culture, the peach symbolizes longevity (people used to offer peaches at birthday celebrations, especially to the elderly) and the bat represents happiness (because the pronunciations of the Chinese words for bat and happiness are very similar).

The Summer Palace suffered enormously during the troubled times of the late Qing Dynasty and was ransacked and destroyed respectively by the Anglo-French allied invasion in 1860 and the eight allied powers in 1900. It was reconstructed by the Chinese royal family, with work done in 1886 and 1903. The garden itself is a masterpiece of ancient Chinese garden art and in 1998 it was listed by UNESCO as a World Heritage Site.

Sun Ce

A famous warlord during the late Han Dynasty, Sun Ce (175-200AD) was the eldest son of Sun Jian, who was killed on the battlefield when Sun Ce was only 16. Sun Ce then succeeded his father to become a local military leader. Modest and tolerant, he won strong support from his people. Consequently he was finally able to establish his own base in the southeast of China with the help of many counsellors and generals, such as Zhang Zhao and Zhou Yu. This laid a solid foundation for the later Kingdom of Wu, one of the three powerful regimes in the Three Kingdoms Period.

Sun Jihai

Sun Jihai (1977-) started his career with Dalian Wanda Football Club in 1995. After three successful seasons he was signed by the English team, Crystal Palace, where he stayed for one season. He was one of the first Chinese footballers ever to play in the First Division. In 2002 Sun signed for Manchester City and became the first Chinese footballer to score in the Premier League.

Sun Wen

The famous female soccer player, striker Sun Wen (1973-) joined the Chinese national team at the age of 17. Her great talent and skill was acknowledged when she led the team in the finals at the 1999 Women's World Cup. Although the Chinese lost to the US in a penalty shootout, she was awarded both the Golden Boot and the Golden Ball for her fabulous performance. In 2000 she was co-holder of FIFA's Woman Player of the Century. She hung up her boots in 2003 and this was seen as marking the end of the golden age of Chinese women's football.

Sun Wu → *Sun Zi*

Sun Wukong

Better known in the West as the Monkey King, Sun Wukong is a legendary character in Chinese mythology. He features especially in the epic novel Journey to the West, in which he escorts his master the Monk Tang (Xuanzang) to retrieve the Buddhist sutras from Tianzhu, or ancient India. Sun Wukong, born from a rock, has supernatural powers. Later, he learns more magic such as the 72 transformations (the ability to transform himself into 72 different kinds of animals and objects, sometimes even other people, from a temple to a fly, a pretty girl to a fish. It's a trick he often uses when fighting against demons (or spying on them). And he obtains a powerful weapon from the bottom of the Eastern Sea, the golden cudgel, which enables him to fight against the best warriors from Heaven during his rebellion against the Jade Emperor. Sun Wukong is finally defeated by the Buddha who imprisons him under a mountain. Guanyin sets him free five centuries later and makes him one of the three disciples of the Monk Tang. Sun Wukong protects his master against all sorts of demons on their journey to India until their mission is successfully completed. For his courage and rebellious spirit Sun Wukong has nowadays become a cultural symbol of the Chinese hero.

A mask of Sun Wukong

Sun Yaoting

Sun Yaoting (1902-1996) is famous for being the last imperial eunuch in Chinese history.

©iStockphoto.com/Ray Roper

A postage stamp honouring Sun Yat-sen

Sun Yat-sen

Known as the Father of the Republic of China, Sun Yat-sen (1866-1925) played an important role in the revolution that overthrew the Qing Dynasty, the Xinhai Revolution, thereby ending China's imperial system which had lasted for over 2000 years. Sun Yat-sen was then elected the first provisional president of the new Republic in 1912. But because of the revolutionary army's military weakness, Sun Yat-sen had to compromise with Yuan Shikai, the leader of the northern warlords, and allow Yuan to become president in exchange for his support in forcing the last emperor to abdicate. Sun Yat-sen's best known political philosophy is the Three Principles of the People, namely the principles of Nationalism, Democracy and People's Livelihood. Sun Yat-sen is probably the only modern political leader who is widely revered in both mainland China and Taiwan.

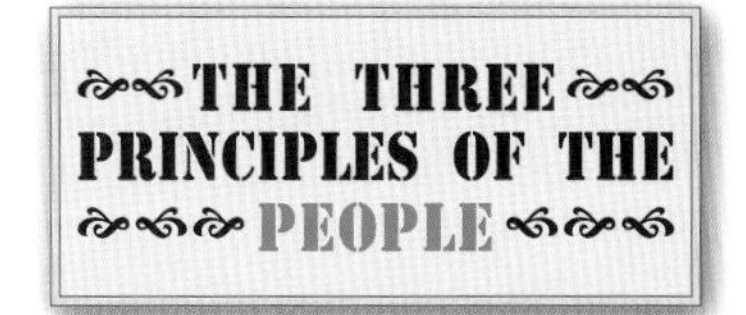

Sun Zi

Sun Zi, also known as Sun Wu, was a general serving in the Kingdom of Wu at the end of the Spring and Autumn Period (770-476BC) and is generally believed to have been the author of *The Art of War*, the earliest and most important Chinese book on military tactics. Throughout Chinese history this book had a great impact not only on warfare but on politics and culture. Today people still put his teachings to good practical use in business and everyday life, for example to gain the advantage in negotiations. Some of the quotes from his book remain popular:

> *All warfare is based on deception.*
>
> *Attack him where he is unprepared, appear where you are not expected.*
>
> *If you know the enemy and know yourself, you need not fear the result of a hundred battles.*

Sunshu Ao

The first known hydraulic engineer during the Spring and Autumn Period (770-476BC), Sunshu Ao (c.630-c.593BC), as minister of the State of Chu, organized the first large-scale construction of dams, reservoirs and irrigation systems, which played a critical role in the development of Chinese agriculture.

Suzhou Gardens

The ancient city of Suzhou, some fifty miles west of Shanghai, contains about sixty gardens. Scholar officials in the Ming and Qing Dynasties created many of the gardens. They dug ponds and built hills, and planted trees and flowering shrubs. Their gardens were like "silent poems" or "paintings in three dimensions", and walking along the winding paths was like unrolling a scroll painting.

One would pause to listen to the wind in the pine trees, to savour the scent of lotus flowers, to admire the reflection of the moon in the water, or to enjoy the garden under snow. Strangely shaped rocks were prized, many from the nearby lake, Taihu.

Buildings and landscape complemented each other. Parties were held for family and friends. In the Qing Dynasty novel *The Dream of the Red Chamber*, these days come back to life.

There are mentions of palace gardens in China as far back as 2500 years ago. And Chinese gardens were the inspiration for the exquisite gardens of Japan. Some of the Suzhou Gardens are now listed as UNESCO World Heritage Sites.

Taipei

The largest city and capital of Taiwan, Taipei had been the administrative centre of Taiwan under the reign of the Qing Dynasty from 1875 to 1895. Then it was occupied by the Japanese from 1895-1945. After 1949 it became the seat of the Chinese Nationalist government.

Taiping Rebellion → *Hong Xiuquan*

Taiwan

Taiwan is a beautiful and prosperous island off the southeast coast of mainland China. Human settlement in the island can be dated back thirty thousand years.

The first historical record of the Han Chinese coming to Taiwan is in the third century AD during the Three Kingdoms Period. In later years Taiwan experienced various changes of fortune. Large-scale immigration to Taiwan started in the Ming Dynasty. In 1642, the Dutch made Taiwan a colony. Zheng Chenggong, a military general at the end of the Ming and leader of the anti-Qing movement, defeated the Dutch in 1662. He established the Kingdom of Tunning in Taiwan as a base to oppose the Manchu invasion in an attempt to restore the Ming. In 1683 Taiwan fell to the Qing forces and remained under the rule of the Qing government till 1895 when China was defeated in the first Sino-Japanese War (1894-1895) and ceded Taiwan to Japan. Japan's rule ended in 1945. The government of the Republic of China (ROC) then claimed Taiwan as part of China's territory. In 1949, defeated by the Communist troops, the ROC government retreated to Taiwan and made Taipei its new capital.

The Communist government of the People's Republic of China, however, has never accepted the Taiwan authority as a legitimate entity and continues to claim sovereignty over the island.

Taiwan has witnessed a continuous economic boom from the 1960s to 1990s with high growth rates and rapid industrialization, and became one of the Four Asian Tigers along with South Korea, Hong Kong and Singapore. With the growing economic exchanges between Taiwan and mainland China, the sovereignty issue remains high on the political agenda of the two governments.

Taiyuan

The capital city of Shanxi Province and one of the most important industrial cities in northern China, Taiyuan was also, in bygone days, a stronghold of strategic importance against invasion by nomadic tribes coming down from the Mongolian Plateau. Taiyuan is also famous for its strong-tasting vinegar.

Taklamakan Desert → *XINJIANG*

Tang Taizong, *a.k.a* ***Li Shimin***

THE GREATEST EMPEROR OF ALL, THE ONE WHO LISTENED TO CRITICISM

Tang Taizong, the second emperor of the Tang Dynasty, ruled from 626-649AD and is thought by many to be one of the greatest emperors in China's history. He was a famous strategist and politician as well as a poet and calligrapher.

As a major-general in his father Li Yuan's army, he performed great deeds during the struggle against the Sui Dynasty and other military rivals and contributed to the founding of the Tang Dynasty. His great abilities and good reputation made his older brother, the original crown prince Li Jiancheng, feel that his future throne was threatened. Tang Taizong realized that his older brother was plotting to kill him. So, together with some followers, he seized the initiative and ambushed his brother at the Gate of Xuanwu. In this battle his two brothers, Li Jiancheng and Li Yuanji, were both killed. In 626 Taizong officially ascended the throne of the Tang Dynasty. During his 23-year reign the country experienced an unprecedented level of success and prosperity in matters civil, political, military and economic. This was the so-called "Reign of Zhenguan" in Chinese history, a period which made the Tang Dynasty one of the most thriving empires in the world at that time.

Unlike most emperors, Taizong viewed his subjects as mirrors in which he could see his own strengths and weaknesses reflected. He had a modest and rational attitude toward such advisors as Wei Zheng – who was famous for daring to criticize imperial governance, even taking issue with Taizong's personal conduct. Taizong also advocated humanist ideas and focused on reforms and policies which would improve the lives of ordinary people. He understood the key role of the common people in the empire's stability and prosperity. Later emperors and historians always quoted his famous saying to illustrate the importance of the common people – the common people are like water and the emperor is like a boat; water can carry the boat but could also sink it.

THE COMMON PEOPLE ARE LIKE WATER AND THE EMPEROR IS LIKE A BOAT; WATER CAN CARRY THE BOAT BUT COULD ALSO SINK IT

Tang Xianzu → *MUDAN TING*

Tang Xuanzong, *a.k.a.* *Li Longji*

Tang Xuanzong (685-762AD), whose personal name was Li Longji and who was also known as Tang Minghuang, was the grandson of Empress Dowager Wu Zetian. At the age of 27, Li Longji ascended the throne of the Tang Dynasty, succeeding his father, Tang Ruizong, and soon changed the title of reign to "Kaiyuan". During the period of Kaiyuan, Tang Xuanzong placed his trust in able chancellors like Yao Chong and Song Jing, and the Tang Empire reached its peak, politically, economically and culturally. This was another golden age in Chinese history.

However, towards the end of Xuanzong's reign, especially in the period of "Tianbao" from 742 to 756, he spent most of his time in the pursuit of pleasure with his favourite concubine Yang Guifei and paid less and less attention to matters of state. He also fell prey to sycophantic and deceitful men

Here are four often quoted lines from Bai Juyi's A Song of Unending Sorrow (telling the story of Yang Guifei and Tang Xuanzong)–

We wished to fly in heaven, two birds with linking wings,
And to grow together on earth, two branches of one tree.
Enduring heaven and earth some time will end,
While this unending sorrow goes on and on for ever.

like Li Linfu and Yang Guozhong (concubine Yang's cousin) – chancellors who dominated the imperial court and corruptly pursued their own personal ends. This growing corruption eventually led to the Anshi Rebellion of 755 when the regional military governor An Lushan rose up against Tang Xuanzong. With the Tang Dynasty collapsing, Xuanzong was forced to flee from An Lushan. His own army, who hated the corrupt Yang family, forced the emperor to kill the chancellor Yang Guozhong and his beloved Yang Guifei. His doomed love affair with Yang Guifei became the theme of a famous poem *Song of Unending Sorrow* by the Tang poet Bai Juyi, a poem that has been passed down from generation to generation.

Tang Zhuang

Tang Zhuang, literally the clothes of the Tang Dynasty, is in fact a modernized version of a fashionable clothing style from the Qing Dynasty (1644-1912). Influenced by the Manchu style costume magua (mandarin jacket), the typical tang zhuang is made of silk with knotted buttons fastening at the front. Tang zhuang caught on as a fashion item during the 2001 APEC summit in Shanghai, where each participant was presented with a tang zhuang jacket and posed for a group photo in it. In daily life, people like to wear the costume for the Spring Festival or for parties.

Tao Tie

Tao Tie is a mythical gargoyle-like figure, often found on ancient bronze vessels, representing greed. It is said to be the fifth son of the dragon and has such an appetite that it even eats its own head.

Taoism

Of all the major religions in China, Taoism (or Daoism) is the only one to have originated in native culture. Its origin can be traced back to the ancient philosopher Lao Zi. Taoism got its name from the Chinese

©iStockphoto.com/Jason Orender

An incense offering in the Man Mo Temple, a famous Taoist temple in Hong Kong

character tao, literally the "way", which bears many abstract interpretations. Taoism regards Tao as the origin of everything in the universe and posits that non-action is the best way to survive. It is a polytheistic religion and Taoists worship deities and immortals in heaven, as well as ghosts in the underworld. The supreme Taoist god is the Three Pure Ones (a trinity) or the Jade Emperor in popular Taoism. Taoists believe that through self-cultivation people can master the "way" of the universe and eventually achieve immortality. Through history, Taoism gradually integrated with elements of Chinese alchemy, astrology, medicine and martial arts. The most common interface between Taoism and ordinary people is probably fortune-telling and feng shui, a Chinese superstition according to which people can improve their fortunes by carefully selecting where to live and where to be buried.

tea

Although tea drinking may have started in China as far back as the 28th century BC, it did not become widespread until the Tang Dynasty when Lu Yu (733-804AD) wrote *The Classic of Tea*, the earliest monograph on tea in the world. In Chinese tea culture, great attention should be paid to the growing of tea plants, the picking and processing of tea leaves, the selection of tea sets and the actual preparation of tea. Tea has permeated into every aspect of Chinese daily life. It is common to have tea served, usually free, before dinner in almost every restaurant. People like to meet friends or have informal business talks at teahouses. Tea can also be used in cooking and herbal medicine. And, if you've wondered where the English word for tea as in the expression "a nice cup of cha" originated, well, we have the Chinese to thank for that.

Tea eggs simmer in a pot in a street market near Urumqi, in Xinjiang province

©iStockphoto.com/Linda Wang

tea egg

The tea egg (or cha ye dan) is a typical Chinese savoury snack commonly sold by street vendors or in night markets. What is it? It's a hard-boiled egg, soaked or stewed in tea and medicinal spices. It is eaten not only as a snack but is also said to be good for the liver and to act against overindulgence in alcohol.

Temple of Heaven

The Temple of Heaven in central Beijing includes perhaps the most famous of all Chinese buildings, the Qinian Dian, a round building with a roof like a blue umbrella topped by a golden point. This was completed in 1420 and rebuilt, after lightning struck it, in 1889. However, it is only part of the complex of the Temple of Heaven, which is more extensive than the imperial palace itself. In Chinese, the Temple of Heaven is called Tiantan, and it is made up of various structures set in wooded parkland.

Tiantan is surrounded by a perimeter wall that is straight on the south like the flatness of the earth and round to the north like the vault of the sky. Ancient cypress trees enclose the structures like a foil of jade.

In the Ming and the Qing Dynasties (1368-1912), the emperor came once a year to Tiantan. On the first day, he underwent ritual purification in a temple and then on the second day he proceeded to a special place, a round platform open to the sky and surrounded by a wall (famous for its echo). It was here on this round platform, the Huanqiutan, that a great central ceremony took place to maintain harmony between China and Tian or Heaven.

©iStockphoto.com/Chandra Menard

The Qinian Dian, or Hall of Prayer for Good Harvests, a perfect example of Ming architecture

In Confucian teaching, harmony in society depends upon proper relationships in the family, between parents and children, between teachers and students, and between rulers and the ruled. The Emperor maintained harmony at the highest level between the nation and the cosmos.

There is a raised walkway leading to the Qinian Dian where ceremonies for good harvests were enacted. In another building, the spirit tablets of emperors and empresses were held.

The Temple of Heaven lies to the south of the Forbidden City. To the north lies the Temple of Earth, to the west a Temple of the Moon and to the east a Temple of the Sun. These date from 1530 and are smaller than the Temple of Heaven.

©iStockphoto.com/Amy Harris

Terracotta Warriors

The Terracotta Warriors, one of the greatest archaeological finds of the 20th century, were discovered in 1974 by local farmers near the mausoleum of Qin Shi Huang (259-210BC) near Xi'an in Shaanxi Province. There are over 8000 life-size terracotta figures of warriors lined up in phalanxes wearing armour and holding weapons. Types of uniform, hairstyle – and even posture – vary in accordance with their military rank. Together with chariots and horses, the scene vividly reflects a real battlefield of that page of Chinese history. The Terracotta Warriors were buried as guards to protect Qin Shi Huang after his death. Listed by UNESCO as a World Heritage Site, the Terracotta Warriors now attract large numbers of visitors to see the so-called eighth wonder of the world.

Three August Ones and Five Emperors

A general term for a group of legendary or mythological rulers before the Xia Dynasty (2100-1600BC), the first Chinese dynasty. The name is also to refer to this mythological period of Chinese prehistory. Despite different versions of their identities, the Three August Ones are generally recognized as Suiren – the discoverer of fire, Fuxi – the brother/husband of Nüwa and the originator of trigrams (used in the ancient Chinese system of divination, I Ching) and Shennong – the father of Chinese agriculture and herbal medicine. The Five Emperors include the Yellow Emperor, Zhuanxu, Emperor Ku, Emperor Yao and Emperor Shun. All of them are said to be the ancestors of the Chinese people.

©iStockphoto.com/Valerie Crafter

Three Gorges Dam

The Three Gorges Dam on the Yangtze River has incurred criticism for the ecological damage it caused and for the large-scale relocation of people. It is the largest hydroelectric power station in the world. It helps control flooding and supplies 10% of China's electricity needs.

Three Pure Ones

The Taoist trinity and the highest gods in Taoism. The Three Pure Ones are: *Jade Pure One* or *Universal Lord of the Primordial Beginning, Supreme Pure One* or *Universal Lord of the Numinous Treasure* and *Grand Pure One* or *Universal Lord of the Way and its Virtue*, who is actually Lao Zi, the founder of Taoism. In Chapter 42 of *The Classic of the Way and Virtue (Daodejing)*, Lao Zi wrote "Tao begets one; one begets two; two begets three; three begets all things". It is from this statement that Taoism developed the Three Pure Ones.

Three Represents

The political theory of Jiang Zemin. Advanced communism represents 1/ an advanced production-based society; 2/ an advanced culture; 3/ the interests of the great majority of the Chinese people.

Three Sovereign Ones → *Three August Ones*

Tian Han

Tian Han (1898-1968) devoted his life to the development of modern drama in China. He was highly active in the theatre and was also involved in political activites. He was also a prolific poet and lyricist, his most famous work being the lyrics of *March of the Volunteers* which was chosen as the Chinese national anthem in 1952. Tian Han died of persecution during the Cultural Revolution.

The first verse of the Chinese national anthem:

Arise, you who refuse to be slaves;
With our very flesh and blood
Let us build our new Great Wall!
The peoples of China are at their most critical time,
Everybody must roar defiance.
Arise! Arise! Arise!
Millions of hearts with one mind,
Brave the enemy's gunfire,
March on!
Brave the enemy's gunfire,
March on! March on! March on, on!

Tiananmen Square

Tiananmen Square in the centre of Beijing is the largest open, urban public square in the world with an area of around 100 acres (a football pitch is about 1.5 acres). It has witnessed many historic movements in the history of modern China. Mao Zedong declared the foundation of the People's Republic of China from the Tiananmen Tower on 1st October 1949. It has become the most recognizable symbol of new China since 1949. The image of Tiananmen Tower is part of the Chinese national symbol.

Tiananmen Square contains a series of tourist sites: the Monument to the Heroes of the People in the middle, the Tiananmen Tower to the north, the Great Hall of the People to the west, the Chinese History Museum to the east and the Mao Zedong Memorial Hall to the south. One interesting cultural phenomenon is that many Chinese tourists come to Tiananmen Square to watch the flag raising ceremony, which takes place each day in the early morning, the most meaningful ceremony, to the Chinese, being the annual National Day flag raising ceremony.

The events of 1989, with the enduring image of student and tank, televised throughout the world, remain a forbidden topic in China. It is seen as a political riot and as a subject only for official and not media comment.

Tianjin

Tianjin is one of the four municipalities directly under the administration of the central government – along with Beijing, Shanghai and Chongqing. Situated on the west of the Bohai Gulf and about 80 miles east of Beijing, Tianjin is regarded as the portal to China's political heartland. It is the third largest city in China and an industrial, trade and educational centre of the north. Tianjin is the home of Beijing opera and some traditional performing arts like xiangsheng (crosstalk) and shuochang (story-singing). It is also famous for its traditional snacks like baozi (filled steamed buns) and mahua (fried twisted dough sticks).

Tibet

The Tibetans are an ethnic group who live mainly in the Xizang Tibetan Autonomous Region (established in 1965) as well as in Qinghai, Yunnan and Sichuan Provinces. In the Tang Dynasty (618-907AD), the Tibetans came into close contact with Han Chinese culture after the marriage in 641AD of the Chinese Princess Wencheng to Songtsan Gampo, the king of Tibet. From the Yuan Dynasty (1206-1368) on, Tibet has been under the administration (albeit sometimes nominal) of the reigning dynasties of China. As a unique cultural community, the Tibetan people have their own language, religious belief, calendar, medicine, art and traditional customs. Some Tibetan people hold that the Chinese government is failing to preserve Tibetan culture and to grant real religious autonomy. Such discontent is intensified by the sensitive predicament presented by the

Tibetan prayer flags with Yamdrok Tso Lake and mountains in the background

issue of the Dalai Lama who fled to India and formed an exile government after the abortive 1959 insurrection supported by the CIA. The Chinese government has never stopped negotiating with the Dalai Lama who, in recent years, publicly reiterated his readiness to accept China's sovereignty over Tibet if his people could enjoy real autonomy in terms of religion and cultural life.

title of reign → *EMPERORS' NAMES*

toffee fruit

Toffee fruit is a famous crispy, sweet and sour snack native to northern China and dating back more than 1000 years. It is normally made of haws coated with rock sugar syrup, strung on a long bamboo stick. A typical Chinese scene is when, with the advancing cold in autumn and winter, pedlars appear on the streets selling toffee fruits. According to traditional Chinese medicine, haws contain a substance that aids digestion. So toffee fruits gradually became a popular folk snack for people of all ages. Nowadays people use a wide variety of fruits like grapes, yams, oranges and strawberries to make toffee fruits.

tofu → *DOUFU*

Tomb Sweeping Festival → *QING MING FESTIVAL*

Tony Leung Chiu-wai → *LIANG CHAOWEI*

Town God

The patron god of a city in Chinese mythology is the Cheng Huang or Town God. This god of local affairs was believed to be able to protect the city from disasters. Since the Tang Dynasty (618-907AD) it has been standard practice to build a Town God temple in every town to guard against evil. You can still find well-preserved Town God temples in cities all over China.

traditional Chinese medicine

This is a medical system that originated thousands of years ago in China. Its treatments include acupuncture, herbal medicine, massage and diet therapy. In traditional Chinese medicine the understanding and treatment of the human body is based on such theories as Yin-Yang and Wu Xing. The human body is considered as a small universe where tissue and organs are connected through a network of channels and blood vessels. The diagnosis starts with an analysis of the entire system and then focuses on the pathological changes. There are four types of diagnostic methods: observe (wang), hear and smell (wen), ask about background (wen) and pulse-reading (qie). (The two wens are in fact different characters when written in Chinese). Most Chinese people don't see traditional Chinese medicine and Western medicine as being contradictory to each other or mutually exclusive. They may see a Western doctor in cases of emergency, for example for acute appendicitis. But they may put their trust in Chinese herbs for treating chronic diseases or keeping healthy. In hospitals dominated by Western medicine, elements of Chinese medicine are also used.

traffic

Traffic during rush hour in big cities is like that anywhere else in the Western world. There is traffic congestion everywhere. A typical additional problem in China is the great number of bicycles, some of which don't follow the rules and make the traffic even worse. Driving in cities is very demanding; you have to pay extra attention to jaywalkers who suddenly appear from nowhere and taxis which stop almost whenever and wherever they want. Sometimes crossing a street without pedestrian crossings can be a near-death experience with a fast flow of cars which don't like to slow down.

©iStockphoto.com/Loic Bernard

But nowadays it is common to see traffic controllers at intersections during rush hour stopping bicycles and pedestrians from crossing against the light.

tri-coloured Tang

A type of glazed pottery from the Tang Dynasty with the three dominant colours of yellow, green and brown, it is famous for its magnificent bright colours and lifelike images.They are now very collectable antiques. Originally Tang Dynasty burial objects, unearthed tri-coloured Tang pieces portray almost every aspect of daily life of the times, with images of people, animals, utensils, furniture and houses. Tri-coloured Tang camels carrying silk or musicians on their backs show typical scenes from caravans moving along the Silk Road in ancient times.

tricycles

Especially in smaller towns, the tricycle is still a common way of getting about.

Tsai Chin, *a.k.a.* ***Cai Qin***

A Taiwanese pop singer known for her mellow and velvety vocals. Tsai Chin (born 1957), a legend of Chinese pop, has won numerous awards. She was at her peak from the late 1970s to the mid 1990s. 2002 saw a revival of her popularity when her song *The Forgotten Times* was featured in the hit film series *Internal Affairs*. Many of her songs, such as *Just Like Your Tenderness*, *Your Eyes* and *Endless Love*, are considered classics.

Tsien Hsue-shen

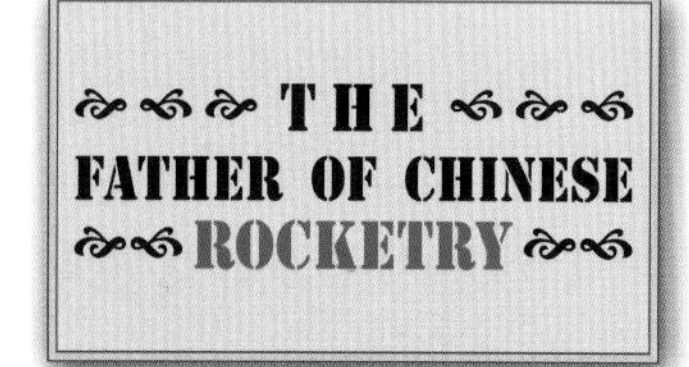

A scientist who was to become known as the Father of Chinese Rocketry, Tsien Hsue-shen (1911-), left the California Institute of Technology with a PhD in 1939 and gradually established himself as a leading figure in US space and missile programmes. Feeling the heat of McCarthyism in the 1950s, he made up his mind to return to China. However, for fear that he could bring highly confidential technology back to China, the US government practically put him under house arrest for a period of 5 years until 1955, when he was finally released. On his arrival in China, he took charge of missile and rocketry programmes and made distinguished contributions to military and technological development.

Tsui Hark, *a.k.a.* ***Xu Ke***

The influential Hong Kong film director and producer, Tsui Hark, was born Tsui Man-kong in 1950 in Vietnam. He studied film in the US then started his television career in Hong Kong in 1977. His début feature film *The Butterfly Murders* (1979) made his name as a director with a unique style. Nicknamed "the Steven Spielberg of Asia", Tsui has made over 50 films, producing blockbusters in all sorts of genres. In 1984 he founded his own production house, Film Workshop, which produced many classics of Hong Kong cinema, such as *A Better Tomorrow* (1986), *A Chinese Ghost Story* (1987) and *The Swordsman* (1990). Tsui practically created most of the popular genres of the 80s and 90s Hong Kong film industry:

heroic bloodshed, ghost romance and martial arts fantasy, to name just a few. Many big stars, like John Woo, Chow Yun-Fat, and Jet Li, all owe their current careers to Tsui. His *Zu Warriors from the Magic Mountain* (1983) launched the modern Hong Kong special effects industry.

Tu Di Gong

Tu Di Gong, or the "local earth god", is, in popular Chinese belief, a god who looks after local matters. It is said that Tu Di Gong, while on earth, was a local tax officer during the Zhou Dynasty (1045-256BC). He treated people fairly and kindly. Three days after his death, his body still looked like a living person and so people began to worship him as a god. Almost every village in China had a temple or shrine for Tu Di Gong, but most were destroyed during the Cultural Revolution. He is also worshipped as a god of fortune and wealth. Farmers still offer sacrifices to him so as to be protected against drought or famine.

Tujia

An ethnic group living in the region connecting Hunan, Hubei, Guizhou Provinces and Chongqing Municipality, the Tujia people are known for their singing and dancing. Their famous Baishou Dance, literally hand-waving dance, is generally associated with occasions such as ancestor worship or praying for a good harvest. They have their own indigenous spoken language, but most of them speak a dialect of Chinese.

Twelve Girls Band

A popular band with twelve female members, the Twelve Girls Band play modern and traditional songs on traditional Chinese instruments, such as the guzheng, pipa, erhu and yangqin. The twelve girls are talented musicians coming from top music schools or Chinese orchestras.

Uygur

The Uygur are a group of Turkic people in Central Asia most of whom live in China's Xinjiang Uygur Autonomous Region. They have their own language and most of them worship Islam. In the first half of the 20th century there were attempts to create a Turkic regime in Central Asia. With the resurgence of Islamic Fundamentalism in Afghanistan in the 1990s some overseas Turkic organizations attempted to instigate separatist activities in China.

Wade-Giles

Wade-Giles refers to a system of romanized Chinese ideograms developed by Sir Thomas Francis Wade (1818-95), the first Professor of Chinese at Cambridge University, and his successor Herbert Allen Giles (1845-1935). In the Wade-Giles system the tones of Chinese characters are indicated by superscript numbers. Nowadays it is generally superseded by pinyin. Most Chinese are unfamiliar with Wade-Giles and there are a number of Chinese names standardly written in the old Wade-Giles system in the West which the Chinese would not recognize. One possible exception is

> Mao Tse-Tung *(Wade-Giles)*
>
> Mao Zedong *(pinyin)*

Wang Anshi

Wang Anshi (1021-1086AD), a famous statesman, thinker and writer during the Northern Song Dynasty (960-1127AD), is best known in Chinese history as an economic reformer. The aim of his reforms was to increase China's wealth and build up a strong army which would be capable of withstanding attacks from the minority races to the north. After being appointed Chancellor, Wang Anshi set about reforming state finance and trade, defence and education. But his policies were boycotted by land-owning conservative officials who had a monopoly over trade and who saw their status coming under threat. On the other hand there were speculators who backed him, seizing the opportunity to accumulate private wealth in the name of national reform. The conservative group eventually found excuses to attack Wang Anshi and expelled him from court.

As well as being an economist, he is noted as a great poet and prose writer who was classed as one of the Eight Giants of Tang and Song Prose.

Wang Chongyang

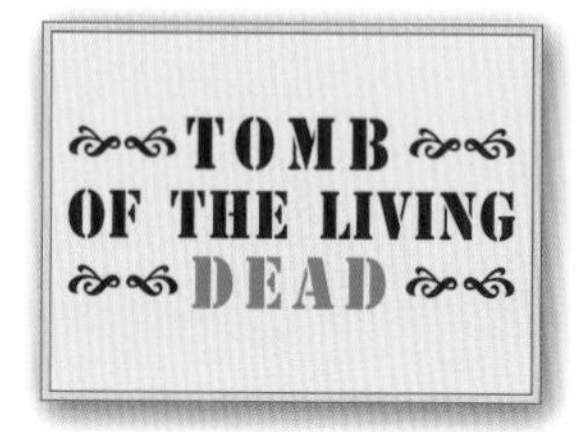

Wang Chongyang (1113-1170AD), a Taoist sage in the late Song Dynasty, was the founder of the *Quanzhen (Complete Perfection)* School of Taoism. Born into a wealthy family, Wang Chongyang had a good education in both literature and martial arts. At the age of 48, he went to Zhongnan Mountain and dug himself a grave called "Tomb of the Living Dead". There, in that grave, he began his hermit life as a Taoist. Three years later he left his grave and began to lecture on his Quanzhen theories. Wang Chongyang thinks that Confucianism, Buddhism and Taoism have a common source and they should be merged together. He recruited seven disciples who are known as the Seven Masters of Quanzhen. The stories of Wang Chongyang and his disciples are well-known among Chinese people thanks to a popular martial arts novel *Legend of the Condor Heroes* written by Jin Yong.

Wang Dayuan

A famous voyager in the Yuan Dynasty (1271-1368), Wang Dayuan (1311-?) made two sea voyages setting out from Quanzhou, a port in the southeastern province of Fujian. He travelled to many places in Southeast Asia and visited India and Sri Lanka. He also sailed as far as North Africa and East Africa. After he returned from his second voyage in 1339, he began to write a book called *The Brief History of Island Countries* (Daoyi Zhilue) to describe his travels. The book has been translated into many languages and is an important work in the history of marine navigation.

Wang Fei, *a.k.a. Faye Wong*

A Beijing-born superstar in Cantopop, she had her heyday in the middle of the 1990s when she released many successful albums, some of which are still regarded as classics. Dubbed Tian Hou (Heavenly Queen) by the media, Wang Fei is also a talented actress. Her excellent performance in *Chungking Express*, one of Wong Kar-wai's stylized films, won her the Best Actress award at the 1994 Stockholm International Film Festival. Targeted by paparazzi, Wang Fei's private life always makes the headlines.

Pop star Faye Wong performing in August 1999

Wang Guowei

One of the few people who could read oracle bone inscriptions, Wang Guowei (1877-1927) was a prominent Chinese scholar who made many contributions to the study of history, philology and literature. He was the first in modern China to apply Western philosophical, aesthetic and literary theories to the analysis and criticism of classical Chinese literature. He also pioneered the approach of combining new archaeological findings (oracle bone inscriptions) with historical texts to study ancient Chinese history. As a Tsinghua University professor, Wang Guowei enjoyed a similar reputation to Liang Qichao. But his imperial affinities were his downfall. Being a stubborn adherent of the Qing Dynasty, he drowned himself in the Kunming Lake in the Summer Palace in 1927 to demonstate his loyalty to the deposed emperor.

ACADEMIC COMMITS SUICIDE BY DROWNING TO SHOW LOVE FOR EMPEROR

Wang Jinxi

Known as the Iron Man, Wang Jinxi (1923-1970) was a worker hero of the Communist revolution. He had endured a hard childhood in the days before Mao rose to power but then found his true vocation in the challenging times when the new China was being forged. In 1960 Wang and his team battled against great hardship and sub-zero temperatures to open up the Daqing oilwell, an achievement which brought Wang legendary status.

Wang Junxia

A former Olympic gold medallist in long-distance events, Wang was a protegée of coach Ma Junren. Her career climaxed in 1993 when the Chinese team of women long-distance runners stunned the world when they won world titles from the 1500m to 10,000m in Stuttgart. Wang took the 10,000m and later that year broke the world records for the 10,000m and 3000m. She also went on to win the World Cup Marathon Championship. The team broke with Ma Junren in 1995 and Wang's form started to fall away. In the 1996 Olympics she won a gold in the women's 5000m and a silver in the 10,000m – and then retired.

Wang Mang

Appointed as a high official by his dowager empress aunt, Wang Mang (45BC-23AD) dominated the last years of the Western Han Dynasty (206BC-9AD), controlling the country through the manipulation of young puppet emperors.

In 9AD he proclaimed himself Emperor of the Xin Dynasty (9-23AD) and attempted to introduce a radical set of reforms including the banishment of slavery and the redistribution of land. Natural disasters, however, brought his short-lived dynasty to an early end and he was eventually murdered by a soldier in a popular uprising.

Wang Shifu → *Xi Xiang Ji*

Wang Xiaobo

The Chinese writer, Wang Xiaobo (1952-1997), achieved posthumous fame when his *Age Trilogy – Golden Age*, *Silver Age* and *Bronze Age* – was published. He has a large following among university students. With their witty and satirical tone, his writings mock the absurdities that prevailed in China under totalitarian rule. His wife, Li Yinhe, a sexologist, referred to him as a romantic knight and bard on account of his unending pursuit of spiritual freedom in his works.

Wang Xiaoshuai

A Chinese filmmaker with a unique style, Wang Xiaoshuai (born 1966) has achieved an international reputation for many of his award-winning films.

His first film *The Days* was selected by the BBC in 1995 as the one and only Chinese film in a list of the top 100 best films. However, Wang Xiaoshuai's real international success started with *Beijing Bicycle*, the Silver Bear winner of the 2001 Berlin International Film Festival. It is about a seventeen-year-old migrant worker searching for his missing bicycle in Beijing. Wang Xiaoshuai's other famous works include *Frozen*, *So Close to Paradise*, *Drifters* and *Shanghai Dreams*.

Wang Xizhi

Wang Xizhi (303-361AD) was a great calligrapher who lived during the Eastern Jin Dynasty (317-420AD). He excelled in every style of calligraphy, particularly in semi-cursive script. Among his works, the most famous is the *Preface to the Poems Composed at the Orchid Pavilion* (Lantingji Xu). Although the original copy is lost, the rubbings and imitations are still regarded as classics. Legend has it that Wang Xizhi learned how to control his wrist when writing from observing how geese move their necks.

Wang Yangming → *NEO-CONFUCIANISM*

Wang Yirong → *ORACLE BONE INSCRIPTIONS*

Wang Yuanlu → *ABBOT WANG*

Wang Zhizhi

Wang Zhizhi (1977-) is a professional basketball player. He has played for various teams in the NBA. Due to a misunderstanding with American basketball officials – as Wang claimed – he was unable to return to China to train with the Chinese national team when his contract in the US ended. Because of this he was thrown out of the Chinese national team in 2002. He was left stranded in the US until 2006 when he publicly apologized for his past mistakes and finally rejoined the national team.

Water Margin

The Water Margin (also known as *All Men Are Brothers* or *Outlaws of the Marsh*) is one of the Four Great Classical Novels. Written by Shi Nai'an (or Luo Guanzhong, according to some scholars) in the 14th century. The novel describes the revolt of a rabble of 108 outlaws (105 men and 3 women) headed by Chao Gai and later Song Jiang who opposed the corrupt regime of the Northern Song Dynasty (960-1127AD). Brimming with fearless heroes, foxy and scheming women and corrupt officials, the story holds the reader spellbound with its intriguing characters and twists of plot. But the rebellious heroism of the 108 ended in tragedy. They accepted an amnesty offered by the imperial court and were then sent to crush another large-scale peasant uprising. Only a few of them survived. The novel gives a fascinating look into 14th century Chinese vernacular literature. It has been adapted into a host of movies and TV series. Stories like *How Wu Song killed a tiger with his bare hands* or *How Lin Chong was framed by Gao Qiu and forced to join the rabble* or *How Chao Gai worked out a scheme to steal the birthday presents for the imperial tutor Cai Jing* are well known to all Chinese people.

Water Splashing Festival → *Dai*

Wei Zhongxian

The most notorious eunuch in the Ming Dynasty (1368-1644), Wei Zhongxian (1568-1627) was a gangster who castrated himself in order to be able to get a position as a eunuch in the imperial palace and so escape his gambling debts. An accomplished flatterer, he gradually won the trust of Emperor Tianqi and so took control of the court. Wei Zhongxian framed and prosecuted many upright officials who were against him and tortured them to death. He also proclaimed himself "Nine-Thousand Years", second only to the emperor who was called "Ten-Thousand Years". After Emperor Tianqi's death, Wei Zhongxian and his gang soon fell from power.

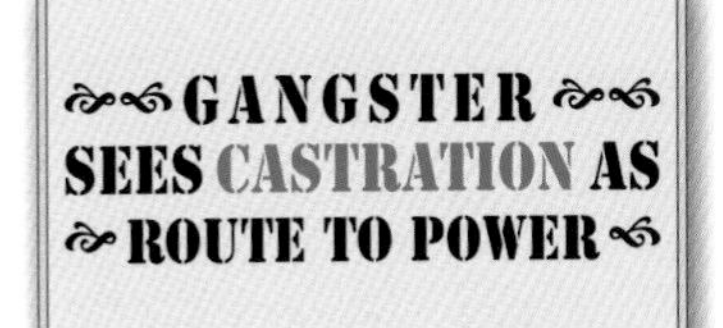

©STRINGER/Getty Images

Premier Wen Jibao meets Tanzanian President Jakaya Kikwete in Dar es Salaam, June 2006

Wen Jiabao

The Premier of the People's Republic of China since 2003, Wen Jiabao (1942-) graduated from the Beijing Institute of Geology and began his career in the Geology Bureau of Gansu Province. In 1986 he was relocated to Beijing and appointed Director of the General Office of the Chinese Communist Party (CCP) Central Committee, a significant move onto the political stage. He was a Vice Premier for about four years, then succeeded Zhu Rongji as Premier in 2003 and was re-elected to this position in 2008. Wen is an experienced technocrat and is known for his candid and modest character. He shows great competence and resolution in his leadership, characteristics which have earned him the respect of both the Chinese people and his colleagues. His popularity was greatly boosted during the 2008 Sichuan earthquake. Wen visited the stricken area only a few hours after the disaster. He was highly praised in the media as "the People's Premier" for his efficiency in directing the rescue work and for his genuine concerns for the victims.

Wen Yiduo

Wen Yiduo (1899-1946) was a famous poet and scholar in modern China, whose theory of poetry had a lot in common with that of Xu Zhimo, giving priority to the formal properties of poetry. His two important collections of poetry are *Red Candle* (1923) and *Dead Water* (1928). During the Sino-Japanese War, Wen Yiduo moved to Kunming in Yunnan Province and became a political activist. While teaching at the National Southwestern Associated University, he denounced the corrupt and dictatorial regime of Chiang Kai-shek, thus incurring fear and hatred from his opponents. In 1946 he was assassinated by secret agents. Chinese school textbooks quote from a speech made by Wen Yiduo to commemorate Li Gongpu, another assassinated democrat:

> *You have killed Li Gongpu, but hundreds and thousands of Li Gongpus will rise up. You are going to lose the support of millions of people....*
>
> *We are committed to this belief: the power of the people will prevail; truth will prevail and truth will exist in eternity.*

Wenchang

Wenchang, the God of Literature, was a patron deity of the Imperial Civil Examination in imperial China. Nowadays there are still many Wenchang Temples or Towers in cities throughout China, most of them listed as Cultural Heritage Sites.

Westerners

How do the Chinese view Westerners?

During the late Qing Dynasty (1644-1912) Westerners were called Foreign Ghosts (Yang Guizi). Here yang literally means "ocean" as the foreigners travelled to China by sea. They were called guizi, literally "ghosts" because i) with their blue eyes and blond hair they looked very different from the Chinese and ii) they were not willing to kowtow when interviewed by the Chinese emperor, and so the Chinese thought that their knees were unable to bend and that they could only jump when they moved, a characteristic of ghosts according to folk legend. The nickname had negative connotations: Westerners were regarded as invaders who only brought war and destruction to China and left behind a lasting sense of humiliation.

After the establishment of the People's Republic of China, and especially during the Cold War and for purposes of political propaganda, the Western world was described as corrupt and riddled with crime, all in sharp contrast to the perfect system of socialism that operated in China. People out there were living in misery and were waiting for the Communists to rescue them.

Chinese views on Westerners, however, changed drastically from hatred and rejection to admiration or even worship after China adopted policies of reform and openness in the latter years of the 20th century. Suddenly exposed to the unknown Western world and overwhelmed by all the new information, people tended to believe that the West excelled in every sphere of society. They held misconceptions about Westerners such as, for example, that Westerners have absolute freedom in matters concerning the press and sex. There was a popular saying in the 1980s that the moon is brighter in foreign countries than in China. With the rapid development of the Chinese economy and its strengthened connections with the West in

©Keystone/Getty Images

Chairman Mao Zedong shakes hands with American president Richard Nixon during the president's visit to China, 1972

business, culture and education, people gradually began to see Westerners in a more objective and realistic way. Maybe the moon is not brighter in the West.

The Chinese have had some amusing slang words for foreigners (Westerners) over the years:

hong maogui red-haired devil (old-fashioned now)

da bizi big nose (now a bit old-fashioned)

lao wai (literally: old foreign)

For many Chinese travelling or working abroad it is the locals and not the Chinese who are the "foreigners" – not an unknown attitude in the West.

White Horse Temple

In Henan Province, this is the oldest Buddhist temple in China, begun in 68AD under the orders of the Emperor Han Mingdi. It is called the White Horse Temple in commemoration of the white horse that carried Buddhist sutras to China from India.

whitening cream

While Westerners go in for fake tans whitening creams are very popular with Chinese women. A whiter complexion can make imperfect features less noticeable and make a woman look more sophisticated.

Wong Fei Hung

A Cantonese martial arts master and a legendary hero. Wong Fei Hung (1847-1924) started learning martial arts at the age of five and opened martial arts schools to recruit new students when he was sixteen. Also a famous physician, he opened a clinic called *Po Chi Lam* to perform acupuncture and offer other traditional Chinese forms of treatment. Stories abound about how he used kung fu to help the weak and fight off thugs. He became a legendary hero. The stories of Wong and his disciples have been adapted into more than 100 martial arts films.

Wong Kar-wai, *a.k.a.* *Wong Jiawei*

A maverick film director and producer based in Hong Kong, his films bear the trademark of his unique visual style and aesthetic and are preoccupied with themes of love, loneliness and alienation in the vibrant but brash metropolis. *Chungking Express* (1994) is perhaps the best among his early movies, which later became a cult hit. His first international recognition came in 1997 when *Happy Together* won Best Director Award for Wong at the Cannes Film Festival. His most acclaimed film in the West is probably *In the Mood for Love* (2000) which was also awarded Cannes accolades. Wong Kar-wai (born 1956), now a regular at international film festivals, is known for not using detailed scripts in film-making and for never taking off his sunglasses in public. He often casts Tony Leung Chiu-wai and Maggie Cheung in his films.

wonton

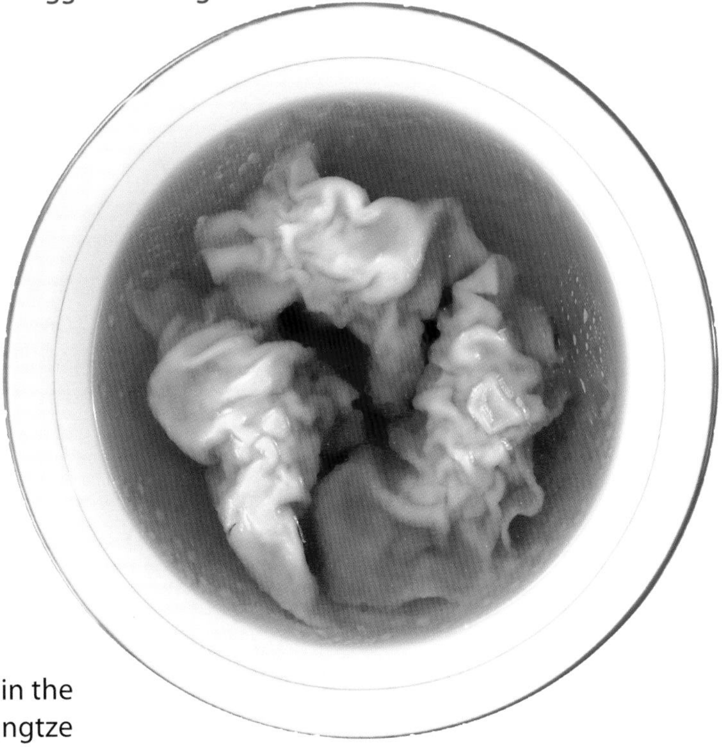

Wonton, a traditional part of Chinese cuisine, is the Cantonese pronunciation of hun tun in Mandarin. They look rather similar to jiaozi (dumplings) but have thinner wrappers and less meat inside. Wonton are usually eaten with soup, jiaozi without soup. Wonton are popular in the south, northerners prefer jiaozi.

Wu

Wu is a dialect widespread in the areas to the south of the Yangtze River, particularly in southern Jiangsu and Zhejiang Provinces and in the city of Shanghai. Wu, the second most widely spoken dialect in China (the first being Mandarin), has many variants, the Suzhou dialect being traditionally considered the most beautiful and representative on account of Suzhou's historical importance and large population. From the 20th century onwards, however, the Shanghai dialect has come more to the fore because of Shanghai's strength in matters economic. After the founding of the People's Republic of China and the subsequent Mandarin promotion campaign, Wu gradually faded out of public use.

Wu Jingzi → *RULIN WAISHI*

©iStockphoto.com/zilli

Wu Qingyuan

A great master of the board game Go, known to the world by his Japanese name Go Seigen, Wu Qingyuan (born 1914) was a veritable Go prodigy, unbeatable in China when he was only 13. He was sponsored to study Go in Japan in 1928 and started on a professional career. At the age of 19, he developed the shinfuseki, a new opening pattern that broke with tradition and turned a new page in the history of Go. Throughout his career he defeated all the leading Go players of the day. He went into retirement in the early 1960s after being injured in a motorcycle accident but continued to make contributions to the Go game through teaching and writing.

Wu Xing

Wu Xing is the name of the five fundamental elements of the universe in traditional Chinese philosophy, namely: metal, wood, water, fire and earth. The theory was used to describe the interaction and interrelationships of everything in the world. It was employed in many fields of early Chinese scholarship such as astrology, traditional Chinese medicine, military strategy and feng shui. The concept of Wu Xing predicates that the five elements are closely related to each other and their relationship can be explained by the Cycle of Birth (sheng) and Cycle of Destruction (ke):

Water produces Wood, but destroys Fire;
Fire produces Earth, but destroys Metal;
Metal produces Water, but destroys Wood;
Wood produces Fire, but destroys Earth;
Earth produces Metal, but destroys Water.

Wu Yusen → *John Woo*

Wu Zetian → *Empress Dowager Wu*

Xi Xiang Ji

Also known as *Romance of the West Chamber*, *Xi Xiang Ji* is one of the most famous Chinese plays written by the playwright Wang Shifu (1260-1336) in the Yuan Dynasty (1271-1368AD). *Xi Xiang Ji* tells the love story of Zhang Sheng , a young scholar, and Cui Yingying, the daughter of the former prime minister at the Tang court. Zhang Sheng falls in love with Yingying when they first meet in an old monastery where Yingying has temporary lodgings. Soon the monastery is besieged by a local bandit who is besotted with Yingying's beauty and wants her for himself. Yingying's mother said that whoever saves them can marry her daughter. Zhang Sheng gets his friend, a general stationed nearby, to drive away the bandits and save Yingying from humiliation. With the bandit out of the way, the old mother, however, goes back on her word because she thinks that Zhang Sheng is too poor for daughter. The two lovers, with the help of Yingying's maid, Hong Niang, find ways to consummate their love secretly. After discovering this, Yingying's mother has to accept that they get married. But she still wants Zhang Sheng to prove his worth by sitting the Imperial Civil Examination. When the results come out, Zhang Sheng ranks first among all the examinees. Thus the story ends happily with the two finally getting married. *Xi Xiang Ji* had long been listed as a forbidden book because it contains premarital sex, which was traditionally considered immoral and indecent.

Xiamen

A very beautiful city in Fujian in southeastern China. Gulang Island in Xiamen is famous for being free of any form of motorized vehicle. Gulang Island also has the unusual claim to fame of having a very high ratio of piano possession per household.

©iStockphoto.com/Ricardo De Mattos

Rush hour in Xi'an; Bell Tower to the right

Xi'an

Xi'an is the capital city of Shaanxi Province. It is the cultural, industrial and educational centre of the Chinese mid-west. Originally called Chang'an, it was the capital of some important Chinese dynasties, the most powerful of which was the Tang Dynasty (618-907AD). It remains a thriving modern city, famous for its software and aerospace industries, its rock music and local culinary specialities (lamb stew with steamed buns, Shaanxi-style pork sandwich, steamed juicy dumpling, glutinous rice cake with jujube). With its rich cultural heritage, Xi'an is one of the most popular tourist destinations in China. The Terracotta Warriors, acclaimed as the Eighth Wonder of the World, top the list of tourist attractions.

Xi'an Incident → *ZHANG XUELIANG*

Xian Xinghai

An influential composer, Xian Xinghai (1905-1945) wrote patriotic songs and music to support the anti-Japanese campaigns during the Sino-Japanese War (1937-1945). In 1938 he went to Yan'an, the political and military base of the Chinese Communist Party and joined the CCP the following year. During his stay in Yan'an he composed his most famous work *Yellow River Cantata*, which was adapted in 1969 into the widely-performed *Yellow River Piano Concerto* for piano and orchestra. He died in Moscow in 1945 at the age of 40.

Xiao Daocheng → *Nan Qi Gaodi and Liusong Houfei Di*

xiao long bao

Xiao long bao, a variant of baozi, is a very popular snack in cities around the Yangtze Delta (Shanghai, Wuxi, Hangzhou). Baozi generally refers to filled steamed buns. Xiao long bao is a miniature baozi with an almost translucent wrapper with a juicy meatball inside. It is traditionally steamed in basket-like containers made of bamboo – hence the name which literally means "bun in little basket". They taste best straight from the bamboo steamer, steaming hot, fragrant and delicious.

Xiaotian → *Erlang Shen*

Xie Jun

A famous chess player who held the title of Women's World Chess Champion twice from 1991 to 1996 and from 1999 to 2001. She is an active popularizer of chess in China.

Xingshi Yinyuan Zhuan

Also known as *The Story of a Marital Fate to Awaken the World*, this is a classical Chinese novel written in the Qing Dynasty by an anonymous author with the pseudonym of Xizhou Sheng. With its minutely detailed and vivid descriptions of social life, it recounts a man's marriage in this life and in the afterlife with a view to illustrating the Buddhist doctrine of karma. The book is highly praised by Hu Shi for its value in studying the evolution of vernacular Chinese and social life under the Qing Dynasty.

Xinhai Revolution

The Xinhai Revolution started with an armed uprising led by several anti-Manchu revolutionary organizations in Wuchang, Hubei Province in October 1911 and culminated in the abdication of Emperor Xuantong of the Qing dynasty (Puyi). It ended the Manchu's imperial rule in China and led to the establishment of the Republic of China in 1912. Sun Yat-sen was elected the first president of the Republican government.

Xinhua

Xinhua is the Chinese equivalent of the news agency Reuters.

Xinjiang

Xinjiang Uygur Autonomous Region, in the far northwest of China, is the largest of China's provinces, almost three times the size of France. Xinjiang, which means New Frontier, was established in 1884. It is a region of extremes: in the far north, where the river Irtysh flows towards the Arctic, winter temperatures can fall to minus fifty degrees centigrade; in the east, where the town of Turfan lies

Desert ruins in Xinjiang Province, on the Silk Road near Jiayuguan

in a depression one hundred and fifty metres below sea-level, summer temperatures can rise to over forty-five degrees.

Southern Xinjiang comprises the Tarim Basin, set between the Tianshan Mountains to the north, the Pamirs to the west and the Tibetan Plateau to the south. The rivers in the Tarim Basin disappear in the sands. Around the edge of the basin are oasis towns. And, in the centre, the forbidding Taklamakan Desert. Demons are said to howl here and towns have disappeared beneath the sands. Taklamakan (in the Uygur language) means "***You can go in, but you cannot come out***".

YOU CAN GO IN BUT YOU CANNOT COME OUT

The old Silk Road passed through Xinjiang, linking China and the Mediterranean. Buddhists from north India, and Muslims and Nestorian Christians from Persia travelled through the Xinjiang towns. Nowadays there is a railway linking Kashgar (or Kashi) in the far west to the rest of China.

Traditionally, sheep and horses were reared in the Tianshan Mountains. The town of Khotan (or Hetian) on the southwest rim of the Tarim Basin was famous for its jade and silk, Hami in the east for its melons, Turfan for sweet grapes.

Today, as China searches for oil to drive its economy, there are oil-wells in northern Xinjiang Province. Urumqi, the capital, thrives on trade with Russia and with Central Asia.

Xishi

Known as one of the Four Beauties of ancient China, Xishi (506BC-?) lived in the state of Yue during the Spring and Autumn Period (770-476BC). It is said that Xishi was so beautiful that even fish in the pond were ashamed of themselves when she passed by and sank to the bottom of the water. In her time, the state of Yue was constantly at war with the state of Wu. King Goujian of the Yue was defeated in a battle, captured and humiliated by King Fuchai of the Wu. Determined to exact vengeance, King Goujian, following his minister Fan Li's plot, offered beautiful women as tributes to King Fuchai to bewitch him. Xishi, as one of the chosen beauties, successfully fulfilled her task. In 473BC the state of Yue finally conquered the state of Wu and King Fuchai committed suicide. According to legend, Xishi, after the fall of Wu, lived a reclusive life with her secret lover Fan Li.

Xizhou Sheng → *Xingshi Yinyuan Zhuan*

Xu Beihong

A famous painter and teacher of art, Xu Beihong (1895-1953) learned traditional Chinese painting from his father when a child. He taught at Beijing University before travelling to Paris and other places in Western Europe to study oil painting and drawing. After his return to China in 1926, he gradually established his status as a leading Chinese painter. Xu integrated Western techniques of perspective and composition with traditional Chinese ink-wash. Best known for his vivid illustration of horses, he was an influential painter who pointed the way for modern Chinese art.

Xu Ke → *Tsui Hark*

Xu Xiake

A famous traveller and geographer in the Ming Dynasty (1368-1644), Xu Xiake (1586-1641) is best known for his *Travel Diaries of Xu Xiake*, which are valued both from a literary and a scientific standpoint. Travelling mostly on foot, Xu Xiake travelled the length and breadth of China. He was robbed three times and often went without food. However, his courage and perseverance helped him conquer the difficulties that he encountered and he doggedly completed his enormous book, recording his travels and observations of local geographical conditions in minute detail. These days there is a fashion for young people to follow in Xu Xiake's footsteps to see the beauties of China.

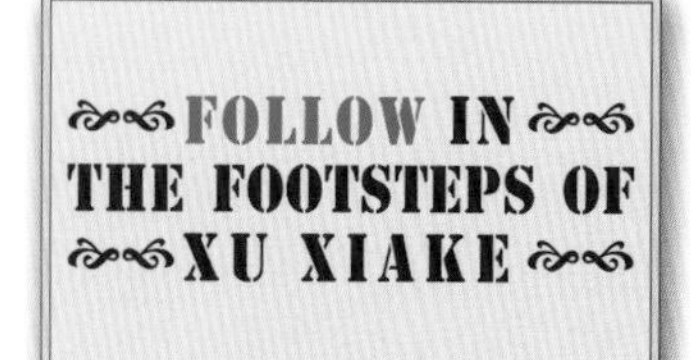

Xu Zhimo

The famous poet, Xu Zhimo (1897-1931), studied at Beijing University before he travelled to the Western world, first Columbia University then Cambridge in the UK. At Cambridge he developed a passion for English romantic poetry and his own work was greatly influenced by it. His poetry is characterized by a lifelong pursuit of aesthetic value, romance and literary freedom. He gradually established himself as a leader of the modern Chinese poetry movement in the 1920s, a movement which embraced Western romantic forms and liberal ideas. His best known poem is probably *Farewell Again to Cambridge*, which is inscribed on a marble stone at the back of King's College, Cambridge.

His love affair and remarriage with Lu Xiaoman, a beautiful writer and painter, was sensational news at the time. The Chinese did not then approve of divorce, particularly when there was no wrong-doing on the part of either party. Xu was killed in a plane crash in 1931.

Very quietly I take my leave,
As quietly as I came here;
Gently I flick my sleeves,
Not even a wisp of cloud will I bring away.

Xuan Wu

As one of the four symbols of the Chinese constellations, Xuan Wu represents the North and the season of winter. Sometimes called the Black Warrior of the North (in Chinese, xuan means black and wu means warrior), Xuan Wu is usually depicted as a black turtle wreathed with a snake, both creatures symbolizing long life. Being a water creature, Xuan Wu is also the god of water.

Xuanzang

Xuanzang (600?-664AD) was a noted Buddhist monk, scholar and translator who helped to develop cultural exchanges between China and India in the early Tang period. In order to get clear about the contradictions and obscurities of Buddhist texts at the time, Xuanzang decided to go on a pilgrimage to India to retrieve the original Buddhist scriptures. In 627, starting from Chang'an (now Xi'an), he set off on an arduous journey through central Asia towards India. He returned to China in 646 with 657 Buddhist sutras and was welcomed by Emperor Tang Taizong. He then devoted the rest of his life to translating the Buddhist scriptures from Sanskrit into Chinese. Xuanzuang also features as a fictional character in the Chinese classic Journey to the West, though in his fictional manifestation he is more often referred to as the Monk Tang or Tang Sanzang.

Xuanzong → *TANG XUANZONG*

Xun Zi

A Confucian philosopher from the Warring States Period (476-221BC), Xun Zi (c.313-238BC), unlike Mencius, believed that man is born with a tendency to be selfish and evil so that education and discipline are needed to rectify his personality. He maintained that benevolent rule should be combined with a rigorous system of justice. Both Han Fei and Li Si were disciples of his and, as proponents of Legalism, deeply influenced Qin Shi Huang's politics. Xun Zi's main ideas are collected in his book *Xun Zi*.

Yan Fu

A scholar and translator in the late Qing period, Yan Fu (1854-1921) is famous for introducing Western thought into China. He was educated in the Confucian classics at an early age. He then learned English, modern sciences and navigation at the Fujian Arsenal Academy. He was selected for overseas training in 1877 and studied at the Royal Naval Academy in Greenwich, England for two years. On returning to China, he became an activist in promoting reform and started to translate many influential Western works into Chinese, including Thomas Huxley's *Evolution and Ethics* and Adam Smith's *Wealth of Nations*. Darwin's idea of natural selection was first introduced to Chinese readers through his skilful translation.

THE TRANSLATOR OF DARWIN AND ADAM SMITH

Yan Xuetong

Professor Yan Xuetong is one of China's most influential academics working in the field of international relations. He has published a series of books and articles about international relations and one of his books – *Analysis of China's National Interests* – won the 1998 China book prize. He is also famous for his predictions. For example, he successfully predicted that the National Party in Taiwan would fall from power and Chen Shuibian would be elected as Taiwan President in 2000. But he apologized in June 2008 on the media for his incorrect prediction of a 2008 Taiwan Strait conflict between Taiwan and China.

Yan'an

Yan'an, in Shaanxi Province, was the political and military base of the Chinese Communist Party. It was here that the Long March ended, the heart and control centre of the Communist Revolution.

Yang Guifei

One of the Four Beauties in ancient China who was known for her fulsome figure, Yang Guifei (719-756AD), originally named Yang Yuhuan, was the favourite concubine of Emperor Xuanzong of the Tang Dynasty. Guifei is the second highest rank for an imperial consort, coming just below the empress. She was the wife of Emperor Xuanzong's son, but Yang's beauty made such an impression on Xuanzong that he took her for his own consort. There are many anecdotes about how much she was favoured by Xuanzong. One of the best known tells how Xuanzong, knowing Yang loved lychees, a kind of fruit only available in the south of China at that time, ordered to have some delivered by the fastest imperial horse messenger service from its southern origin over 600 miles away to his capital Chang'an. Because of her honoured status in court, many of her family members also became powerful – her cousin, Yang Guozhong, was promoted to the rank of chancellor.

Statue of Yang Guifei in Xi'an

Emperor Xuanzong and Yang Guifei had great trust in an influential general, An Lushan, who half-jokingly honoured Yang as his mother. However, An Lushan, because of conflicts with Yang Guozhong, started a rebellion in 755. A civil war broke out. When An Lushan's forces approached Chang'an, Emperor Xuanzong fled with Yang Guifei. When they came to Mawei Station, the imperial guards rebelled. Believing it was the Yang family who had caused all this turmoil, they killed Yang Guozhong and demanded that the emperor execute Yang Guifei, the person they saw as the root cause of all the unrest. So Xuanzong had no choice but to have his beloved Yang Guifei strangled. It is also said that she was forced to commit suicide. He spent the rest of his life grieving her loss. Their love story has been retold in many poems, novels and plays.

Yang Liping

A famous dancer from the Bai ethnic group who is generally known as the "Princess of the Peacocks", Yang Liping (1958-) showed an extraordinary aptitude for dancing at an early age though she had never had any professional training. In 1986 the dance show "The Soul of the Peacock", both choreographed and performed by Yang, captivated millions of Chinese TV viewers and helped her reap various awards. Later she became a member of one of China's most prestigious troupes – the Central Song and Dance Ensemble of Nationalities. Her performances on stage are dynamic, highly aesthetic and lyrical.

Yang Liwei

China's first astronaut, Yang Liwei (1965-) graduated from the No. 8 Aviation College of the PLA's (People's Liberation Army) Air Force in 1987. In January 1998 Yang was selected as a candidate for China's first manned spaceflight programme and underwent five years of rigorous training. On 15th October 2003, Yang was launched into space aboard the Shenzhou 5 spacecraft. China, after Russia and the US, had become the third nation to successfully send a human being into outer space. Yang is regarded as a national hero and was promoted to major-general in 2008.

Yang Liwei waves after emerging from the Shenzhou 5 capsule in Inner Mongolia, October 2003

Yang Zhenning, *a.k.a.* ***Chen Ning Franklin Yang***

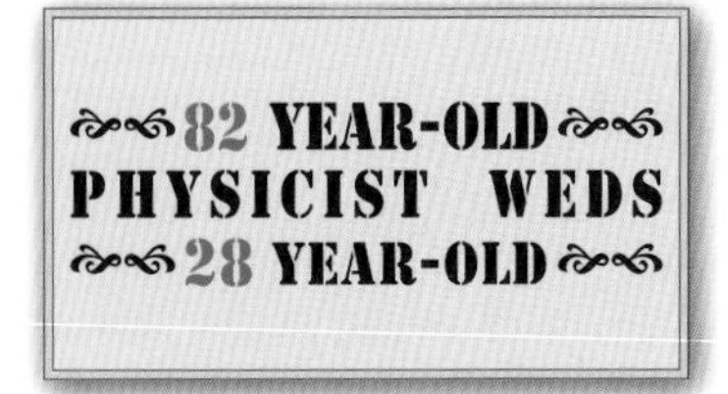

Yang Zhenning (1922-) is the first Chinese-born American Nobel Laureate and a world-renowned theoretical physicist. He received his bachelor and master's degrees from National Southwest Associated University in Kunming. In 1945 he continued his doctoral studies at the University of Chicago where he met Li Zhengdao and started a 16-year collaboration in the fields of parity and particle physics research. They shared the 1957 Nobel Prize for Physics. From 1965, he has been engaged in research at various prestigious institutes and universities. His second marriage with a 28-year-old in 2004 at the age of 82 caused a big stir in China.

yangqin

A type of dulcimer played by hitting the strings in pairs with a bamboo hammer held in each hand. The tone sounds a bit like a harpsichord.

Yangtze River

The Yangtze is the longest river in China and the third longest in the world. It rises in the Tibetan plateau and flows for nearly 4000 miles eastwards through 11 provinces and municipalities. The river reaches the wealthiest region, the Yangtze River Delta which includes Shanghai, southern Jiangsu Province and northern Zhejiang Province, before it drains into the East China Sea.

Yanluo

In Chinese mythology Yanluo is the god of death and ruler of the underworld. Every dead soul is brought to him for judgment by Ox-Head and Horse-Face, the two fearsome guardians of hell. The deserving are rewarded with a better future life or even resurrection from the dead. Those who have done bad things are sentenced to torture and a miserable future. With too many cases to deal with, Yanluo was divided into ten, acting as the judge of the ten halls in hell. In popular belief, therefore, Yanluo is more of an office than an individual god. Legend has it that some worthy officials were rewarded by being given the post of Yanluo when they died.

©Adrian Dennis/Getty Images

Yao Ming towers above other athletes at the closing ceremony of the 2008 Beijing Olympic Games

Yao Ming

Standing 7 feet 6 inches (229cm) tall, Yao Ming (born 1980) is currently the tallest player in the NBA. He first played for the Shanghai Sharks in the Chinese Basketball Association (CBA) and then entered the 2002 NBA draft. He was selected number-one player overall by the Houston Rockets, after playing for them for six seasons. Yao Ming's role in the Chinese national men's basketball team is also unsurpassed. His outstanding performances helped the Chinese team reach the quarter-finals at the Athens (2004) and Beijing Olympic Games (2008).

yaoguai

Yaoguai are malevolent animal spirits or fallen celestial beings that have acquired magical powers through the practice of Taoism. Their burning desire is to achieve immortality. In Journey to the West, the demons seek this by abducting the holy man, Xuanzang and trying to eat him.

Ye Jiangchuan

A former top chess player and chief coach of the Chinese national team, Ye Jiangchuan (1960-) won the national championship seven times between 1981 and 1996 and in 1999 he became the first Chinese player to have a FIDE (World Chess Federation) rating of over 2600. Ye, as Xie Jun's coach, played an important role in her success.

Ye Jianying

A prominent general in the Chinese Communist Party, Ye Jiangying (1897-1986) was one of the founders of the Huangpu Military Academy, the training ground of many outstanding military leaders for both the Nationalist Party and the CCP. Ye was instrumental in Mao Zedong's rise to power and directed many major battles before the CCP finally took control of China. In 1955 Ye Jianying was made a marshal. After Mao Zedong's death, Ye, as the Chairman of the Standing Committee of the National People's Congress, played a decisive role in crushing the Gang of Four and supporting Hua Guofeng in ending the Cultural Revolution. He retired in 1985 and died one year later in Beijing.

Yellow Emperor

The Yellow Emperor is one of the legendary Three August Ones and Five Emperors in Chinese mythology and considered the ancestor of the Chinese people. Also a cultural hero, he has been credited with the invention of the principles of traditional Chinese medicine, and of many other things such as the Chinese calendar, the wheel, armour and weaponry, the compass and coins.

Yellow River

The Yellow River, China's second longest river (only the Yangtze is longer) rises on the northern slopes of the Bayankela Mountains in Qinghai Province and flows for some at 3400 miles through nine provinces and autonomous regions before it empties into the Bohai Sea (not every year now though: sometimes it does not reach the sea). The Yellow River is known as the cradle of Chinese civilization (China's pride) because of the flourishing agricultural communities that grew up along its course. But it is also called China's

CHINA'S SORROW AND CHINA'S PRIDE

©iStockphoto.com/Qian Jin

Hu Kou Falls on the Yellow River

sorrow because of the disastrous floods that have frequently occurred down the centuries with great loss of life.

Yi

The Yi are an ethnic group who live mostly in southwest China. The largest community of the Yi people is in Liangshan Yi Autonomous Prefecture in Sichuan Province. There are a lot of smaller communities scattered around Sichuan, Yunnan, Guizhou and Guangxi. The Yi people have their own spoken and written language (called Yi Yu). The most important Yi celebration is The Firebrand Festival which falls on the twenty-fourth or twenty-fifth day in the sixth month of the Lunar Calendar. The festival, originally connected with fire worship, is a carnival when people put on their best clothes and sing, dance and enjoy various activities, such as cockfighting (still legal but not common), horse racing and wrestling.

Yin-Yang

The concepts of Yin and Yang in Chinese philosophy explain how things work in the universe. They represent two opposite sides of interrelated things or phenomena in the natural world. For example, the side facing the sun is yang and the opposite side is yin. While yin would be dark, passive, downward, cold, contracting and weak, yang would be bright, active, upward, hot, expanding and strong. The continual movement of these two energies is inherent in all things, when yin is waxing, yang is waning, and vice versa. The yin-yang theory holds that the development and changes of everything in the universe result from the unity or opposition between yin and yang. The concepts are widely used in traditional Chinese medicine. The organs of the body are seen to be interrelated in the same ways as other natural phenomena in the universe. Illness is seen as a disturbance in the balance of yin and yang. Therapy thus relies on accurate diagnosis of the source of the imbalance.

Yiwu

Yiwu in Zhejiang Province is almost certainly the world's biggest cutprice market, where over 30,000 stallholders offer every imaginable item at knockdown prices, including imitation designer goods galore. The place functions as a wholesaler for discounters worldwide.

Yongle → *Ming Chengzu*

Yongzheng → *Qing Yongzheng*

Young Pioneers → *photograph at education*

Most schoolchildren between the ages of 7 or 8 and 14 are members of the Young Pioneers. You can recognize Young Pioneers by the red neckscarves they wear to school.

The first children in a class to join the Young Pioneers are model students recruited by their teachers. These then go on to recruit other members of the class they consider suitable, so children are generally very keen to be chosen, as the brightest and most popular students tend to be the ones who get chosen first.

The Young Pioneers choose their own leaders from among the class, and take part in a variety of voluntary activities, such as helping the elderly and keeping their neighbourhood tidy. There are also political study activities, organized by the school's Communist Party, which usually centre about important current events.

Membership of the Young Pioneers ends at 14, at which point most children go on to join the Communist Youth League.

youtiao

Youtiao (literally oily tails) is the name for long deep-fried twisted strips of dough usually eaten for breakfast. Youtiao is also known as you zha gui, literally oil-fried devil, in Cantonese. There is a story that, in the Southern Song Dynasty (1127-1279), the patriotic general Yue Fei was framed and executed by the notorious official Qin Hui and his wife. The outraged and indignant people fried two long strips of dough, woven together, one representing Qin Hui and the other his wife. Since in Cantonese, hui and gui (devil) are close in pronunciation, the food began to be known as you zha gui (oil-fried devil). Youtiao is normally taken together with congee or soy milk.

Yu Dafu

Yu Dafu (1896-1945) was a famous writer and poet. He was educated in Japan. He is well known for founding the Creation Society, a literary society that promoted vernacular Chinese and modern literature. In this he worked together with other influential writers and intellectuals such as Guo Moruo, Zhang Ziping and Tian Han. His most famous short story collection *Sinking* (1921) shocked the Chinese literary establishment with its frank self-analysis in descriptions of his own sex life. During the Sino-Japanese war he mostly worked as an anti-Japanese propaganda writer and activist. He later moved to Singapore. In 1942 when Singapore was taken by the Japanese, he fled to Sumatra where he was said to have been murdered by Japanese gendarmes in 1945.

Yu Hao

An outstanding architect in the Song Dynasty (960-1279), Yu Hao's special expertise lay in building wooden pagodas. During the Song Dynasty timberwork architecture had reached a high level of structural and stylistic development. Yu Hao's greatest contribution was in compiling the *Mu Jing* (*Timberwork Manual*), an important classical architectural work highly praised by Shen Kuo in his *Dream Pool Essays*. The work has not survived the passage of time, but is known to posterity through Shen Kuo's writings.

Yu the Great → *Da Yu*

Yuan Chonghuan

Yuan Chonghuan (1584-1630) was an eminent general and a patriot in the Ming Dynasty (1368-1644). He was commander-in-chief of Ning Yuan, a strategic city at the frontline of defences against the Manchu invasion. In the first Battle of Ning Yuan, Yuan Chonghuan defeated the Manchu army with the successful use of artillery, wounding the Manchu leader, Nurhaci, who died eight months after the battle. Huang Tai Ji, the son and successor of Nurhaci, was also unable to conquer Ning Yuan even though he outnumbered them. So, in order to get rid of Yuan, Huang Tai Ji managed to make Emperor Chongzhen believe that Yuan Chonghuan had made a secret arrangement with the Manchu to overturn the Ming Dynasty. Although he had no solid evidence for this assertion, the emperor arrested Yuan Chonghuan and had him and his entire family executed. Many people believe that his death was a factor leading to the collapse of the Ming Dynasty.

Yuan Longping

Yuan Longping (1930-) is an agricultural scientist famous for developing high-yield hybrid rice varieties. His contribution to China's strategic solution to the problem of food shortage and the worldwide fight against famine cannot be overestimated. Yuan was acclaimed as the Father of Hybrid Rice. In the 1970s he started his painstaking research which led to the development of "super hybrid rice", a variety which can yield 10 tons per hectare. He was awarded China's State Supreme Science and Technology Award in 2001 and was made the 2004 World Food Prize laureate by the UN Food and Agricultural Organizaion. His breakthrough has helped China to solve its food shortage problems within the space of three decades.

Yuan Shizu, *a.k.a. **Kublai Khan***

Better known in the West as Kublai Khan, grandson of Genghis Khan, this eminent Mongolian ruler was the founder of the Yuan Dynasty, the first minority regime to unify and rule over all China. Yuan Shizu conquered the Southern Song Dynasty in 1279 and became the emperor of all China. He adopted Chinese ways in politics and matters cultural and appointed Han Chinese as his official advisors. He furthered economic development by repairing and constructing dams and irrigation systems. He was a militaristic and aggressive person and made a series of (abortive) attacks on adjacent countries such as Japan and Vietnam. During his reign the empire developed relationships with parts of Europe and Central Asia. Many traders, travellers and scholars (like Marco Polo) came to China during his rule.

Circa 1260, Kublai Khan, Mongol Emperor of China. Marco Polo spent twenty years at his court.

Yue Fei

Yue Fei (1103-1142 AD) was a patriotic general and a national hero of the Southern Song Dynasty (1127-1279AD). Born in a poor family, he rose to become an accomplished general who fought against the invading Jurchen armies of the Jin Empire. It is said that Yue's mother tattooed four characters jin zhong bao guo (serving the country with the utmost loyalty) across his back before he left home to join the army, a famous anecdote to show his patriotism. A brilliant commander, he won a series of victories and recovered most of the territory previously taken by the Jurchen, a nomadic tribe from the north. Facing the formidable Yue army, a Jurchen commander exclaimed, "It is easier to shake the mountain than to shake Yue Fei's army." Thanks to Yue Fei and a contemporary general Han Shizhong, the weak regime of Southern Song was able to stay in power. But his emperor, Song Gaozong, afraid of Yue Fei's popularity and seeing him as a threat, ordered him back to the capital, where he was thrown into prison and eventually executed on a groundless charge of treason. The next emperor of the Southern Song cleared Yue Fei of the charges and honoured him as a "Loyal Hero".

Yunnan

A province lying along the southwest frontier of China sharing borders with Burma, Laos and Vietnam. Its capital is Kunming. Ethnically diverse, Yunnan is home to over 50 ethnic groups, accounting for nearly 40% of its total population. Its cultural diversity and beautiful natural scenery make it a popular tourist destination for people from all over the world.

Terraces with young crops near Tiger Leaping Gorge in Yunnan Province. The snow-capped peaks of Jade Dragon Snow Mountain can be seen in the distance.

Zao Jun

Zao Jun, or the Kitchen God, is one of the most popular Taoist gods in China. Traditionally, people would put his portrait above the fireplace in the kitchen. It's believed that Zao Jun returns to Heaven on the 24th day of the 12th lunar month when he files a report for the Jade Emperor on the activities of every household in the past year. Since Zao Jun's report decides who will be rewarded and who punished, every family, on the evening of the 23rd, would make offerings and burn incense, a ritual called "seeing Zao Jun off", so that he wouldn't badmouth them in front of the Jade Emperor. These days people do this as part of the ceremony of welcoming the New Year.

Zhang Ai-ling → *Eileen Chang*

Zhang Dai

A great essayist born in the Ming Dynasty (1368-1644), as a young man Zhang Dai (1597-1679) was something of a playboy and bon viveur. He wrote over thirty books though only a few have survived, amongst which most famously are *Sailboat at Night*, *Reminiscences in Dreams of Tao An* and *Search the West Lake in Dream.*

Zhang Daqian

Zhang Daqian (1899-1983) was one of the greatest masters of traditional Chinese painting working in the 20th century. He learned to paint in his early years by imitating the works of ancient masters. Such are his skills that many an expert is hoodwinked by his forgeries. He admired the art of the Tang Dynasty so much that he spent nearly three years in Dunhuang copying the Buddhist frescoes in the Mogao Caves. This experience was fundamental to the development of his unique style. He left China before the Communist takeover and travelled around the world. He was regarded in the West as a master of Oriental art. He finally settled down in Taipei and died after finishing his masterpiece the *Lushan Landscape (Lushantu)* in 1983.

Zhang Fei

An intrepid general of the Kingdom of Shu in the Three Kingdoms Period (184-280AD), Zhang Fei (?-221AD) was one of the sworn brothers of Liu Bei, Lord of Shu and was depicted as a legendary warrior in *Romance of the Three Kingdoms*. With only 20 guards, he held out against Cao Cao's 5000 soldiers at Chang Ban Po. His blood-curdling howl so frightened the enemy general that he fell off his horse and was killed. Known for his loyalty to his lord and strength as a warrior, he was very ill-tempered and treated his subordinates and his troops very harshly, which often got him into trouble. Zhang Fei was murdered by his deputy generals when he was asleep.

Zhang Guorong, *a.k.a.* Leslie Cheung

A great actor and superstar in Cantopop, Leslie Cheung (1956-2003) was too special an artist to be neatly categorized. With his delicate features, sexy voice and smouldering charisma, his glamour would overshadow that of the actresses co-starring with him. He remained alluring to both men and women even after he acknowledged his homosexuality, a brave thing to do in a society intolerant of gays. His most famous part is that of a gay opera star known for his elegant performance of female roles in Chen Kaige's *Farewell My Concubine* (1993). A versatile actor, he can be hilarious in a comedy and macho in an action movie. His best performances, however, are complex personalities such as the dashing and heartless playboy in *Days of Being Wild* (1991) or Tony Leung Chiu-wai's abrasive lover in *Happy Together* (1997). A natural in front of the camera and on stage, he knew how to lend his beauty to a character or an extravaganza show. In his last concert series (2000-2001), the successful yet controversial *Passion Tour*, he tried the nerves of the audience and media with unconventional costumes designed by Jean-Paul Gaultier, wearing red high heels, a long wig and a beard. He was a golden boy in the eyes of his fans and chose a drastic way to keep the image alive forever. Leslie Cheung jumped from the Mandarin Oriental Hotel in the city centre of Hong Kong on 1st April 2003, leaving a suicide note that said he had been suffering from depression.

©Liu Jin/Getty Images

Hong Kong's king of pop, singer Leslie Cheung on stage during a solo concert in Shanghai Stadium, September 2000

Zhang Heng

A mathematician, geographer, artist and literary scholar who lived from 78-139AD in the Eastern Han Dynasty. His greatest contributions were in the field of astronomy. In 123AD he worked out corrections to the calendar to bring it into line with the seasons. He was the first person in China to construct a rotating celestial globe. Writing about his theory of the universe, he said, "The sky is like a hen's egg, and is as round as a crossbow pellet; the Earth is like the yolk of the egg, lying alone at the centre." He is best known in the West for his invention of the seismograph. Zhang Heng also proposed the square root of 10 for π. On top of all this he was a great poet and painter.

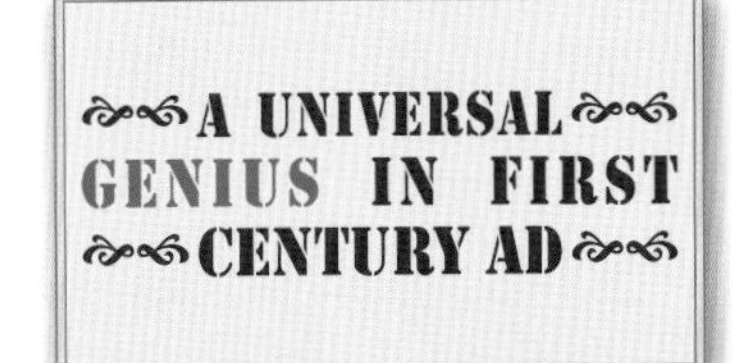

Zhang Manyu → *MAGGIE CHEUNG*

Zhang Qian

An outstanding diplomat, Zhang Qian (c.164-114BC) was dispatched by Han Wudi as the imperial envoy to the state of Yuezhi in the Western Regions (now Central Asia) in the 2nd century BC. His mission was to form a military alliance with Yuezhi to fight against the Xiongnu, a powerful nomadic tribe which threatened the western borders of the Han Dynasty. But, when crossing Xiongnu territory, he was captured and imprisoned for 10 years. During this time, Zhang Qian married a Xiongnu wife, but he never forgot his duty as a Han envoy. Finally he managed to escape and continued westward until he successfully reached Yuezhi. When Zhang Qian eventually made it back to Han, he gave a detailed report to the emperor about the civilizations in the Western Regions and was honoured by being appointed to the position of palace counsellor. In spite of all the difficulties encountered in his first mission, Zhang Qian was later sent on a second mission, this time to Wusun, another Western Region state. As a pioneer in establishing communications between China and Central Asia, Zhang Qian initiated the trade link which became known as the Silk Road.

Zhang Sanfeng

A semi-mythical Taoist sage during the end of the Yuan Dynasty (1271-1368) and the beginning of the Ming Dynasty (1368-1644), Zhang Sanfeng was a great martial artist and founded the Wudang School of martial arts at the Taoist monastery in the Wudang Mountains. It is said that he took inspiration from a fight between a crane and a snake and developed the concept of Neijia Kung Fu (internal kung fu), especially T'ai Chi Ch'uan (shadow boxing), which features gentle actions but great underlying power.

Zhang Weiying

Professor Zhang Weiying is a well-known Chinese economist specializing in state-owned enterprise reform and industrial organization research. He took a PhD in economics at Oxford University in 1994. Professor Zhang was the first scholar in China to propose dual-track pricing. He also argued that the government should step back and let free market forces determine economic development. His opinions were widely reported by the Chinese media and factored into Chinese economic reforms in the 1990s. In recent years, people began to criticize Professor Zhang's views on economic reform in view of the negative effects of privatization, such as unfair social distribution.

Zhang Xianliang

The writer and poet Zhang Xianliang (born 1936) was labelled a rightist for his published poem *Song of the Great Wind* during the anti-rightist campaign initiated by Mao Zedong in 1957. At the age of 21 he was sent to prison and then to a labour reform camp where he was kept for 22 years until 1979 when Deng Xiaoping rose to power and started to rehabilitate the wrongly charged rightists. After he was released he began to write novels based largely on his experiences during his imprisonment. His most famous novel is probably *Half of Man is Woman* (1985). This was a controversial bestseller in the mid 1980s. A semi-autobiographical story, it depicts a man's life in the labour camps and his sexual difficulties after release, suggesting the theme that Chinese intellectuals have been emasculated as a result of political and cultural suppression. Another novel *Grass Soup* (1992), based on the notes he kept in his diary when in the labour camp, describes how humanity can be destroyed by frightening mass complicity and how small but moving acts of kindness can keep hope alive.

Zhang Xueliang

Zhang Xueliang (1901-2001), the eldest son of the warlord Zhang Zuolin in northern China, took control of Manchuria in 1928 after his father was assassinated by the Japanese. He soon proclaimed his support for the Kuomintang government, a selfless deed facilitating the reunification of China. In 1931 the Japanese army invaded Manchuria. Zhang Xueliang, who was said to be following the orders of Chiang Kai-shek, pulled his armies back from the front lines without any resistance. His discontent with Chiang Kai-shek's non-aggressive policy against Japan was intensified when he was ordered to attack the Communist military force based in Yan'an. After meeting with several influential figures in the Communist Party, he leant towards their view that the whole nation should be united into a National Anti-Japanese Front regardless of party and ideological differences. In 1936 Zhang Xueliang, together with Yang Hucheng, another patriotic military general, started a military mutiny and arrested Chiang Kai-shek in Xi'an. Chiang was compelled to agree to form an alliance with the Communist Party. This is known as the Xi'an Incident. To show his personal allegiance to Chiang, he unwisely accompanied Chiang back to Nanjing where he was placed under house arrest. He didn't regain his freedom until 1990, after the death of Chiang Kai-shek's son and successor Chiang Ching-kuo. He then emigrated to Hawaii and died at the age of 100.

Zhang Xueyou, *a.k.a.* ***Jacky Cheung***

ONE OF THE FOUR HEAVENLY KINGS OF CANTOPOP

A megastar in Cantopop and a Hong Kong actor, Zhang Xueyou (1961-) started his career after winning a singing contest in Hong Kong in 1984. Since then he has released dozens of albums. Tagged as one of the "Four Heavenly Kings" of Cantopop, he is credited with numerous hit songs throughout Chinese-speaking communities. Being the biggest selling Chinese pop singer, Zhang received the title of "Chinese Artiste of the World" twice at the World Music Awards. His recent work on the Cantonese musical *Snow Wolf Lake* has been highly acclaimed by audiences and critics. Also a talented actor, he has been cast in a great many films and has won two Best Supporting Actor Awards, one at the Hong Kong Film Awards (1988) and the other at the Golden Horse Awards in Taiwan (1990).

©China Photos/Getty Images

Jacky Cheung performs during the musical Snow Wolf Lake on August 27, 2005 in Wuhan, Hubei Province

Zhang Yimou → *photograph at* Gong Li

A world-famous filmmaker, Zhang Yimou (1950-) was listed as one of the "Fifth Generation" directors, along with Chen Kaige, Tian Zhuangzhuang and Wu Ziniu, who were largely responsible for the revival of the Chinese movie industry at the end of the Cultural Revolution. Zhang started out as a cinematographer. His debut film *Red Sorghum* won him the Golden Bear at the 1988 Berlin Film Festival. It marked the beginning of his successful collaboration with actress Gong Li and his award-encrusted career in cinema. His films are sometimes criticized in his home country for portraying the ugly side of China. But they are also known for their unique use of colour, gorgeously photographed images and their vivid depictions of intense emotions as people struggle with inner conflict. *The Story of Qiu Ju* and *Not One Less* brought him two Golden Lion Awards at the 1992 and 1999 Venice Film Festivals, *The Road Home* a Silver Bear in Berlin in 1999. In recent years, Zhang's films have become commercial on a grand scale. He made three big-budget epic films that broke box office records in China. In 2008 Zhang Yimou directed the opening and closing ceremonies at the Beijing Olympics.

©Pedro Ugarte/Getty Images

Zhang Yining returns the ball to her compatriot Wang Nan (not pictured) during their women's singles gold medal table tennis final at the 2008 Beijing Olympic Games

Zhang Yining

Top female table tennis player and Olympic champion, Zhang Yining (1981-), having dominated this sport for more than five years, has been No.1 in the ITTF (International Table Tennis Federation) ranking for women's singles since January 2003. She only temporarily lost her No. 1 rank at the beginning of 2008. In her career, she has won altogether 16 world championships for women's singles, doubles and team events. She is one of only three female table tennis players in the world, along with Deng Yaping and Wang Nan, who have ever won championships at the three most important international events – the World Cup, the World Tournament and the Olympics.

Zhang Ziyi → *photograph at Zhou Xun*

An internationally recognized actress (1979-), Zhang Ziyi shot to stardom with her first role in Zhang Yimou's *The Road Home* (1999), which won the Silver Bear Award in Berlin. Her fame continued to increase – especially in the West – after her cooperation with Ang Lee in the Oscar Winner *Crouching Tiger, Hidden Dragon*. This runaway success paved her way to Hollywood. In 2005 Zhang starred in *Memoirs of a Geisha*, for which she was nominated for a Golden Globe Award and a BAFTA.

Zhang Zizhong

A patriotic general in the Second Sino-Japanese War (1937-1945), Zhang Zizhong (1891-1940) participated in the famous Battle of Taierzhuang in 1938 and won an important victory against the Japanese forces. In 1940 the Japanese assembled some 300,000 troops for the Zaoyi offensive aimed at gaining control of river traffic on the Yangtze. With only two regiments, Zhang Zizhong led his men in a courageous act of resistance and sacrificed his life for his country.

Zhao Gao

As Qin Shi Huang's favourite eunuch, Zhao Gao (259-207BC) was responsible for the collapse of the Qin Dynasty (221-206BC). After Qin Shi Huang's death, Zhao Gao conspired with Li Si, the prime minister, to alter the emperor's will. Fu Su, the virtuous crown prince was forced to commit suicide, and his younger brother, later called Qin Er Shi, succeeded to the throne in his place with the connivance of Zhao Gao, who turned the new emperor into his puppet. It is said that Zhao Gao, who was taking control of the court, once asked the court officials to call a deer a horse in front of Qin Er Shi. Those who didn't would be eliminated. The Chinese idiom zhi lu wei ma (calling a deer a horse) is derived from the story. It means distorting the truth, confounding right and wrong.

CALLING A DEER A HORSE

Zhao Gao levied heavy taxes on the Chinese people and treated them cruelly, causing farmers across the land to rise up in revolt. He was so power-hungry that he even murdered Qin Er Shi, his own puppet emperor. He finally met his end at the hands of Fu Su's eldest son, Ziying, who killed Zhao Gao and his entire family in revenge for Zhao Gao's having forced his father to commit suicide. But the removal of Zhao Gao came too late to prevent the downfall of the Qin Dynasty.

Zhao Gou → *Song Gaozong*

Zhao Kuangyin → *Song Taizu*

Zhao Yun

One of the "Five Tiger Generals" of the Kingdom of Shu in the Three Kingdoms Period (184-280AD), Zhao Yun (?-229AD) was known for his courage and heroism in the battle of Chang Ban Po. Coming under attack from Wei troops led by Cao Cao, Liu Bei (Zhao Yun's emperor) fled with his soldiers, abandoning his wives and son. Zhao Yun charged back into the enemy ranks and saved their lives. In the Battle of Hanshui, Zhao Yun bravely fought against Cao Cao's army, which greatly outnumbered his own. With courage and clever strategy, he defeated the enemy's mighty attack. He was therefore praised by his lord Liu Bei as the "General with the Might of a Tiger". Featured as a handsome and fearless warrior, he became a household name after the popularity of the *Romance of the Three Kingdoms.*

Zhao Zhenkai → *Bei Dao*

Zhejiang

Zhejiang Province is a coastal province south of Shanghai, larger than Ireland, with a population of about forty million. It is named after the Zhe River, the old name of the province's largest river, the Qiantang. The inhabitants of Zhejiang say that it is "7 parts mountain, 1 part water, 2 parts fields". The jagged coastline with all its many bays, headlands and islands is famous for fishing. Once isolated communities retain their own dialects, and traders down the coast used to communicate in pidgin English. Hangzhou, the capital city, is the southern terminus of the Grand Canal.

Zheng He

The greatest explorer of his time, Zheng He (1371-1433) was originally a eunuch of the Emperor Yongle in the Ming Dynasty (1368-1644). Emperor Yongle had seized the throne from his nephew Zhu Yunwen, who was said to have then fled abroad after the palace coup. Zheng He was dispatched by Emperor Yongle to lead a fleet to sail overseas and search for Zhu Yunwen. From the year 1405 to 1433, Zheng He and his fleet set sail on seven expeditions starting from Taicang in the province of Jiangsu. His voyages took him to over 30 foreign countries, mostly in Southeast Asia, though the farthest flung places he reached were the Red Sea and the East Coast of Africa (now Somalia).

Compare the size of Zheng He's ship with one used by Columbus!

The scale of Zheng He's fleet was unprecedented. It consisted of some of the biggest ships in the world, far bigger than anything else that existed at that time, ships equipped with advanced navigation systems and capable of carrying over 27,000 sailors and soldiers. His was a peaceful, diplomatic purpose and Zheng He never posed a threat to any country that he visited, in spite of the mighty navy that he commanded. Instead, he helped to promote trade and cultural exchanges between China and those countries. Zheng He is a Chinese national hero and is also remembered as an envoy of peace and a pioneer of navigation.

SHIPS WITH ADVANCED NAVIGATION SYSTEMS AND EACH CARRYING OVER 27,000 SAILORS AND SOLDIERS

Zheng Yi Sao → CHING SHIH

Zhong Kui

A mythological ghost-catcher in Chinese folklore, Zhong Kui is said to be a scholar of the Tang Dynasty (618-907AD) who achieved the title Zhuangyuan, the top honour in the Imperial Civil Examination. But he was stripped of this title. Why? Simply because he was so ugly. Indignant and outraged, Zhong Kui committed suicide. After his death he became the demon-expelling god in the underworld. Legend has it that the Emperor Xuanzong of the Tang Dynasty once became very sick because of disturbing dreams in which he saw a ghost. One night, Zhong Kui came into the emperor's dream and swallowed the ghost that was haunting him. The Emperor Xuanzong then recovered from his illness. After that, he had Zhong Kui's image painted and printed, and asked people to put it up in their homes to ward off ghosts. The custom exists to this day.

Zhongshan Zhuang

The Zhongshan Zhuang, or Zhongshan suit or Chinese tunic suit, is a form of "national dress" introduced by Sun Yat-sen, Zhongshan being a name he used to hide his identity from the authorities when in danger of persecution.

It was customary in ancient times to change the national costume whenever a new dynasty replaced the old one. Thus, after overthrowing the Qing Dynasty, Dr. Sun Yat-sen followed his Nationalist Party's proposition and asked designers to modify a casual style of dress into this tunic – four pockets and a turned-down collar, fastening right down the centre with five buttons. Simple and tasteful. The suit, adapted from Japanese student wear, features a jacket with four pockets and trousers.

Sun Yat-sen, Chiang Kai-shi and Mao Zedong, three political leaders in modern China, all used it as formal dress on important occasions. Mao seemed to have a special liking for it: he made public appearances either in a Zhongshan suit or in military uniform. In the Western world it is also widely known as the Mao Suit.

Zhongnanhai

Zhongnanhai, to the west of the Forbidden City, is the residence of the highest-ranking leaders of the People's Republic of China and the administrative headquarters of the central government. It houses the Central Committee of the Communist Party, the State Council and the Military Commission of the Party Central Committee. Zhongnanhai (literally: Central and South Lake) is a compound built around two lakes – Central Lake and South Lake – and displays examples of imperial garden architecture such as the Hall of Diligent Government and the Garden of Plenty.

But these days Zhongnanhai is more important for its political significance than its architectural grandeur. It symbolizes the top Chinese leadership and the highest echelons of the administration of the People's Republic of China and has a resonance parallel to that of the Kremlin or the White House. However, compared with its Western counterparts, Zhongnanhai remains mysterious to outsiders. Apart from a period from 1977 to 1985 when people could purchase tickets to visit some parts of South Lake, Zhongnanhai is strictly off limits to the general public.

Zhou Enlai

THE PEOPLE'S PREMIER

Zhou Enlai (1898-1976) was a staunch supporter of Mao Zedong and helped Mao establish his military authority during the Long March. In 1936 he played a pivotal role in the Xi'an Incident and succeeded in establishing a political coalition with the KMT against the Japanese. He worked as the CCP's liaison officer with the Nationalist government until 1946 when the political union broke up and civil war began. Zhou served as the Premier of the PRC from 1949 till his death in 1976. An outstanding diplomat, he was also Chinese foreign minister from 1949 to 1958. He was credited with promoting Sino-foreign relationships and tempering anti-communist hostility in the Western world. He helped to break the ice in Sino-US relations by welcoming US President Richard Nixon to China in 1972. He put forward the famous "Five Principles of Peaceful Coexistence" which was acknowledged as an important guideline in the settlement of international disputes. A pragmatic and moderate statesman, he managed to mitigate the damage done by the Red Guards and took steps to protect as many intellectuals and officials as he could from persecution during the Cultural Revolution. His death on 8th January 1976 triggered large-scale public mourning in Tiananmen Square. This turned into a protest against the central authorities under the rule of the Gang of Four. Zhou was known as the "the People's Premier" and is greatly admired by the Chinese people for his charisma, his dedication and wisdom.

Zhou Enlai, September 1973

Zhou Huajian, *a.k.a.* ***Emil Chau***

Zhou Huajian (1960-), born in Hong Kong, was an extremely popular singer in Taiwan, Hong Kong, mainland China and in other Chinese communities in Southeast Asia during the mid 1990s. He first signed on at Rock Records in 1985 as an assistant producer, and two years later his first hit album *Direction of the Heart* was released. Up to now he has released more than 40 albums in Mandarin, Cantonese and English. He was also active in raising money for charitable and philanthropic purposes.

Zhou Jielun → ***Jay Chou***

Zhou Xingchi, *a.k.a.* ***Stephen Chow***

A well-known Hong Kong comedian and filmmaker characterized by a Mo Lei Tau style (nonsense humour), Zhou Xingchi (born 1962) has starred in and directed over 50 movies since the late 1980s. His works have won him numerous awards and honours. His most famous productions are the two *A Chinese Odyssey* films, a love story which is sad yet full of hilarious moments and based on stories from the Chinese classic Journey to the West. The two films, though not box office successes, surprisingly became cult classics among university students in mainland China when the DVD version was released. Some lines in the movies are still widely quoted in the media and by his fans. His later films like *Shaolin Soccer* and *Kung Fu Hustle* have attracted a lot of attention in the West.

Zhou Xuan

A popular singer and actress in the 1930s and 40s, Zhou Xuan (1918-1957), born as Su Pu, was raised by foster parents. She took Zhou Xuan as her stage name when she joined a song and dance troupe in Shanghai at the age of 13. After she won second place in a singing competition in Shanghai, people began to nickname her "Golden Voice". She shot to stardom in cinema in 1937 when she played a singing girl in the hit film *Street Angel*. The two theme songs she sang, *Four Seasons Song* and *The Wandering Songstress*, are among her most memorable songs and have enjoyed long-lasting popularity. As the first pop diva in modern China, her personal life was as dramatic as any of her scripts. A failed marriage, two illegitimate children fathered by two lovers and several suicide attempts made headlines in the gossip columns. She suffered a nervous breakdown in 1951 before her last film was completed. She passed away in a mental asylum in Shanghai at the age of only 39. Her tragic early death elevated her status from movie star to legend. There have been books, films and television series retelling the story of her colourful yet ill-fated life.

Zhou Xun

Chinese actress and singer, Zhou Xun (1976-) was seen as one of the most promising young film actresses in the early 2000s. Her most impressive and successful performance is probably to be found in Chen Kexin's film *Perhaps Love* in 2005, which won her Best Actress at the 2006 Hong Kong Film Awards. She was cast as Huang Rong in *The Legend of the Condor Heroes* in 2002, a TV adaptation of one of Jin Yong's most acclaimed novels. She is also a popular singer and has released albums titled *Summer* (2003) and *Come Across* (2005).

Zhou Xun (left) and Zhang Ziyi at the Palazzo del Casino in Venice

Zhou Yu

An outstanding military strategist of the Kingdom of Wu during the Three Kingdoms Period (184-280AD), Zhou Yu (175-210AD) is best known for his leadership in the Battle of the Red Cliff (208AD) fought between the Kingdom of Wei and the alliance of the Kingdoms of Wu and Shu, the result of which was crucial for the future balance of powers among the three kingdoms. Adopting Huang Gai's tactic, the allied force led by Zhou Yu defeated Wei's fleet by the use of fire.

SHOULD ONE NOTE OF THE TUNE BE WRONG, ZHOU YU WILL NOTICE

In Romance of the Three Kingdoms, Zhou Yu is depicted as a narrow-minded man who is jealous of the great strategist, Zhuge Liang's talents. In reality, however, he was intelligent and open-minded. Generally considered as a handsome young man, Zhou Yu was also a musician and there was a saying at the time: "should one note of the tune be wrong, Zhou Yu will notice."

Zhu Da

Also known as Bada Shanren (八大山人), Zhu Da (c.1626-c.1705) was a famous 17th century painter and calligrapher. After the collapse of the Ming Dynasty, Zhu Da became a Buddhist monk to demonstrate his loyalty to the defunct Ming court. He would usually sign his drawings with the characters for Bada Shanren. When put together vertically, 八大 looks like both 哭 (ku, meaning cry) and 笑 (xiao, laugh), and 山人 looks like 之 (zhi, it), so altogether it reads "crying over it and laughing at it". Perhaps Zhu Da intended to use his nickname to express his divided feelings about his own fate and that of the nation. Zhu Da excelled at drawing flowers, birds and landscapes. The exaggerated strokes of his paintings speak of his indomitable spirit.

Zhu De

A great military leader and statesman of the Chinese Communist Party, Zhu De (1886-1976) was the founder of the Red Army, the predecessor of the People's Liberation Army (PLA). He took part in Sun Yat-sen's Nationalist Movement in the 1910s. Later he led his troops to join with Mao Zedong's guerrilla forces in the Jinggang Mountains where China's first Soviet-style regime was established. He was appointed Commander-in-Chief of the Communist forces for the Sino-Japanese War (1937-45) and the Chinese Civil War (1946-50) and retained this post until 1954. He was also in overall command during the Korean War in the 1950s. For a long time his name was closely linked with Mao. The two had a very close relationship and people often called them collectively "Zhu Mao". In 1955, he was made a Marshal. When the Cultural Revolution started he was denounced as a Big Warlord and a Black General. Thanks to his prestige and the support of Zhou Enlai, he narrowly escaped the political purge, but had to disappear from political life. He died in July, 1976, two months earlier than Mao.

Zhu Que

The Zhu Que, literally "Vermillion Bird", is one of the four symbols of the Chinese constellations, representing the element fire, the direction south, and the season summer. In Chinese myth, the Zhu Que is an elegant, noble bird with fiery red feathers. It is usually associated with the phoenix.

Zhu Rongji

Zhu Rongji (1928-) was an outstanding statesman and former Premier of the PRC (1998-2003). A graduate of Tsinghua University, his administrative skills and economic insight helped him get elected Mayor of Shanghai in 1988. In 1991 he was appointed Vice-Premier and in 1998 Premier. He was one of the most popular Chinese leaders. People approved of his strong stance against corruption and nepotism. He also won international respect for maintaining stable economic growth in the face of the Asian economic crisis at the end of the 1990s. He retired from office in 2003 and was replaced by Wen Jiabao.

Zhu Xi

Zhu Xi → *Neo-Confucianism*

Zhu Yuanzhang → *Ming Taizu*

Zhu Ziqing

The famous Chinese essayist and poet, Zhu Ziqing (1898-1948), graduated from Beijing University in 1920. In those days Beijing University was the centre of the New Culture Movement and Zhu became one of the trailblazers of modern Chinese literature. For most of his life he was dedicated to teaching and literary creation. A prolific writer, his greatest accomplishment lies in his prose works. Essays like *Moonlight over the Lotus Pond, Retreating Figure* and *Green* are often found in textbooks for literary criticism and appreciation. His best known poem is *Destruction* (1922). Zhu strongly condemned America's collaboration with the Nationalist government and signed a statement declaring he would accept no American aid. Shortly before the fall of the Nationalist government, with the economy in ruins, inflation soaring and food scarce he remained true to his word and his moral principles. He died of hunger, although US aid was available.

Traditional costume of the Zhuang minority group

©iStockphoto.com/btrenkel

Zhuang

An ethnic group with the second largest population (second only to the Han Chinese). Ninety percent of Zhuang people live in Guangxi Zhuang Autonomous Region, with the rest scattered in Yunnan, Guangdong and Guizhou. The Zhuang people have a long history as an agrarian society. They have their own indigenous language called Zhuang Yu, but they do not use it as much as they do Chinese.

Zhuang Zi

An influential philosopher in the Warring States Period (476-221BC), Zhuang Zi (c.369-286BC) is regarded as the successor of Lao Zi and one of the founders of Taoism. His book *Zhuang Zi*, a classical Taoist text, contains many fables which hint at philosophical questions. In the famous story *Zhuang Zi dreamt he was a butterfly* he raises a question of theory of knowledge.

In general, Zhuang Zi's philosophy is that of a sceptic. He also proposes that people should live a quiet, withdrawn life and not compete with others. In this way disappointments will be avoided. He argued that, since man's life is limited, while the extent of knowledge is unlimited, it would be foolish to waste a limited life in pursuit of unlimited knowledge. Zhuang Zi enjoyed great popularity among the literati who were disillusioned with the darkness of politics and society and saw in him an escape into a private life of self-cultivation and spiritual freedom.

Zhuang Zi dreamt he was a butterfly
Zhuang Zi woke up and wondered:
am I Zhuang Zi who was dreaming he was a butterfly?
or am I a butterfly who is dreaming I am Zhuang Zi?

Zhudi → *Ming Chengzu*

Zhuge Liang

A great military strategist in the Three Kingdoms Period who later became a symbol for intelligence and tactics in Chinese culture.

zhuyin, Taiwanese notation system

Consisting of 37 letters and 4 tone markers, this is a phonetic system for transcribing Chinese and is used by people to learn to read, write or speak Mandarin. It has the same pronunciations as pinyin, hence there is a mostly a 1-to-1 mapping between the two systems. The only difference is that zhuyin uses symbols whereas pinyin uses the roman alphabet.

For example:

zhuyin	*pinyin*
ㄅ	b
ㄆ	p
ㄇ	m
ㄈ	f
ㄚ	a
ㄛ	o
ㄜ	e

zodiac

The Chinese zodiac has a repeating 12-year cycle, each year associated with a particular animal: tiger, rabbit, dragon, snake, horse, goat, monkey, rooster, dog and pig, rat, ox. Every animal sign has its own qualities and characteristics, according to which the Chinese are able to tell you the strengths and weaknesses of a person born in a particular year. However, this does not mean that people born in the same year will share exactly the same qualities, as there are also other animal signs assigned by month and hour of the day in regard to the traditional Lunar Calendar. For example, a person might appear on the outside to be a dragon, but he might also be a horse on the inside as well as being a closet ox. In addition to the different days within a month, there are millions of combinations which make Chinese astrology a study of statistics. How is it used? It is a tradition to consult specialists when marriages are arranged to see whether the two people match as a couple. The younger generation may not do this anymore, but it is still believed in by lots of people. In daily life, the Chinese have their own special way of asking someone's age. They simply ask for a person's zodiac sign and put it into a cycle of 12 years. With a bit of common sense, they will work out the person's age within a few seconds.

tiger	rabbit	dragon	snake	horse	goat
1938	1939	1940	1941	1942	1943
1950	1951	1952	1953	1954	1955
1962	1963	1964	1965	1966	1967
1974	1975	1976	1977	1978	1979
1986	1987	1988	1989	1990	1991
1998	1999	2000	2001	2002	2003

monkey	rooster	dog	pig	rat	ox
1944	1945	1946	1947	1948	1949
1956	1957	1958	1959	1960	1961
1968	1969	1970	1971	1972	1973
1980	1981	1982	1983	1984	1985
1992	1993	1994	1995	1996	1997
2004	2005	2006	2007	2008	2009

Remember: the year starts at Spring Festival not January 1st.

tiger

Tigers are incredibly kind and sensitive, but can also be extremely blunt and short-tempered. Brave, but at times rather selfish. Honest to the last, the tiger is a creature of principle and will always stand up for what he believes in. However, the tiger is also extremely sensitive to criticism. The tiger is a deep thinker, but can also be a ditherer.

rabbit (or hare)

A quiet and obliging creature, the rabbit is almost always a pleasure to have around. Being extremely sentimental, however, it sometimes earns itself a reputation for being superficial. The rabbit is a thorough and efficient worker with an excellent memory and a good head for figures. The rabbit is often successful in business, but can lose out through being overcautious. Rabbits have expensive tastes in food and the fine arts.

dragon

The dragon is a very outgoing creature, full of life, proud, self-confident and ambitious, but also rather impulsive. Although highly intelligent, the dragon is also a perfectionist, which means that others sometimes find dragons rather demanding. Dragons often prefer to remain single throughout their lives.

snake

The snake is a wise and romantic creature and has much to offer. Unfortunately, however, snake's quiet and reserved nature often causes a failure to communicate feelings successfully. Relationships are important to the snake, but the snake is indecisive, and will often have many relationships before settling down. The snake has a knack for remaining calm in even the most stressful of situations. Snakes are very good at controlling their finances.

horse

The horse is noted for being energetic and open-minded. Horses are quick-witted and many of them are eloquent speakers. They are not good at self-discipline and can sometimes be arrogant.

goat (or ram)

The goat is a very gentle and peaceful creature. Full of imagination and creativity, they are usually good at artistic work. Though they appear to be sensitive and shy, they can be inwardly determined and rebellious.

monkey

The monkey is a witty and humorous creature who gets along well with others. Monkey likes to compete and is very ambitious. Sometimes cunning and snobbish, monkey can be something of a social climber.

rooster

Roosters are talented, intelligent, persuasive, have a good sense of humour and are known to be very hard workers. They are often flamboyant but can be moody and overly outspoken. Good with money matters. If (and it's a big if) roosters can establish a stable relationship, they tend to be very loyal. Roosters enjoy solitude.

dog

The dog is born under the signs of loyalty and obedience. They can keep calm in a crisis even though they have a short temper. They have sharp tongues and can be a bit stubborn and eccentric. Dogs work well with others and are good leaders. They prefer being with people on a one-to-one basis and usually fail to mix well at social gatherings.

pig (or boar)

The pig is a simple and honest creature, full of passion and intelligence. They can be a bit naïve and emotional, trust others too easily and can sometimes be cheated. They also tend to be self-indulgent and materialistic.

rat

The rat is intelligent and charming, observant and imaginative. However, being something of a social drifter, many of the friendships rat makes turn out to be short-lived. The rat is a hard worker, but not a risk-taker. Rats tend to be critical, something which often lands them in a lot of trouble.

ox

A resolute and hardworking creature, the ox is considered dependable and capable of being a good leader. But sometimes ox can be stubborn and narrow-minded.

zongzi

Zongzi, a traditional Chinese food, is usually a pyramid-shaped dumpling (with or without fillings) made from glutinous rice wrapped in bamboo or reed leaves. Fillings vary from region to region and can be both sweet and savoury. Either steamed or boiled, zongzi is an essential and principal food at the Dragon Boat Festival.

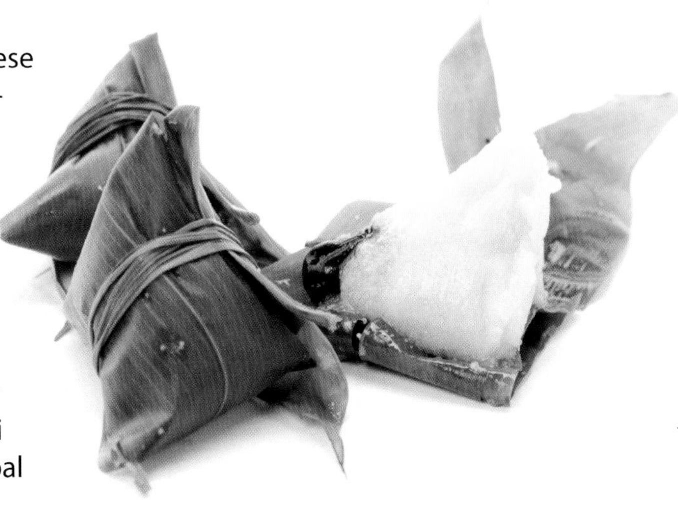

Chinese language books published by Lexus

"Foreign languages are truly doors which we must open."

Mao Zedong

If you want to start learning to speak and understand Chinese, why not open the door of the Chinese Classroom.

ISBN 978-1-904737-117

ISBN 978-1-904737-148

If you want to start getting to grips with the written language, you could do worse than step into the Chinese Classroom, Book 2.

If you are going to travel to China, a Chinese Travelmate could open doors of friendship for you.

ISBN 978-1-904737-063